BECOMING CHRISTIAN

BECOMING CHRISTIAN

Dimensions
of Spiritual Formation

Bill J. Leonard, editor

Westminster/John Knox Press
Louisville, Kentucky

© 1990 Bill J. Leonard

Unless otherwise indicated, scripture quotations are from the Revised Standard Version of the Bible, copyrighted 1946, 1952, © 1971, 1973 by the Division of Christian Education of the National Council of the Churches of Christ in the U.S.A, and are used by permission.

Scripture quotations marked NEB are taken from *The New English Bible,* © The Delegates of the Oxford University Press and The Syndics of the Cambridge University Press, 1961, 1970. Used by permission.

Scripture quotations in chapter 13 marked NIV are from *The Holy Bible, New International Version.* Copyright © 1973, 1978, 1984 International Bible Society. Used by permission of Zondervan Bible Publishers.

Book design by Gene Harris

78650756

First edition

Published by Westminster/John Knox Press
Louisville, Kentucky

PRINTED IN THE UNITED STATES OF AMERICA

9 8 7 6 5 4 3 2 1

Library of Congress Cataloging-in-Publication Data

Becoming Christian : dimensions of spiritual formation / Bill J. Leonard, editor. — 1st ed.
          p.   cm.
    Includes bibliographical references.
    ISBN 0-664-25119-6

    1. Spiritual formation.   2. Spiritual formation—Baptists.
3. Baptists—Membership.   I. Leonard, Bill.
BV4511.B43   1990
248—dc20   90-31441
                                                        CIP

To the students of

The Southern Baptist Theological Seminary—

past, present, and future

Contents

Foreword

In his letter to the Ephesians, the apostle Paul writes:

> And his gifts were that some should be apostles, some prophets, some evangelists, some pastors and teachers, for the equipment of the saints, for the work of ministry, for building up the body of Christ, until we all attain to the unity of the faith and of the knowledge of the Son of God . . . to the measure of the stature of the fulness of Christ; so that we may no longer be children, tossed to and fro and carried about with every wind of doctrine. . . . Speaking the truth in love, we are to grow up in every way into him who is the head, into Christ, from whom the whole body, joined and knit together by every joint with which it is supplied, when each part is working properly, makes bodily growth and upbuilds itself in love.
>
> Ephesians 4:11–16

Those words not only describe the church's ministry, they describe the nature of spirituality for all the people of God. At its best, the church of Jesus Christ is a crucible of spirituality guiding persons in faith and ministry for the "edifying" of the entire body of Christ. This book represents an effort on the part of a diverse group of church women and men to encourage Christians in the pursuit of the spiritual life.

As members of the faculty of The Southern Baptist Theological Seminary, the contributors take seriously their task in preparing persons for ministry in the church and in the world. At its best the seminary promotes both scholarship and spirituality. Faculty members and students together participate in the perfecting of the saints, the work of the ministry, and the edifying of the body of Christ. This book is one way of informing that spiritual legacy in the seminary and the church. We believe it is important in several ways.

First, spirituality informs every facet of the church's life. It is not limited to certain sacred moments when the people of God are being identifiably pious or "spiritual." The church expresses its spirituality when it preaches the good news and when it maintains soup kitchens, when it prays for the sick and when it lobbies for better medical care, when it reads the book of Psalms and when it opens day care centers. Through spirituality, the church of Jesus Christ seeks to conform to the "measure of the stature of the fulness of Christ." Christ is the center, the model for the church's spiritual identity.

Second, spiritual maturity is inseparable from theological maturity. As Paul perceives it, becoming Christian means growing up in the faith so that we are no longer children, tossed about by "every wind of doctrine," easily manipulated by every new ecclesiastical fad or super apostle who appears on the scene (2 Cor. 11:13–14). The rigors of theological investigation and study are also a part of spiritual pilgrimage. Spiritual maturity in the seminary and the church is characterized by such ideas as freedom, sacrifice, devotion, openness, creativity, innovation, commitment, prayer, community, and a sense of the prophetic. Spirituality leads to theological maturity.

Third, spirituality leads to action—a caring response to human need. Mature spirituality is expressed in servanthood. It opens our eyes to those around us and challenges us to respond to the human predicament. That is often easier said than done. Just as churches can hide behind pulpits and pews to avoid sacrifice and servanthood, so theological schools can focus on lectures and libraries, thereby avoiding the call to put spiritual insight into practice. In a day when many of us spend much of our time talking about the Word of God, we would do well to remember that Jesus spent much of his time living out God's love, offering tangible response to the outcasts of his society.

A pastor friend of mine returned from a tour of mission sites in the Far East and made the rounds of local churches, showing slides of his trip and urging people to support Christian mission. He had one particularly poignant photo of a little girl, dressed in rags and obviously underfed, staring into a bakery window on a Hong Kong street. He used the slide to encourage persons to pray for needy persons. After one presentation an observer asked, "What did you do about the little girl?" The pastor suddenly realized that he had done nothing. He had taken a picture and walked away. He had used the picture to make certain spiritual observations, but he had made no response to the human being right in front of him.

Christian spirituality should bring us closer to Christ, enabling us to reach out as he did to the broken, hurting people all around us.

This book is an exercise in spiritual exploration. It is intended to aid pilgrims in becoming Christian, "to grow up in every way into him who is the head, into Christ." Perhaps it will help us to experience God's presence and express God's love, in the church and in the world.

Roy Lee Honeycutt
President
The Southern Baptist Theological Seminary

BECOMING CHRISTIAN

Introduction

This book is a collection of essays written by members of the faculty of The Southern Baptist Theological Seminary, Louisville, Kentucky, that explore the nature of Christian spirituality. With one exception, each chapter reflects the work of two faculty members representing diverse disciplines in the schools of Christian Education, Church Music, Social Work, and Theology. The manuscript grew out of a three-year program of faculty development in the study and pursuit of the spiritual life, funded through a grant from the Lilly Foundation. During this three-year period the faculty was divided into small groups, each focusing on specific issues related to the role of spirituality in Holy Scripture, history, worship, ethics, ethnicity, education, the arts, and in the personal stories of specific individuals. The faculty also participated in a retreat during which each group reported on its experiences. Participants reflected on the meaning of spirituality for the seminary, for the church, and for personal religious life. The retreat was a valuable occasion, culminating in a worship event that included the washing of feet, that ancient (and Baptist) celebration of servanthood and community. The entire process helped to create a renewed commitment on the part of faculty and administration to pursue spiritual development in the classroom and in other areas of seminary life.

This book also reflects our concern to address questions of spirituality as members of the Church of Jesus Christ, apostolic and universal. While all the contributors belong to the evangelical Free Church tradition of the Baptists, the articles are intended for use by persons within various Christian communions. No one church or denomination has a corner on the gospel. We are all catechumen, learners together on the spiritual journey. Whatever our particular traditions, Christian spirituality involves our "response to the grace of Christ before the challenge of everyday life in a given historical and cultural environment."[1]

Founded in 1859, The Southern Baptist Theological Seminary is itself heir to a wide variety of approaches to spiritual development. The Regular Baptist tradition provided an ordered piety centered in Calvinism and a concern for intellectual integrity and heart religion. The spirituality of the Separate Baptists stressed immediate contact with God through dramatic conversion and spontaneous religious enthusiasm, a spirituality shaped by the revivalistic evangelicalism of the American frontier. Both traditions placed great importance on personal piety and direct experience with God. Both insisted that Christian experience began in an encounter with divine grace and was nurtured through Bible study, prayer, and service to God. The church was a community in which sinners were brought to faith and where new believers were guided in the pursuit of Christian discipleship. That heritage informs the seminary's task to prepare men and women for ministry in the church and encourage them in cultivating the spiritual life.

Since its move from Greenville, South Carolina, to Louisville, Kentucky, in 1877, the seminary has benefited from the spiritual pluralism of the Kentuckiana area. Students and faculty alike find spiritual insights and encouragement at the Benedictine Archabbey in St. Meinrad, Indiana, and the Abbey of Our Lady of Gethsemani in Trappist, Kentucky, as well as at Bellarmine College, Spalding University, and Louisville Presbyterian, Lexington (Disciples), and Asbury (Methodist) seminaries. For years, Southern Seminary faculty and students have tried to take advantage of the many opportunities for spiritual direction and exploration available in the Louisville area. In 1964, for example, Thomas Merton wrote from the Abbey of Gethsemani, "I want to give up retreats. Yet, already a letter has come from the Baptist Seminary begging me not to stop my talks. I was touched by it. No one could be more sincere and less political than Glenn Hinson, who wrote it."[2] Dr. Hinson, one of the contributors to this volume, continues to guide students at Southern Seminary toward a deeper appreciation for the devotional life.

The essays included in this volume are not written by "experts" in Christian spirituality. They are prepared by members of a community of sinners who have experienced God's grace in Jesus Christ and are continuing to discover grace together. Our concern is with that holistic spirituality which impacts every facet of human life. In a real sense, we are ever *becoming* Christian, recognizing the presence of God in the unexpected places of life, learning to practice that Presence in struggle in celebration. We confess that we see only "through a glass darkly." No one person comprehends the totality of the gospel; thus we need the insights and encouragement of other spiritual guides. At its best, perhaps, Christian spirituality is the promise of wholeness that is to come and the grace to live with the absence of wholeness along the way.

Louisville, Kentucky   Bill J. Leonard
Advent 1989

PART ONE

Theological Dimensions
of Christian Spirituality

1

Mapping
the Spiritual Journey

Dan R. Stiver and Daniel O. Aleshire

These days, it seems all kinds of people are yearning to be "spiritual." New Agers and evangelicals, Roman Catholics and secular humanists, all have a desire for authentic spirituality. The concept of spirituality has attracted such a diversity of opinion, however, that confusion overwhelms definition. Even among people with common religious images, the meaning of spirituality is slippery and individualistic. When a small class of first-year seminary students was asked, "What does spirituality mean to you?" the answers revealed very different perceptions. One student said that he felt most spiritual when he was involved in direct ministry to the needs of people in the inner city. Another announced that he was taking a year's leave from seminary for a personal retreat to discern God's will for his life. A third expressed a sense of closeness to God through involvement in the life and programs of a typical evangelical congregation. These responses reflect the confusion and underscore the difficulty of defining spirituality. Is one of the three options most correct? Is each option appropriate for that individual but not for others? Is each one seriously flawed? What does "Christian spirituality" mean?

Evangelical Christians need usable answers to these questions. Other Christian traditions have attended carefully to the character and practice of Christian spirituality, but evangelicals have given more attention to piety than to spirituality. We know a great deal about the fruit of the Spirit but very little about a spiritual way in the world. This book is the attempt of one community to contemplate the meaning of spirituality. Our concern is not generic spirituality; it is Christian spirituality. And, even more particularly, our questions explore the meaning of Christian spirituality for Christians who have not dealt a great deal with this reality. Our writing uses analogy and metaphor and reflects our personal witness and experience. What Baptists, as evangelical Christians, have lacked in contemplation they have always compensated for with experience. This chapter seeks to map the territory of Christian spirituality. It does not give an exact picture of the road or the contours of the countryside, but it does provide clues for finding and staying on a route. The map is based on the work of a group of professors at The Southern Baptist Theological Seminary and the subsequent reflection of the faculty as a whole. The group was assigned the task of defining spirituality and, at the end of a rather torturous journey, concluded that "Christian spirituality involves transforming responsiveness of the whole person individually and corporately to God, the 'Beyond in our midst,' and participation in God's continuing creation and redemption in and through Jesus Christ."[1]

As the definition is exegeted in sections of this chapter, one overriding caution has attended the effort. However spirituality may be defined, it remains mystery. It is mystery in Gabriel Marcel's sense that, the more one explores it, the more one simultaneously understands and does not understand.[2] On the surface and in its depths, spirituality is a mystery. It is enigmatic, inscrutable, and indescribable. It is also familiar, personally experienced, and intimately embraced. Such a mystery evokes reflection while it defies assessment. Mystery calls for a response other than complacent ignorance. To say something is mystery does not mean it is completely incomprehensible. Reflection can point to the error of false assumptions, such as confusing spirituality with a reclusive temperament or the legalistic practice of religious duty. Reflection can identify a path into and through the mystery, even though it cannot solve the mystery.

With this caution firmly rooted, this chapter contends that: (1) the center of spirituality is relationship to God, (2) God is the source and goal of spirituality, (3) there are multiple ways in which people respond to God, (4) spirituality is linked to transformation, and finally (5) spiritual disciplines have an important role in the practice of spirituality. Each section is more reflective than descriptive, and more connotative than denotative. Like this volume as a whole, our efforts seek a faithful way of knowing in which true ideas are confirmed in the heart.

The Center of Spirituality

Spirituality can be conceived as a web that forms a Christian way of being in the world.[3] All aspects of life are included in the web of spirituality; all of its parts affect and are affected by all other parts. Spirituality cannot be regarded simply as an aspect of the Christian life; it *is* the Christian life. Such an inclusive characterization creates the need to find a center. Where is the center of spirituality, and how can it be identified?

Everyday Images That Point Toward the Center

Sometimes, commonsense usage of a word is an instructive guide to understanding it. "Spirituality" is a word often used in the company of words such as faith, salvation, and reconciliation. It is also used in the middle of common phrases. Sometimes, people will say, "Now *there* is a spiritual person," or, "Doing this will help you grow spiritually," or, "There is so much spirituality in that person." These phrases suggest that a spiritual person is one who does what it takes to be spiritual; that to grow spiritually refers to the means by which spirituality is nourished (prayer, meditation, Bible study); that spirituality is evidenced in virtues embodied in the spiritual person, such as love, joy, and peace, and other "fruit of the Spirit" (Gal. 5:22–23).

If everyday expressions can point toward the center, spirituality must have something in common with faith and salvation. Spirituality entails effort; it uses strategies by which it is nurtured; it evidences itself in specific qualities. None of these precisely describe the character of spirituality, but they have a way of pointing toward the center of the mystery. They grab attention but cannot focus it. What, then, can both include these everyday expressions and experiences and also focus them and transcend them?

Relationship with God

The center of spirituality, we would argue, is a relationship with God. This emphasis is central not only to the evangelical tradition, but also to the entire spectrum of spirituality in the church. A relationship with God is no cozy experience of God as a good buddy. On the contrary, it points to the centrality of Jesus' own "Abba" relationship to God in the Synoptic Gospels; to the intimate images of "abiding in Jesus" and the Holy Spirit as "Paraclete" (comforter, counselor) in the Gospel of John; and to the language of "in Christ" and "knowing" God in Paul's letters. It reflects the emphasis on union and communion in the mystical tradition and is congruent with the power of Brother Lawrence's image of "practicing the presence of

God."[4] Spirituality may mean many things, but it cannot be understood apart from a deep sense of communion with God. The communion may be peaceful and serene, or it may be turbulent and disquieting. In either case, the center of spirituality has personal and relational dimensions. While this relationship may not be a sufficient condition for authentic spirituality, it is fundamentally necessary for it. A relationship with God forms the center of the web of spirituality from which all other aspects are channeled and shaped. The relationship is experienced both individually and corporately. It is not just a personal relationship, nor is it merely the relationship one experiences as part of a group.

Locating the center of spirituality provides a point of reference within the mystery. If the center is relationship to God, then God is best understood as the source of spirituality; virtues are seen as fruit or outcomes of this relationship; deeds of ministry are best construed as expressions of this relationship; and the spiritual disciplines are vehicles for nurturing that relationship.

God as Source and Goal of Spirituality

The startling message of the gospel is that God initiates something in our lives. Spirituality is not grasping and groping after God. It is no more an individualistic accomplishment than is salvation, sanctification, or bodily resurrection. It rests on the prior initiative of God, who draws near to us that we might draw near to God (James 4:8). God is the source of spirituality. Karl Barth expressed the priority of God's initiative in writing of faith as "acknowledgment." Faith is a response to the one who has gone into the far country in search of the spiritless.[5] Faith acknowledges God as the ground and the goal of the Christian life. Such an emphasis does not minimize the importance of the human response or of the need for discipline and effort. It does rule out self-congratulatory smugness or superiority.

While spirituality requires human responsiveness, its source is in the initiative of God. Henri Nouwen's image likens this process to the opening of clenched fists.[6] The wooing of the Spirit of God invites fists to relax so that people can begin to face God and the world with opening hands. The hands open because of the gentle persistence of a grasping of God, not by human efforts to clutch the divine. As a result, the prime virtue of spirituality is humility.

God is not only the source for spirituality, God is also goal.

Paul Tillich acknowledged that his concept of "ultimate concern" is an abstract translation of the true first commandment: Love God with all your heart, soul, mind, and strength (Mark 12:28–29).[7] God becomes the source for the human capacity to love and the most noble object of that loving. Nothing less than God is worthy of this love, despite surface attractiveness or enticing qualities. The human tendency to replace loving God with loving something else causes persons to flee from the only legitimate source of the transcendent in life. Tillich contended that relating to God is a matter of life and death, of our being and non-being.[8] "Having God," as Søren Kierkegaard put it, is not something one can put off or be detached about. A person who is truly concerned about God "counts every delay a deadly peril."[9]

God's priority in spirituality has several implications. First of all, it *encourages* us to continue down paths, even when the going is arduous. God beckons. God seeks us before we seek God. God wills us to be spiritual, and we can take heart that God will provide the resources we need to follow the spiritual path.

God's priority also *enables* us. Sometimes people cry out in the words of the father who desired healing for his son, "I believe; help my unbelief!" (Mark 9:24). Sometimes people are not even sure if they want to believe. At other times people desire to follow God but do not know how. God's priority suggests that God will empower and enable people in the midst of these problems. Spirituality occurs in the mystery of the wind blowing where it will, in the middle of all kinds of human lives, gently opening clenched hands.

God's priority *guides* us. There is a direction in the spiritual journey. It is not just a walk with God, it is a path that leads somewhere. The destination is none other than Jesus Christ, the human face of God.[10] Dale Moody points out that our movement should be from the image of God in creation, in which all begin, to the image of God in Christ, in which all are invited to end.[11] So, in the language of Hebrews, we "run with perseverance the race that is set before us, looking to Jesus" (12:1–2).

God's priority also *cautions* us. A common human tendency is to run ahead of God's guidance. If our spirituality is dependent on God's initiative, we must wait upon God and learn to trust in God and resist our craving for certainty. People need to be willing to be surprised by God.[12] Spirituality is one area of our lives that we cannot bring under the rule of what Tillich called technical reason.[13] The tendency of technical reason is to dominate, but the rhythm of the spiritual life is to "wait upon the Lord."

Responding to God's Initiative

Since God takes the initiative, the human side of spirituality is response. Spirituality is a web or network and is best understood as a person's response to God in all the relationships of life. Spirituality is a Christian way in the world that is dominated by relationships.[14] Because spirituality is relational, it reflects a variety of individual responses to God, it breeds a unique kind of knowing, and it has its own trajectories of growth.

Individual Responses

Understanding spirituality in relational terms provides an insight about the diversity evident in the student responses described at the start of the chapter. Each answer reflected a response to God; and, as such, each embodied an appropriate aspect of spirituality. One student responded through service with the poor; another, through a retreat to wait on God; another, through the work of typical congregational life. Some are active responses, others passive. Universalizing any one of them, however, would result in a one-sided, deformed spirituality. Spirituality is a web spun between poles. It integrates all aspects of the Christian life while recognizing individual tendencies and calling. Not all persons are called to solitude, but some surely are. Not all are called to giving their lives to inner-city ministry, but some surely are. However, all are called to respond, and that response spins ever-expanding webs of relationship.

Spirituality includes many capacities for human responding, including intellect, emotion, and will. Loving God with the mind is a spiritual event, as Thomas Aquinas demonstrated.[15] Part of the response involves the affective dimension of the self, as people love, hope, and grieve in their lives of faith. Above all else, mystics such as Teresa of Lisieux and St. John of the Cross were Christians exploring the heights and depths of the emotions of spirituality.[16] Another aspect of the response engages the will, as in Kierkegaard. Each of these dimensions is involved in spirituality. None is negotiable.

All people think, feel, and will, but individuals combine these aspects of personhood in different ways and express them in different manners. Humans thus take common resources for responding to God and compose an endless variety of improvisations with them. The relationship one person has with God differs from the relationship another person has because the people are different and relationships are influenced by the people who form them. God may ever changeless be, but the God who is at home with the infinite accommodates to as many unique persons as seek the Presence. Spirituality never requires us to abandon being ourselves, with all our gifts and limitations. We may experience the despair of longing to be someone else, as Kierkegaard pointed out,[17] but we must resist this temptation since spirituality always partakes of the uniqueness of human personalities. Barbara Kelsey relates how she tried for many years to follow her husband Morton's kataphatic (imagistic) way of spirituality until she realized that she was fulfilled via the apophatic (emptying) way. Morton Kelsey concludes that these two major ways of spiritual contemplation, the apophatic and kataphatic, appeal to different personality types with different life experiences.[18]

The Spirituality of Knowing

Spiritual knowing is relational knowing in which ideas do not have force apart from their connectedness to God, to people, and to life. Relational knowing never treats information like a commodity to be owned and sold. It embraces the known tenderly. It is the kind of knowing in which persons live with openness to the known, are receptive to its truth, are vulnerable before it, and can be changed because of it.[19]

Spiritual knowing involves what Kierkegaard called subjective truth.[20] This truth is neither whimsical nor undependable but has a personal nature to it. Spiritual truth is life-changing. It evokes decision, change, and transformation. In both the Old and New Testaments, truth is anchored to repentance in which the individual turns from sin and toward God.

Spiritual knowing, as a relational phenomenon, involves human emotions. As words and symbols are the language of rational thought, emotions are the language of relationship. They are its vocabulary and its genre. Emotions must be tutored,[21] and people must learn to love the right things. Augustine distinguished Christians by their expression of the right love: they loved God rather than the world.[22] The very wellsprings of the heart change in the process of spiritual growth. William Law was right:

> If religion has raised us into a new world; if it has filled us with *new ends* of life; if it has taken possession of our hearts, altered the whole turn of our minds, and changed the whole stream of our affections; if it has given us new joys and griefs, new hopes

and fears; if all things in us are become new; if "the love of God is shed abroad in our hearts by the Holy Ghost . . . given unto us" (Rom. 5:5), and this "Spirit . . . beareth witness with our spirit, that we are the children of God" (Rom. 8:16), then are we Christians, not in name only, but in truth; then we do believe in the Holy Jesus, and we shall "rejoice in the day of Christ that we have not run in vain, neither laboured in vain" (Phil. 2:16).[23]

Spiritual knowing also involves doing. There is a knowing that accrues from deeds done and the reflection that follows their doing. We may not always be motivated to pray. We may not always feel like praying. We may not be sure what our prayers mean. But we pray. Not infrequently, our very action teaches our hearts to want to pray and our heads what prayer means. Spirituality involves the virtues of courage and tenacity that are expressed in deed. Dietrich Bonhoeffer, Martin Luther King, Jr., and Mother Teresa have embodied a spirituality of action.

Trajectories of Spiritual Growth

Because spirituality involves thinking, feeling, and acting, and because people think, feel, and act differently at different points in life, spirituality will change over time. James Fowler has argued persuasively that faith grows qualitatively more than quantitatively.[24] Mature expressions of faith differ from less mature ones more in terms of kind and nature than in size and amount. Growth in the spiritual life is more like the growth of caterpillar to butterfly than kitten to cat. The process of growing always entails the trauma of shedding skins, encountering pain—even dealing with darkness.

Spiritual growth is grounded in the Christian doctrine of sanctification. The God who begins a good thing works to bring it to maturity. The God who works in human lives like a master artisan does not finish until beauty and function have been crafted into a unity. Sanctification is the way in which the continuing initiative of a hardworking God interacts with the faithful human response. Sanctification reminds us that growth does not take place because people have made a spiritual effort or have followed a formula of religious devotion. Just as spirituality begins with God's initiative, it continues by the effort of that same God. Spiritual growth is sometimes wonderful, sometimes terrible. It involves moments of purification, illumination, and union.[25] A spiritual map alerts the reader about dark nights of the soul and times of spiritual leanness. In an era of positive thinking, of quick results, and the equation of growth with happiness, some people are surprised and dismayed by the obstacles and dangers that accompany spiritual growth. Fortunately, moments of illumination and even ecstasy are also common to authentic spiritual growth.

The trajectory of spiritual growth is influenced by more than the changes in personal characteristics, however. Spirituality is also shaped by its cultural and historical contexts. Christianity is incarnational: the Son of God came in a particular context, as a particular person, in a particular time. It is not surprising, then, that the incarnational character of Christian spirituality reflects the contexts and times in which people live. Tradition shapes us as we shape it.[26] Urban Holmes suggests, for example, that apophatic or self-emptying forms of prayer seem to predominate in times of social upheaval.[27] Because traditions of faith fashion our response to God, people do well to attend to the spirituality of their own religious tradition first and then draw on other, less familiar forms. Glenn Hinson calls Baptists, for example, to return to the mainstream spiritual tradition, but at the same time he confesses:

> If my own experience is typical, however, none of us can ignore or abandon our own tradition and plunge headlong into the Christian mainstream, as I once thought possible. We had best wade back through our own stream, even if it is but a trickle, and meet the larger stream where ours joins it.[28]

Transformation

Spirituality exists in the midst of influences, but influences do not determine its course; they do not control its energy. The blowing of the spirit often becomes a gale that overturns significant aspects of a tradition. The new constantly appears again. Responding to the initiative of God inevitably leads to transformation. God is not satisfied with any spot or wrinkle. Transformation jettisons prejudices and unsettles the bad to prepare for the good. Jesus' parables always had a way of "shattering worlds."[29] The presence of God in our lives leads to new horizons, new habits, new responses. It means that we become more like Christ, a process that continues even beyond this life (Phil. 3:12–16).

The transformation occurs within individuals, but it extends into corporate dimensions as well. For example, a part of being spiritual is being political. The life of faith brings people into community, and people live in community with public virtues, not merely personal ones. The kingdom of God in Christ's teaching reminds us that spirituality has significant moral and social dimensions. Langdon Gilkey argues that the future kingdom is not pie in the sky by and by but is both norm and lure for the present.[30] Jesus' parable of the sheep and the goats is a sober reminder that social ministry, as it is called today, is a minimum requirement for the gospel, not some modern-day addition (Matt. 25:31–46). Urban Holmes cautions:

> John of the Cross has a low estimate of people who suffer from what he calls the "spiritual sweet tooth." These are individuals who like to dabble in prayer, getting an occasional "thrill," and posing as holy people. They are ascetical dilettantes, who go from one spiritual director to another, quote the latest books on prayer, and subtly boast of spiritual epiphenomena. They were common in John's day. They persist today.[31]

Spirituality is meant to be earthy and express itself as cups of cold water for the thirsty, shelter for the homeless, and justice for everybody. The transforming character of Christian spirituality brings together what has all too often been torn asunder: inner contemplation and outward action.[32] Linking the Abba relationship to the kingdom of God, as Jesus did, makes such a divorce hardly believable—if it had not occurred so often.

Spiritual Disciplines

The spiritual life, and the disciplines associated with it, are among the more ancient interests of Christian people. They have recently been explored and reevaluated by Protestant Christians. Despite Protestant fears about all forms of works righteousness, an increasing number have discovered the necessity of disciplines that nourish the spiritual life. Glenn Hinson has suggested that it is time for us to be honest about the spiritual impoverishment of much of the Protestant tradition and, while clinging to what is good, also seek a corrective.[33] How do spiritual disciplines fit into the web of spirituality as we have discussed it in this chapter? How important or necessary are they?

The most obvious feature of classical spiritual disciplines is variety. This diversity unerringly reminds us that God's wind "blows where it wills." Spirituality can never be the subject of controlling reason and cannot be nourished in the variety of human lives by only one method. Surefire methods or guaranteed techniques should create suspicion. The variety of spiritual disciplines is necessary because different persons relate to

God in differing ways. The variety does not mean anything goes, however, because not every activity has potential as a spiritual discipline. Spirituality is nurtured by those disciplined practices that help people live a life that is more centered, focused, open, and receptive to God. While the disciplines may vary, there is strong consensus that some sort of discipline is necessary to travel the spiritual path. Spiritual disciplines should not be confused with being spiritual, but they should be recognized as catalysts for spiritual transformation. On the other hand, spiritual disciplines can become overbearing legalism, as Richard Foster has warned.[34] They can also ready us for the transforming work of God.

Since spirituality is elusive, it is not possible for people to engage in a program of spiritual disciplines that axiomatically causes spiritual maturity. Spiritual growth is not readily obtained by the organized efforts of growth by objective. We may intentionally focus on particular aspects of our lives at certain points, but spirituality as a whole is a way of being, a way of responding to God and the world. It is more than a particular set of actions or body of knowledge. We become spiritual by the grace and initiative of God, not merely as an act of our own choosing. Spirituality is a result of abiding in Christ and, like the biblical vineyard, is nurtured by time, pruning, unexpected rains, and occasional weeding. If the Christian life were a race, it would be a marathon, not a sprint. If it were a house, it would be built of stone to last for centuries, and not of wood that lasts the life of a thirty-year mortgage. The growth that comes by grace and spiritual disciplines is not one that appeals to a quick-fix, three-simple-step society. It is the one that leads to "much fruit." (John 15:5).

Conclusion

A map is a handy possession on a journey. It provides a source of orientation, outlines the direction of one's journey, and offers a rough idea of the terrain. But the road itself often exhibits conditions that do not show up on the map. Maps seldom note the landmarks. An intersection may not be as obvious "on the way" as it appears on the map. A map indicates the ways travelers can choose, but it does not tell them which way is best.

Although Jesus may be "the way," we do not all carry the same cross or walk the same steps. We all may arrive at some of the same intersections, but we do not necessarily need to make the same turns. Having a map is not enough. Besides a map, we need to carry the gospel of grace and forgiveness, as well as of power and direction. And if spirituality is centered on a relationship to God, we need most of all at the beginning what is desired at the end: the presence of God—Counselor, Guide, Savior, Companion, Friend.

2

The Bible
and the Spiritual Pilgrimage

Pamela J. Scalise and Gerald L. Borchert

As the guide of the people of God, the Bible provides dynamic testimonies and powerful insights into the nature and characteristics of life as spiritual pilgrimage. While we may be tempted to think of pilgrim people such as Abraham, Moses, Peter, and Paul as the heroes of the Bible, it is imperative for us to recognize the genuine humanity of all those who belong to the company of the committed, Israelite and Christian alike.

The Holy Scriptures are brutally honest about the nature of the human condition. The Old Testament hero David, revered as "a man after God's heart," is described, warts and all, as given to intrigues, passions, and failures. Nor do the New Testament writers try to cover up the frailties of even the most prominent apostles. In Simon Peter, for example, we discover a disciple given to high moments of commitment but also to cowardice, betrayal, and racism. The people of the Bible are clearly described in their humanness for all to read. In a real sense, therefore, the hero of the Bible is God, not the frail people of God. As the writer of Hebrews suggests, God's people are runners in a marathon of life (Heb. 12:1–2). In every age, they are weak and frail pilgrims on a spiritual journey. They require directions along the way. They need God's saving mercy and grace to forgive and transcend human frailty. They require a sense of vision and hope that provides the divine perspective in the midst of the mundane realities of life.

Throughout the Holy Scriptures, spirituality itself is seldom an isolated category. It is, however, implicit in such issues as faithfulness, love, obedience, and patience. Spirituality is inherent in those qualities that contribute to the development of an authentic pilgrim, a woman or a man of God.

Because spirituality permeates the Bible, any attempt to sur-

vey biblical teaching and spiritual pilgrimage is indeed a difficult task. This chapter makes no attempt to summarize the
entire scope of biblical spirituality. Rather, it attempts to intro-
duce some of the great biblical themes that are related to spirituality by focusing particular attention on two specific books—
Psalms and Ephesians. Through the medium of the book of
Psalms we discover a broad spectrum of themes that relate to
the spiritual life of the people of God. Indeed, we realize that
the psalms themselves are diverse expressions of the spiritual
dimension of human personality. Similarly, in Ephesians we
discover the intricate relationship of all the aspects of a Christian's life in the quest for spiritual maturity. Theology and life
are not isolated categories. For Christians, they are united in
daily spiritual pilgrimage. These two spiritual handbooks provide insights into the dimension of spiritual life in the Bible.
Perhaps these models for studies in spirituality will encourage
the reader to examine other biblical texts for additional perspectives on the nature of the spiritual life.

The Psalms and the Old Testament

The Old Testament is an essential resource for spiritual
growth. While the spirituality of ancient Israelites is distinct
from Christian spirituality, the two perspectives are related to
each other by common scripture and by devotion to the same
God. The Old Testament came into being over the course of
several centuries, in the context of various forms of political
and social existence, and against the background of the many
religions of the ancient Near East. Yet the people whose spiritual life is reflected therein were bound together by faith in the
one Lord who Christians confess to be also the God and the
Father of our Lord Jesus Christ. The Old Testament is a true
witness and revelation of God and an authentic resource for
Christian spirituality.

The diverse forms of spiritual expression and experiences with
the presence of God that are recorded in the Old Testament may
be grouped around the two dimensions of surprise and stability.
The ancient Israelites knew God through the divine surprises of
creation and election, theophany and call, and in the holy stability of sacred times and places, worship ritual, and Law-governed
community life. Spiritual growth took place both in the com-
memoration and expectation of God's acts of redemption and in
the commitment to holy living, conformed to the righteousness
of God. Numerous threats to spiritual living are also described in
the Old Testament. The faithful encountered enemies, doubt, de-

spair, failure, suffering, disobedience, apostasy, and even the hiddenness of God, but victory could be won by submitting to the Lord, who is both surprising and constant.

More than any other Old Testament writings the psalms have served as a spiritual resource for Christians. We sing them in worship and pray them in times of distress. The book of Psalms was the prayer book of the church from its beginning; most of the psalms are prayers addressed to God. The psalms as canonical scripture are part of God's initiative toward us. Dietrich Bonhoeffer writes joyfully of the psalms: "This is pure grace, that God tells us how we can speak with him and have fellowship with him."[1] Praying and meditating on the psalms are part of transforming responsiveness to God.

One who prays or sings the psalms stands before God as a responsible person but not as an isolated individual. The Old Testament records psalms as the prayers of individuals on occasions of personal crisis (for example, Hannah in 1 Samuel 2, Jonah in Jonah 2, and the thirteen psalms associated with particular episodes in David's life). Many of the psalm-prayers are composed in the first person singular. Even psalms assigned to individuals by their setting or grammatical form, however, are connected to the prayer tradition of Israel by their content and structure—Hannah gives thanks for her son by praising the Lord as creator and ruler of human destiny (1 Sam. 2:3–8), Jonah vows to make a thanksgiving sacrifice at the Temple (Jonah 2:9), and David claims to be righteous according to divine ordinances and statutes (Ps. 18:22–23). The one who takes a psalm on the lips or into the heart prays as part of the people of God.[2]

In their form, content, and setting, the psalms reflect the diversity of Old Testament spirituality. They may, therefore, provide a vehicle for Christians to understand and appropriate the rest of the Old Testament as a source of spiritual guidance and nourishment. The sketch of Old Testament spirituality that follows draws its examples primarily from the psalms, but it also points beyond them to other passages that give evidence of related aspects of the transformation of human life in the presence of God.

God the Creator

Spirituality in the Old Testament begins with the acknowledgment of God, the one Lord who created humanity, loved and chose Israel, forgave sinners, and called individuals to special service. God's desire is that all peoples shall know that "I am the Lord."[3] The Old Testament exists to make God known. The revelation of the divine name to Moses at his call,

"I AM WHO I AM" or "I WILL BE WHO I WILL BE" (Ex. 3:14), is an invitation to watch and see what the Lord will be and do. It is also a commitment on God's part to be known in a personal way by human beings. *To know and acknowledge God, and to be known by God,* creates an intimate divine-human relationship that is the core of spirituality.

In the Old Testament, "knowledge of God yields knowledge of self."[4] To know God as creator, covenant maker, redeemer, and Lord is to know oneself as creature, beloved, member of the people of God, saved sinner, and servant. The spiritual journey is a voyage of discovery. In communion with God one discovers God and self.

The psalms celebrate God as creator and as the one who continues to sustain and direct the workings of the universe (for example, Psalms 95:1–5; 148; and 104, which parallels the account of the creation in Genesis 1). Creation power demonstrates that the Lord cannot be compared with the deities of other nations (see Ps. 89:5–18; Hos. 2:8; Isaiah 40 and numerous passages in the following chapters). The heavenly bodies lead forth in a song of praise (Ps. 19:1–6) in which all God's human creatures are invited to join (see Psalm 117; Isa. 42:10–13 and passim).

Praise of God, the Creator, leads to acknowledgment of one's creatureliness (Psalms 8:3–4; 139; 144:3–4). There are limits to human strength and knowledge (for example, Isa. 40:30; 55:9). Even the steadfast integrity of Job was overwhelmed by his encounter with the Creator (Job 38:1—42:6). The final limit on human creatures is our mortality (Pss. 90:10; 103:14–16). Ecclesiastes meditates on how to live in the face of inevitable death and counsels, "Remember also your Creator" (Eccl. 12:1).[5] The awareness of God's presence up to and beyond the boundaries of human existence compels us to recognize our total dependence on God's love and power (for example, Ps. 18:16–19) and weans us away from the worship of mere creatures, including ourselves.

The Lord's creativity extended to the making of the nation of Israel. In the Old Testament, the Israelites knew themselves fundamentally as a people who had been loved into existence and had been chosen by God (for example, Psalm 100; Deut. 7:6–8). Beginning with Abram, who followed God's leadership into an unknown future, the Old Testament story of God's grace includes the glorious array of divine initiatives and the full range of human responses. God cared for Israel by providing leaders, opening wombs, rescuing from enemies, giving food and water, winning battles, healing diseases, judging sin,

inviting repentance, forgiving sinners, and especially in faithfully standing by them. Israel responded, sometimes with loyalty and obedience, but often with rebellion and sin. Israel
came to know God as both just and merciful (Ex. 34:6–7; Ps.
103:8; Nehemiah 9). Numerous psalms offer praise and thanksgiving for Israel's personal history with God (for example,
Psalms 105; 135; 136; Ex. 15:1–18), especially in the face of
repeated unfaithfulness (Psalms 78 and 106).

The psalms and other Old Testament prayers show how individuals may understand their own personal experience with
God to be one facet of God's dealings with Israel. Worshipers
bringing their firstfruits to the sanctuary give thanks for the
harvest by reciting Israel's salvation story (Deut. 26:1–11).
The psalmists know that their own prayers are answered in the
same way that God has cared for Israel (for example, Psalms
22; 40; 66; 77; 130). Habakkuk waits faithfully for an answer to
his prayer by praising God for past deliverance (Habakkuk 3).
Daniel confesses Israel's continual sinfulness, recalls God's
constant justice, and then brings his prayer on behalf of Jerusalem,"not . . . on the ground of our righteousness, but on the
ground of thy great mercy"(Dan. 9:18). These examples may
guide Christians to pray and meditate on psalms and other
prayers in such a way that the Old Testament story becomes
part of their own personal stories.

Communion with God

In the presence of the holy and righteous Lord, the Israelites
knew themselves to be sinners who were unworthy to enjoy fellowship with God (for example, Ps. 143:3; Genesis 3; Ex. 20:18–
19; 33:5; Judg. 6:22–23; Isa. 6:1–7). Nevertheless, God's gracious gifts include the means to make this communion possible.
The first of these gifts is the Law. In the Old Testament, the Law
is as much a manifestation of God's character as any of God's
saving acts. Because the Israelites had been given the Law, they
knew the will of God and could do it (Deut. 30:11–14). Three
psalms reflect on the blessings of having and living by the Law
(Psalms 1; 19:7–14; and 119). The Law in general and the purity
laws in particular taught Israel how to prepare to meet God in
worship (for example, Leviticus 15; cf. Ex. 19:10–15 and the
way God protects Moses in Ex. 33:21–23). Obedience to the
Law, however, did not purchase admission to God's presence.
Only God could forgive sin and declare a person righteous
(Psalms 5; 51; 130:3–4; cf. Gen. 15:6). This righteousness reck-
oned to faithful persons is also a divine gift.

The Temple stood as evidence of God's decision to dwell among the people (Ps. 132:13–18; 1 Kings 8:10–13). Worship at the Temple was a means of enjoying the blessings of God's presence. The psalms emphasize the protection and security of Zion amid the threats from surrounding nations (Psalms 46; 48) and personal enemies (Psalms 23:5–6; 27:4–6; 84; 121). Many Israelites succumbed to the temptation to trust in the Temple and its cult rather than in God (for example, Jeremiah 7). At its best, however, "The Temple is the world as it ought to be . . . in which God's reign is unthreatened, and his justice is manifest, in which life is peaceful, and every Israelite is without blemish"[6] (Psalms 15; 24; 84:10–12; 121; 133). In the ritualized encounters with God at the Temple, the relationship between holy God and humble worshipers was experienced with particular intensity. Each act of worship, from bringing an offering to singing a hymn of praise, may be understood as a deed of devotion and submission to the sovereign Lord.[7] Without this personal commitment, however, worship is false and empty (for example, Ps. 51:15–17; Amos 5:21–24).

The goal of spirituality in the Old Testament is complete love and obedience to God. This aim is defined in terms of the covenant relationship, which calls for unswerving loyalty to the Lord (Ex. 20:1–6). Both Jewish and Christian tradition identify Deuteronomy 6:4–5 as the Great Commandment (Mark 12:29–30): "The LORD our God is one LORD; and you shall love the LORD your God with all your heart, and with all your soul, and with all your might."

Love and loyalty to God are demonstrated by living, loving, and thinking in obedience to divine Law. The Law embraces all areas of life, so that even the most mundane activities may be done to honor God (such as measuring grain in Lev. 19:35–37). The blessings of a life filled with the presence of God are received only when one lives in harmony with other persons. Peace and unity among husbands and wives (Gen. 2:18–25; Song of Solomon), parents and children (Ex. 20:12), neighbors (Lev. 19:18), Israelites and foreigners (Lev. 19:33–34), and the nations of the world (Isa. 2:2–4) are essential aspects of Old Testament spirituality. By means of the Law, God guided Israel on the path of spiritual growth toward the full blessings of life with God (Psalms 1; 119:105; Deut. 30:15–20; cf. Prov. 9:1–6).

Spiritual Disciplines

In a sense, the Law makes a spiritual discipline of every area of life about which it gives instruction. Devotion to God through obedience to the Law transforms a person. Four particular disciplines that are relevant for Christians may be mentioned:

1. *Praise.* Praise is joyful, and often spontaneous, but the practice of praise deepens devotion to God by constantly calling to mind God's glory and goodness.

2. *Study and meditation on God's word.* The revelation of God in and through the word is a gift that leads persons to repent, to be reconciled to God, and to reform their lives according to God's will (for example, Josiah in 2 Kings 22–23).

3. *Tithes and offerings.* Giving up a portion of the produce of field and orchard reminds one that God is the source of food and enables one to imitate and participate in God's care for the needy (Deut. 14:22-29).

4. *The sabbath.* Sacred times serve as reminders that the world and history belong to God, not to human beings. Sabbath observance recalls God's work of creation (Ex. 20:8–11) and the blessing of work assigned to human beings (Gen. 1:28). Abstaining from work on the seventh day not only commemorates God's rest but teaches that a person is not defined exclusively by his or her work. Our identity as human beings comes from God, not from our jobs (Gen. 1:27). The sabbath also celebrates the exodus from Egypt, when God delivered the people of Israel from their slave labor for Pharaoh in order to serve God (Deut. 5:12–15), and reminds us that all persons may enjoy the blessings of God's rest (Deut. 5:14).

According to the Old Testament, spiritual life is a pilgrimage undertaken with trust and hope in God in spite of the dangers that threaten from without and within. The pattern of Israel's history with God is repeated in the lives of individuals. God's people cry out in distress, and God delivers them. Sometimes one can do nothing but stand and wait, like Israel at the Red Sea (Ex. 14:13–14). The psalms of lament, trust, and thanksgiving demonstrate again and again how the knowledge of God as creator, redeemer, and sovereign engenders hope and trust that God will once again overcome all enemies (for example, Psalms 42; 71; 107; 124). Communion with God leads to complete dependence upon the Lord and unshakable confidence in God.

Ephesians and the New Testament

The New Testament is an inspired and inspiring collection of ancient literary works that deal with many issues related to the Christian life. As such, it is a treasury of resources for spiritual formation. It is impossible in one chapter to do justice to the great resources available in the New Testament. Rather, the focus here will be on one book, Ephesians, as a model for biblical studies into the nature of Christian spirituality.

In following this approach, coauthor Gerald Borchert used a method that he developed in a variety of earlier works to demonstrate a particular theme through focal texts. In writing on *Assurance and Warning,* he discussed 1 Corinthians, John, and Hebrews.[8] More recently, in *The Crisis of Fear,* he and Edward E. Thornton used a number of specific texts from the Old and New Testaments as models for various and particular aspects of fear.[9] In the present study, the framework of Ephesians has been chosen as a guide to essential elements of Christian spirituality. If the psalms are a prayer book, Ephesians is a guidebook to the nature of the spiritual life.

The Christian as a Child of God

Many commentators have noted that Ephesians emphasizes the glory of God and the unity of the church.[10] It also has a great deal to say about what it means to be a Christian and the necessity for pursuing the Christian life with spiritual vigor. Almost hidden in the middle of this book is a message for the readers to *remember from where they come* (2:11–22). They were once treated as outcast Gentiles who did not belong to God's people. They were foreigners to the experiences of the psalms, hopeless aliens who may have recognized a transcendent force in the world but had no knowledge of a personal God (2:12). Yet in Christ Jesus these foreigners and motel dwellers in relation to the realm of spirituality (2:19) have been accepted as those who belong to the one people of God (2:13–16). Now they have become legitimate citizens, partakers in the spiritual resources of Israel's God and fully qualified members of God's household (2:19–20). The first lesson in spirituality, then, is to understand something about who you are: a child of God. If you regard yourself as a second-class citizen, spiritual pilgrimage will be exceedingly difficult.

Second, the quest for spirituality also deals with the question of *why Christians are acceptable.* The beginning of Ephesians provides some perspective. The first chapter starts with what seems a hymn of praise to God (1:3–10). This hymn affirms four important things God has done for Christians. First, it places them in an awesome cosmic setting in which they learn that they have been chosen, not merely from the days of Abraham but from the very beginning of the world (1:4). Second, they were destined to fulfill the divine purposes as God's sons and daughters through Jesus Christ (1:5–6). Third, God abundantly forgave their sins through Jesus' own self-giving death (1:7–8). Fourth, God has brought all these matters together so that Christians might understand the genuine purpose of wholeness for the world in Christ (1:9–10). In discussing spiritual development, therefore, it is crucial for North American Christians, the heirs of post-nineteenth-century individualism, to realize that they are not simply self-sufficient determiners of their own existence but that their lives are linked to God's eternal purposes in history.

Yet the question of spirituality is not to be answered simply as the responsibility of God. There is another side to the issue. While Christians are the beneficiaries of God's activity in history, they have also been assigned a *responsibility of living* to the praise of God (1:12). Indeed, a foundational relationship with God implies: (1) that they have heard the word of truth—the gospel, (2) that they have believed, and (3) that they have been marked by the presence of the Holy Spirit in their lives (1:13).

The apostle[11] knew that Christians were not perfect and that spiritual growth was not automatic. Therefore, like a concerned parent who is unable to accompany a child to college, the absent Paul turns to prayer as the means for dealing with his concerns. In typical Pauline fashion he begins with a reflection concerning their faithfulness and love and thanks God for his memories of them (1:15–16). Like any good parent, he prays that they might have true wisdom and knowledge (1:17–18). It is particularly enlightening in regard to spiritual formation to recognize what he wants them to know. First, he wants them to know the great hope that relates to their vocation as Christians. Second, he encourages them to recognize their marvelous inheritance as people of God (1:18). Third, he prays that Christians might know the incredible power that is within them, a power that was evidenced in the resurrection and enthronement of Christ Jesus (1:19–21).

"My father, Leo Borchert, never tired of reminding me that in Jesus Christ I was 'a child of a king,'" Gerald says. "Those words have been very influential in my own pilgrimage as a Christian. They do not tell me primarily 'who' I am but 'whose' I am. They remind me of my hope and speak to me of my spiritual inheritance in Christ.

"As a teacher, building on the foundation of my father's advice, I never tire of reminding my students that we are people of the resurrection, people who have been touched by the greatest power in the world and who are followers of the Christ under whose feet all things lie in subjection. The resurrection and enthronement of Christ are the watershed of spiritual power in the lives of Christians."

As Christians, however, we are on pilgrimage toward spiritual maturity and need to be reminded of the journey that is ours. Thus Paul reminded his readers that they had once been dead in their sinful ways (2:1). Once they actively followed the directions of the devil, like all disobedient children (2:2). Once they sought self-gratification as a goal for their lives and accordingly yielded to their desires (2:3). But God's love through Christ changed that pattern by bringing them to life and joining them with Christ as people of the resurrection and of victory (2:4–7). These truths continue to apply today.

It is in this context that some of the best-known verses of Ephesians appear. "For by grace you have been saved through faith; and this is not your own doing, it is the gift of God—not because of works, lest any man should boast" (2:8–9). Therefore, just as in the great texts of Romans (Rom. 3:27–31 and 11:17–25), Paul reminds us that we have no reason for boasting about our accomplishments or our spirituality. By grace, we have been joined to the people of God. Our relationship to God is a gift (Eph. 2:8–9). But it is a gift that carries with it a demand or a responsibility. That responsibility is to allow God's transforming work to proceed in us to the point that we produce good works or the fruits of transformation (2:10). The spiritual pilgrimage, therefore, is not simply the quest of a mystic to dwell in isolation and contemplate the vision of God[12] (though contemplation is surely important to spiritual life). The pilgrimage of spirituality is to lead to effective transformed work, and this objective has been God's purpose from the beginning (2:10). It was God's purpose with Abraham (Gen. 12:2), and God's goal is to bless the whole world with a new perspective. At this point Paul called on his readers to remember their past as aliens and to be aware of their present as fully accepted members of God's household, the theme with which this study began (Eph. 2:11–22).

Called to Accountable Living

Paul knew, however, that Christians would have difficulty being truly authentic even with their transformation and their divine commission. So he reminded them that it was his task even as a suffering and imprisoned minister to call them to an accounting (3:1–13 and 4:1). His call, however, is not that of a stern judge. It is the call of a loving parent who cares a great deal for a growing child.[13] Thus he expresses his concern first in another prayer and then in instruction.

This prayer, a model of his loving concern for his spiritual children, is a threefold petition that summarizes his desire for them. First, he asks that they may receive inner strength, without which it will be difficult to live correctly. Second, he prays that Christ may dwell deep in their hearts, for without God it will be difficult to love correctly. Third, he requests that they be empowered to understand the greatness of God and the overflowing love of Christ, without which it will be difficult to think correctly about God and to be filled fully with God's presence (3:14–19). The prayer concludes with a powerful ascription to God, which affirms that God is able to do far more than the apostle could ever begin to ask. In the journey of the spiritual life, prayer is always an important element. But human prayer is never the measure of God's will. To learn this lesson is an important step for Christians in their pilgrimage toward discovering an authentic vision of God.

Instructions for Christian Living

With chapter 4 the apostle details his instructions, which provide important insights into a mature spiritual life, the worthy calling of a Christian (4:1). First, Paul touches on the style of the Christian life, calling Christians to the way of humility (cf. Phil. 2:5–11). Lowliness, meekness, long-suffering, and forbearance (4:2) are not qualities of weakness but of spiritual strength and discipline. They are desperately needed in our own day when egotism and self-centeredness seem rampant in the church among its ministers.

Second, Paul calls on Christians to be zealous to keep "the unity of the Spirit in the bond of peace"(4:3). Paul must have known that Christians do not do very well with peace, unity, or cooperation. Therefore, he reminds them that there are only one God, one Christ, one Spirit, one genuine theology, one church, one way to enter, and one hope (4:4–6). But Christians do not seem to learn that peace and unity are genuine characteristics of spiritual maturity or that fussing is a sign of immaturity. Merely talking about peace or organizing committees to discuss peace when there is little intention to achieve genuine peace causes Christians to undermine the authenticity of spirituality. It can even create a kind of pseudospirituality.

The goal for adequate leadership in the church (4:11–12) is the use of genuine loving truth, which heals hurts and brings authentic growth to the church (4:15). Alienating and evil ways (4:14; 18–19) are not to be practiced by Christians, because such is not the way one comes to Christ (4:20).

Paul next (4:17–5:20) calls on Christians to adopt a new morality as the embodiment of spiritual life (4:24). What was once called a "new morality" in America was hardly new.[14] It was the old morality of the world, and it has existed since human beings first rebelled against God. The quest for spiritual maturity will never succeed if Christians attach themselves to the self-centered and indulgent ways of the world. Christians, even Christian ministers, may appear to be spiritually mature, but if they play with the ways of the world their lives will be like a house of cards waiting for a great collapse. Among his many instructions, therefore, Paul calls on Christians to speak authentically (4:25); to avoid sinning when angry (4:26); to stop stealing, including stealing other people's reputations (4:28); to reject immorality (cf. 1 Cor. 6:18), uncleanness, and covetousness (Eph. 5:3); to relinquish all types of evil talk, cutting words, and bad humor, a practice not unknown among Christians (5:4); to put an end to worldly activities such as drunkenness (for inspiration Christians were to seek inspiration from the Holy Spirit, not from earthly stimulants, 5:18–20). Why was it necessary for Paul to deal with these issues? Because they are intrinsic to the human condition in every age. True spiritual development involves the whole person—thoughts, morals, attitudes, actions, and relationships.

Indeed, it certainly involves a person's relationships! Unlike the household codes of the ancient world, which concentrated on wives, children, and slaves, Paul's instructions also deal with husbands, fathers, and slaveowners. Paul calls for spiritual transformation at the heart of every relationship.[15] He calls on husbands to love wives as much as Christ loved the church (5:25). Christ died for the church! That affirmation has significant implications for the marriage relationship. Likewise, to fathers Paul writes, "Do not exasperate your children, but raise them with careful discipline and instruction in the context of the Lord's leading" (see 6:4). As Christ is the spouse of both Christian husbands and wives (members of the church), so the Lord is really the parent of both fathers and children. The letter to the Ephesians calls for a totally transformed set of relationships, a way of relating to people different from the pattern of the world. It is indeed the way to spiritual maturity.

Spiritual Confrontation

As Paul draws this letter to a conclusion, he is aware of the fact that the pattern he has set forth is very difficult to achieve. Spiritual maturity is not gained easily, because the pilgrimage of the spiritual life is a battleground on which the Christian confronts the spiritual forces of the devil (5:11–12). In this battle the Christian needs every ounce of divine support available (5:10–11).

Accordingly, Paul summarizes the nature of the spiritual battle by describing the Christian in the quest for spiritual maturity as an ancient warrior. This illustration is one of the most powerful word pictures in the Bible. Christian soldiers are protected at the midsection with truth or authenticity. Covering their hearts like a breastplate is righteousness or genuine goodness. Their feet are wrapped with peace so that everywhere they go they walk peaceably. In front is faith, protecting them like a shield from the doubts and temptations thrust upon them by the devil. The assurance of salvation protects their heads like a helmet. In their hands is the sword of the Spirit. These six elements are vital for Christians in their spiritual warfare against the forces of evil. But there is still a seventh aspect, which completes the description.

This seventh part of the Christian's weaponry was well illustrated by John Bunyan in his famous *Pilgrim's Progress*. There he pictured his hero, Christian, in the armor of the warrior from Ephesians.[16] As Christian fought with Apollyon, the devil's representative, he became terribly frightened by the enemy's power. He was ready to flee when he noticed that there was no armor on his back. Then he realized that to flee from the devil would mean death because there would be nothing protecting him from behind. Therefore, Christian turned again to face his enemy with a fearful cry and a prayer to God for help and strength. God answered by strengthening Christian's spiritual will. As a result, Christian won this battle and was able to continue the pilgrimage to his promised goal.

Bunyan's story portrays the final aspect of the spiritual struggle. All the spiritual armor we possess will fail if the inner person is weak and flees the spiritual battle. Therefore, the Christian is summoned to pray in every situation of life (6:18). This continual reliance of the Christian upon the presence of God through the Spirit is essential to spiritual growth and development. Thus, strength in the inner person is crucial to the struggle against the spiritual forces of evil. To the person in quest of spiritual maturity, the cry of dependence upon God is the sine qua non of the life in the Spirit.

Accordingly, it is clear from Ephesians that spiritual development does not come easily. It is a struggle, a battle. But it is a struggle worth all of life because its end is the glorious inheritance that is readied for the saints (1:18). Christians are children of a king. May each of us continually desire to accept God's grace in Christ and to live dependently as children of God, our spiritual king, imitating our Lord and walking in love (5:1).

Conclusion

Obedience and humble dependence upon God are undoubtedly the foremost characteristics of true biblical spirituality. The biblical writers understand that the people of God will regard the holy God as requiring faithful, authentic life, that human sin and disobedience will be confronted honestly by God's followers, and that spiritual development will come from God's loving mercy and grace in the lives of his obedient people. The Bible clearly sets standards of excellence while recognizing human frailty. Between the standards and the reality of human weakness stands the gracious, beckoning God who has provided the means for the atonement of sin and divine companionship on the pilgrimage of life.

The divine presence has been recognized throughout the history of God's people. It was evident in the traveling tent and the moving ark of the pilgrim Israelites, and in that most holy place, the Temple in Jerusalem. It was present in Jesus Christ, the Word made flesh, crucified, buried, and raised victoriously from the dead (see John 2:19–21 where Jesus identifies himself with the Temple). Today it is known in the presence of the Holy Spirit, the Paraclete, who dwells within the heart of the Christian believer. Dependence on this presence and obedience to the will of the "present one" are foundations from which authentic spiritual growth proceeds. From these flow spiritual qualities such as humility, praise, sincerity, patience, purity, integrity, goodness, and love (see Psalm 15; Phil. 4:8–9; Gal. 5:22).

But spiritual growth must not be viewed superficially as a way of life easily achieved. It is beset by the problems of human inconsistency and the temptations of the spiritual forces arrayed against God. In the spiritual battle of life, however, the dependent cry for God's assistance sounds again and again throughout life, as God's pilgrim people cry for help and learn daily that God is surely a refuge, our means of support even in the most trying times of life (Ps. 46:1–3). Indeed, in all of life God is the source of stability in the midst of his people (46:4–7), who struggle for peace, security, and spiritual maturity.

The Bible asserts that the spiritual pilgrimage of God's frail people is possible because God cares what happens to those who turn to God for help. Indeed, God has demonstrated the ultimate nature of divine concern by giving Jesus, the Son, to be both the Savior of the world and the impeccable model of self-giving, obedient spiritual maturity (John 4:42; Phil. 2:5–11; see also Isa. 42:1–4).

3
Spirituality and Worship

Hugh T. McElrath and Bill J. Leonard

"Church services and bad theater last longer than anything else in the world."
—Ingmar Bergman, filmmaker[1]

"Awake, O sleeper, and arise from the dead, and Christ shall give you light."
—Ephesians 5:14

To suggest that Christian worship, at least in its corporate, Sunday-to-Sunday expression, can be a powerful means of enlivening the human spirit may indeed seem an audacious claim. Much present-day public worship seems predictable at best, boring at worst, an endless verbal assault of hymns, prayers, and sermons expressed in various liturgical forms, aimed at appealing to specific regional, ethnic, and socioeconomic subgroups. The various denominations themselves seem confused as to the meaning of worship and its impact on spirituality. Contemporary Roman Catholics debate the benefits of liturgical renewal begun with Vatican Council II and evident in the introduction of the vernacular mass and the loss of Latin. Many so-called "mainline" Protestants, facing continued decline in worship attendance, wonder if anybody is listening. While some evangelical churches attract large crowds, their worship often seems less an encounter with the divine presence than a weekly media event—Jesus saves; film at eleven!

In the midst of these modern dilemmas, however, Christian worship remains a major source of spiritual nurture and vital religious experience for many persons in various traditions, an essential element in the practice of the presence of God. In private and public worship, Christian people seek God in adoration and praise, confession and reconciliation. Indeed, there is no genuine Christian spirituality that does not involve worship.

An analysis of the relationship of spirituality and worship is no easy task, since neither can be defined and distinguished with precision. Worship incorporates spirituality, and spirituality requires the experience of worship. Both have to do with things mystical and intangible. Both involve "traffic" with the transcendent God whose ways are "past finding out." The relationship between worship and spirituality is truly an intricate one. As Paul Hoon observes, even "to think about worship is itself to be a worshiping act."[2]

We begin with some definitions. Spirituality has many meanings. It can describe elements of individual experience with God and the diverse ways of expressing that experience. Spirituality may also be understood as a constant state of spiritual being, a continuing process of experience with the divine. Indeed, spirituality is "being" above all. It involves a "transforming responsiveness . . . individually and corporately, to God."[3] This "state of spiritual being," therefore, results in "doing" the work of God in the world in one way or another. This description of the nature of spirituality may also apply to the nature of worship. Above all, worship is a response to the gracious initiative of a loving and merciful God. In worship, "being" also precedes "doing." Genuine worship is not simply an obtuse, otherworldly contemplation of things transcendent. It eventuates in receiving the spiritual encouragement necessary for participation in what God is doing in creation and redemption. As Donald Hustad suggests, worship is "a full confrontation with the self-revealed God of the Scriptures, with ample opportunity to respond."[4]

Through both the spontaneity and order of worship, persons become more aware of God's presence and are confronted with God's call to obedience and action. Through prescribed times and unexpected moments, personal and corporate spirituality is nourished and deepened.

Both worship and spirituality are centered in the Word of God. At worship the people of God gather around the Word of God, spoken and enacted, in proclamation and silence. What is the Word of God? It is the presence of Christ coming to us. It is the presence of God made known through written word (Holy Scripture) and the living Word (Christ) both mediated through the enlivening power of the Holy Spirit in the hearts and minds of individual believers and the believing community. Through encounter with the Word of God the spiritual life is nurtured.

Broadly speaking, therefore, spirituality involves a "composite of actions, prayers . . . and deeds of witness in which Christians engage by way of responding to God in faith."[5] This spirituality is nurtured in and through the church, the community of faith. Thus spirituality is a significant element of worship, and worship is intricately related to spirituality. Yet the two are not always coterminous.

The Problem of Balance

Worship and spirituality alike reflect important paradoxes that confront Christians with the problem of balance. First, worship and spirituality involve both individual and corporate religious experiences. In one sense, the spiritual journey is intimate and personal, plumbing the depths of individual consciousness and self-awareness. Persons who embark on such a life must decide that it is indeed the "pearl of great price," worth having at the expense of all else. It can be a lonely life of solitude, as evidenced in the lives of many significant, inner-directed Christian persons. Likewise, individuals are called to praise and worship, even though others do not seem to hear or understand. Worship and spirituality may involve certain experiences with God that cannot and should not be disclosed. Indeed, one of the greatest images of the biblical story and the history of the church is the lone individual calling out to God, determined to experience God's presence whether or not anyone else believes or follows.

At the same time, Christian worship, like Christian salvation, is inseparably bound to community. To be Christian is to belong to a people, the people of God, the communion of saints, the church of Jesus Christ. Spirituality cultivates in each person a way of understanding the self in relation to the "family of God." As theologian E. Frank Tupper notes, "Family imagery stamps the pages of the entire New Testament, sustaining the appropriateness, even necessity, for understanding the church on a familial model."[6] As "family," the New Testament church cultivated communal worship in awe and mystery as well as personal worship in the intimacy of the home.[7]

Thus the corporate and the individual are intricately related. Paul Richardson writes that "corporate worship provides direction for the individual who worships alone, but whose worship, even in solitude, is as a member of the body of Christ."[8] No spirituality—or worship, for that matter—is experienced entirely in solitude. We belong to the one body of Christ, past, present, and future.

Second, worship and spirituality involve both spontaneity and order. They reflect the freedom and unexpectedness of the Spirit as well as the ordered life of spiritual rigor and discipline. These qualities have divided the church almost from the beginning. Those who look for spontaneity complain that order shackles Spirit to human forms, which too easily deteriorate into "corpse cold" rituals. Those who seek order suggest that the Spirit is not the author of confusion and that when spontaneity reigns, fanaticism, even chaos, is not far behind.

Reinhold Niebuhr acknowledged this division when he observed that Protestantism's protest against order and ritual often led to its destruction. He writes that there "may be brief periods of religious spontaneity in which the absence of such discipline does not matter. The evangelism of the American frontier may have been such a period. But this spontaneity does not last forever. When it is gone a church without adequate conduits of traditional liturgy and theological learning and traditions is without the waters of life."[9]

Black churches often provide a creative environment for cultivating spontaneity and order in the spirituality of the worshiping community. At first glance, these churches seem a seedbed of spontaneity where individuals express themselves freely in response to the urgings of the Spirit and the preacher. More extensive investigation, however, reveals that the boundaries of spontaneity are often clearly set and recognized by the gathered congregation. Certain actions and responses are appropriate only at certain points in the service. Spontaneity and order are maintained by and through the community of faith. Cultivating both qualities enhances worship and spiritual experience for the people of God.

Third, effective worship nurtures both summer and winter spirituality. In his book *A Cry of Absence,* historian Martin E. Marty distinguishes between these two types of spirituality. The former reflects the joy of Christian living. For those who model a summer spirituality, "the rites with which one passes through life have to represent emotionally violent turns from the old self to the born-again new being."[10] Winter spirituality—less appreciated, perhaps, but no less valid—is the spirituality of darkness. Marty writes that "not every believer can move easily into the rhythms of country-and-western Christianity with its foot-stomping, exuberant styles. Those styles may come naturally and be authentic to people in some regions and ranks. Must they be the same for everyone?"[11] He calls for peaceful coexistence between the advocates of these different spirituality types and joins with Roman Catholic theologian

Karl Rahner in urging the church to respond to those whose faith is "not strengthened by a spirituality of the charismatic type."[12]

Worship, therefore, allows room for both spiritual conditions in the varied experience of the gathered community. It recognizes that spirituality cannot be mass produced and that every individual who unites with others in common prayer brings innumerable needs, struggles, and crises to the moment of worship. Too much "summer" can produce spiritual superficiality and foster unnecessary guilt in those who cannot offer immediate praise. Too much "winter" can create cynicism and deepen despair. Yet to ignore either is to minimize the depth of human experience with life and with the Spirit.

The great paradox in worship and spirituality is evident in the life and teachings of Jesus. To worship is to lose oneself, to relinquish something of the self—identity, pride, future, even freedom—for the sake of the gospel, the life of loving response to God and humanity. Yet the willingness to relinquish self is the very means by which the self is rediscovered, as the fragmented individual moves toward wholeness and community. Worship is the occasion for losing self—alone and in community—and the occasion for finding it again.

The Form and Style of Worship

Worship and spirituality do not exist in a vacuum. They are shaped by the times, cultures, and experiences of a changing world. Trends and practices in worship come and go in response to the sociological, political, and theological needs of the historical moment. In the 1970s, for example, the emphasis turned to Christian action and the celebrative aspects of corporate worship. There was great emphasis on the incarnational elements of worship and spirituality. Worship practices often seemed preoccupied with celebration here and now in all its finite human dimensions. Worship was often "overhumanized," with primary concern for divine immanence to the neglect of transcendence. In music and cultic action such worship often gave way to overfamiliarity and sentimentality, self-indulgence and hypocrisy.

In the 1980s the emphasis turned toward greater concern for transcendence and the otherness of God. Increased attention was given to inwardness and spiritual worship as a corrective to overfamiliarity with God and the overemphasis on the human. Students and practitioners of worship renewed their commitment to discover worship that would speak to both the immanent and the transcendent elements of the divine/human relationship.

Truly the Spirit is elusive. The seeker is ever amazed at the genuine spiritual experience evident within the broad and diverse context of the Christian community. The spiritual graces blossom in a variety of worship styles and approaches. At the same time, no one worship tradition or method assures spiritual growth and encounter with the Spirit. Indeed, those who claim that theirs represents the truly biblical form of Christian worship, or that form which alone God has chosen to bless, may cultivate a state of spiritual arrogance that is not conducive to a life of faith. The Spirit comes in many worship experiences, which appeal to a variety of individual tastes. In fact, individuals may find the spiritual life nurtured within different worship contexts at different times in their lives. Recognizing that fact and providing various forms of worship is an important contribution of the local congregation. One brief illustration must suffice.

For many years, Trinity Church on the Green (Episcopal) in New Haven, Connecticut, maintained a variety of worship styles in its weekly worship schedule, each aimed at appealing to the diverse spirituality of its parishioners. The first Sunday morning service—usually held around 8 A.M.—was a brief service of prayers and lessons from the *Book of Common Prayer*. It centered on the quietness of early morning prayer in a simple ritual. The second service, held around 9 A.M., was more of a "people's service," concerned with immanence and community and allowing for greater participation and informality. A special hymnbook of spirituals and folk hymns was used, often accompanied by guitars and drums. At Communion, the congregation gathered at the chancel to share bread and wine, celebrating the family of God in spontaneity and intimacy. At 11 A.M., the church worshiped ("as God intended Episcopalians to worship") with more elaborate liturgy and a choir of men and boys. In these three types of services the church recognized that spirituality is cultivated in a variety of liturgical forms. Indeed, parishioners might participate in different services at different points in their own lives and in response to their personal tastes, schedule, and needs.

Few congregations offer such diversity, however, and Christians often must move from one church to another in order to encounter a variety of liturgical experiences. Nor can one form of worship be all things to all Christians. Congregations must struggle to provide worship that best reflects the integrity of their liturgical, spiritual, and ethical understanding of the gospel. Yet within those traditions there can be many diverse opportunities for practicing the presence of God.

In an intriguing and sadly neglected article, Richard A. Baer, Jr., suggested that various liturgical forms may indeed produce a common spiritual benefit. He observed that "Quaker silence, Catholic liturgy, and Pentecostal glossolalia" created a setting that permitted "the analytical mind—the focused, objectifying dimension of [the] intellect—to rest, thus freeing other dimensions of the person . . . for a deeper openness to divine reality."[13] In each of these distinctive experiences the worshiper discovers a vehicle for transcendence as the rational elements of human nature are allowed to "rest" and the nonrational side of life is permitted to function with greater freedom. Through the familiarity of liturgy, the discipline of silence, and the "playfulness" of glossolalia, the individual may overcome inhibitions, restlessness, and self-consciousness, thereby moving into another spiritual dimension. Baer observes that those persons who insist on being fully in control of their inner selves insulate themselves from experiencing the divine.[14] Spirituality may be nurtured through a variety of worship forms and expressions.

The Contents of Worship: The Nurture of Spirituality

Diverse expressions of worship nonetheless may contribute to common spiritual experiences. Whatever the form, worship should nurture basic spiritual graces through prayer, silence, word, and sacrament. Different elements of the church's worship life nurture individuals in broad, holistic spirituality. Individual practices are pieces of a mosaic that combine to create a whole context for spiritual encounter. Each service provides various segments by which spiritual graces may be cultivated. Not all segments of one service are equally beneficial, all the time. Worshipers may be touched by one element of a given service rather than the entire event. A brief survey of the contents of worship surely includes the following.

Prayer—the Voice of Silence

You Evangelicals don't know anything about worship. You meet in churches with all the aesthetic appeal of a barn. You ignore God and sing not about him but about how "happy, happy, happy" you feel. Instead of quieting your hearts before the Lord when you come to the sanctuary, your pastors tell you, "Say a friendly hello to at least three people around you." And your song leaders are always telling you to sing louder, as if you were in a contest with the church next door. No, you Evangelicals just have a "church service." It's like having a party, talking and laughing and making speeches about each other and completely ignoring the one who is supposed to be the guest of honor.[15]

This caricature of evangelical worship may also point to the flaws in the spirituality of one of the church's largest traditions. Evangelical religion may be so eager to talk *about* God that it undermines the opportunity to talk *with* God. Prayer is the essence of spiritual worship. All worship, public and private, begins and ends with prayer. Worship begins with the invocation of the presence of God, not as a prescribed formula but as a grateful recognition that God is present with God's people.

In reality, God's presence cannot be invoked. God is already present in every place and every acknowledgment of presence. Perhaps the real invocation comes not when the worship service officially begins but in the silence of the heart, as each person prepares for worship. Silence, however, is often threatening to modern men and women. Our audiovisual age often contributes to our inability to use silence as an effective medium of spiritual experience. One of the great temptations for worship leaders is to bombard their congregations with sound. Musicians feel compelled to explain the history or interpretation of hymns before they can sing them. Preachers—the worst offenders—feel it necessary to say what every segment of worship means, lest some in the congregation fail to understand properly. Organists play filler music in order to alleviate "dead time" in worship services. Silence in the congregation becomes an occasion for shuffling feet, adjusting clothing, or checking out the crowd.

Fred Craddock writes of modern society, "No doubt the fact that we are bombarded with words has contributed to the decay of meaning."[16] He cites Max Picard's comment that "when language is no longer related to silence, it loses its source of refreshment and renewal and therefore something of its substance. . . . By taking it away from silence we have made language an orphan."[17] The modern church must renew its efforts to cultivate a sense of silence within the worship life of its people. Such education in the use of silence may be developed in various ways.

First, the weekly worship folder can be used to provide spiritual direction. It may contain suggestions for silent meditation and reflection on hymn texts, scripture, prayers, poems, or other materials that direct worshipers toward particular ideas or methods of contemplation. Printed materials may simply encourage worshipers to remember that their primary reason for worship is to experience the presence of God, to listen and wait silently on the Spirit.

Second, the order of worship can also provide opportunities for silence. Some churches make use of the "discipline of silence" prior to spoken prayers as an occasion for individual meditation. Some worship leaders also use so-called bidding prayers, which guide the focus of congregational prayers but also leave opportunity for silent reflection. This allows the congregation to direct its prayers to the needs of the world, the church, and the local community as well as to their own individual concerns.

Through the corporate use of silence, Christians may also learn how to experience silence in daily meditation. Public worship can provide a model by observing silent prayer as part of one's continuing spiritual experience. For it is in daily life that modern individuals are most assaulted by sound. In public worship we learn the importance of centering down, focusing our thoughts and cares on God. What begins in the gathered community should continue in the life of the individual. Silence does not happen easily. It is learned and cultivated, but it is also essential to the life of the Spirit. As Frederick Buechner observes, "Before the Gospel is a word, it is silence. . . . It is life with the sound turned off so that for a moment or two you can experience it not in terms of the words you make it bearable by but for the unutterable mystery that it is."[18]

Spiritual Participation in Congregational Action

Søren Kierkegaard's famous analogy of public worship as drama in the presence of God has been used by many writers and preachers to describe the nature of Christian worship. Kierkegaard attacked the liturgical indifference of many in the church of his day by insisting that genuine worship was a drama in which the congregation served as the "actors" while God was the real "audience." Musicians and preachers were merely "prompters" who encouraged the community of players.[19] While this analogy may be helpful in placing the responsibility for worship with the congregation, where it rightfully belongs, it does not go far enough. Kierkegaard did not make clear just what actions are appropriate for the worshiping community.

Since God is the audience, God observes much more than the outward actions of the people in singing, praying, and speaking. God discerns the interior actions of the heart. The real drama, therefore, takes place in the hearts and lives of the worshipers as they enter into corporate prayer, confession, and praise. Sometimes this inner-directed element of worship is intentional as persons willingly cultivate the presence of the Spirit and seek to open their lives to the activity of God. This involves a conscious effort to use the forms of worship to encounter the divine presence. It is a disciplined attempt to discover God in the continuing experience of worship. At other times, however, the Spirit overtakes the individual when least expected, in some unanticipated moment of divine grace. Sometimes we come to worship too distracted by the cares of the world to direct our spiritual nature toward God. At such times we may be overtaken by grace.

In that well-known journal entry of May 24, 1738, John Wesley recounts how he went "very unwillingly to a society in Aldersgate Street. . . . About a quarter before nine, while he was describing the change which God works in the heart through faith in Christ, I felt my heart strangely warmed."[20] So Wesley experienced—reluctantly—the heartwarming presence of God in worship. Sometimes the presence of God comes with our intentional spiritual preparation; sometimes it comes when we, like Wesley, are unwilling participants in worship itself. God may confront the people in, or in spite of, the order of worship and the desires of the heart.

Spirituality and the Music of Worship Among the fine arts, music is perhaps the most compatible vehicle for spiritual expression and experience. It is also the most intangible of the arts. Unlike the visual arts, which are static arts that can be observed and enjoyed repeatedly, music is experienced for the moment and then it is gone. Like the Spirit, the power of music moves where it will and we do not know "whence it comes or whither it goes" (John 3:8). Therefore, music is that art form especially suited to the ways of the Spirit. It has long been regarded as the language of the soul. Like spirituality, music is an elusive but powerful means of encountering the Spirit.

The relationship of music and spirituality is evident in Holy Scripture. At creation, "the morning stars sang together" (Job 38:7). The ark of the covenant was carried to Jerusalem amid musical expressions of joy (1 Chron. 15:16). The announcement of the advent of the Christ was made by a heavenly choir singing "Glory to God in the highest" (Luke 2:14). God's heavenly throne itself is described as surrounded by endless song (Rev. 4:8).

The Contradictory Nature of Church Music Although music can have a powerful bonding effect on those who sing together within the worshiping congregation, it can also be divisive. The diversity of musical tastes and backgrounds that are brought to worship can contribute to bewilderment and conflict as well as to spiritual experience. The kinds of music selected for performance—hymns, anthems, and other musical selections—can sometimes be a cause for disagreement among participants who associate certain types of music with appropriate spiritual response. Such preferences and conflicts are illustrated in the attitude of one evangelical chorister who insisted that she would not sing one word of Beethoven's "Hymn to Joy" until she was assured that the composer was "born again"!

Introducing congregations to new musical experience requires a willingness to subordinate individual differences of taste and the adoption of a charitable spirit of experiment and adventure. It reflects a willingness to use traditional music—which varies from denomination to denomination and congregation to congregation—as well as an openness to new musical forms through which the Spirit may speak. At its best, this exercise in Christian forbearance results in the music's becoming a vehicle of spiritual unity and common worship. In spite of their differences, the family of faith that "sings together, clings together." Those who "play together, stay together."

How, then, does new and unfamiliar music presented in corporate worship affect those who are hostile toward certain unfamiliar forms or styles of music? How does one who is spiritually mature but musically uninformed listen to music performed in the worship service? Must all music presented in worship appeal to the tastes of all the members of the worshiping congregation? Two observations seem essential. First, music certainly cannot speak to each member of the congregation all the time, every time it is presented. Such an effort would reflect both musical immaturity and spiritual insensitivity. It would also create a form of musical expression that settled for the lowest common denominator of musical and spiritual encounter. Second, it creates a theology of church music as congregational entertainment rather than music as an offering to God from and within the community of believers. Music's highest service to worship is as the very act of spiritual devotion—an offering to the glory of the One who is the Creator of all beauty and goodness. Ideally, the music written by the Christian composer is itself an offering to God. The re-creation of the composition in public worship is—or should be—the offering of the people of God—performers, musicians, or congregations—to the glory of God. Those who simply listen have a responsibility to offer such music back to God in adoration and praise. Likewise, the spiritually mature congregation will learn to worship the divine Recipient of a particular musical offering instead of depending on the music itself to inspire them to worship. They will look beyond mere entertainment to the worship of God as the central element of all genuine spiritual encounter.

If music making and music listening in worship are to be considered spiritual "sacrifices of praise," the musical works involved must be offerings of excellence. Those musical artists whose creative integrity demands that their work be the result of dedicated imagination must be affirmed, because thereby in some sense the Creator is glorified. "Every time we hear . . . something truly imaginative, we should applaud God . . . the giver 'of every good and perfect gift' who is the source of the tremendous surge and urge within each of us."[21]

At the same time, however, the spiritual musical concerns of the persons in the pews should not be overlooked. Congregations need both the spiritual adventure of new music forms and the spiritual security of the familiar. Both qualities work together in worship to enhance spiritual maturity. Musicians who wish to be spiritually responsive to the body of believers will also manifest humility in their use of materials. Such humility may involve a willingness to rein their muse occasionally and choose various types of music to address the varied needs and tastes of a particular congregation.

Praying the Hymns Congregational hymn singing also offers a special opportunity for both the expression and enhancement of spirituality. Many significant hymns of the faith are addressed to God as prayers of praise, thanksgiving, confession, supplication, and petition. Considered only as a musical activity, singing such hymns in corporate worship may be pleasurable or mundane. There is no doubt that many Christians find singing in public worship a pleasant activity simply because they like to sing or enjoy certain tunes. They appreciate it purely as a musical experience. Other worshipers, less interested in or adept at music, may find congregational singing less pleasurable.

Yet the music of Christian worship is more than merely a happy pastime or a required ritual. Hymns are the prayers of the people sung together in the presence of God. To sing the hymns of the church is to participate in the prayers of the church. As we sing these prayers together, we can know that we belong to Christ and to one another and that our spiritual lives are renewed.

Conclusion: Worship and Memory

For those who desire to worship in spirit and truth, the interior life must be open to the special remembrance that a heightened sense of worship brings. To worship is to remember. It is to remember that we belong to a people who have cried out to the Lord in generation after generation. It is to remember that where the spiritual life is concerned there are no self-made men or women; we are all debtors to those who have gone before. To remember is to pray, and prayer is the language of spirituality. In corporate worship we remember God and what God has done for us, even in the incarnation of Jesus Christ. At worship we not only look for new insights into the gospel, we are reminded of those ancient truths we have long known but easily forget. At worship we remember the ancient promise: "They cried unto the Lord in their trouble, and he delivered them out of their distresses" (Ps. 107:6, KJV).

4
Ethical Maturity and Spiritual Formation

Paul D. Simmons and Larry L. McSwain

Christian ministry is a multifaceted reality. It is being that grows from the call of God and doing the will of God through witness to the world and service among the people of the world. It is intensely *private* as the individual minister struggles in prayer and solitude to understand the will and heart of God. It is essentially *public* as the functions of Christian service are accomplished in corporate worship and in the interactions of small groups, through the structures of public organizations and in relationships with individuals in need. It is *personal,* for the individual for whom Christ died is the primary object of all ministry action. It is *structural,* for in ministry "we are not contending against flesh and blood, but against the principalities, against the powers, against the world rulers of this present darkness, against the spiritual hosts of wickedness in the heavenly places" (Eph. 6:12).

This interactive holism was best portrayed in the ministry of Jesus himself. The text he chose for his inaugural sermon at Nazareth (Isa. 61:1–2) integrates these multiple elements into one declaration of purpose. It declares:

> The Spirit of the Lord is upon me, because he has anointed me to preach good news to the poor. He has sent me to proclaim release to the captives and recovering of sight to the blind, to set at liberty those who are oppressed, to proclaim the acceptable year of the Lord.
>
> Luke 4:18–19

"The Spirit of the Lord is upon me" describes the ontology of ministry. Mission defines the outcome of such being. Spiritual empowerment is the essence of ministry. What follows is the consequence of such empowerment:

Proclaiming good news to the poor and blind
Liberating the captive and oppressed
Preaching messianic hope for the present age

The tasks of spiritual formation for ethical actions are two-fold. First, the primary focus of formation is on the development of the truly spiritual person whose being is rooted in the will of God. Second, the consequent actions that are products of genuine spirituality must be an agenda of the formation task. Training in the "how" of ethical conduct must be integrated with understanding the "what" of ethical being.

In reality, every disciple of Jesus Christ is called to the same pilgrimage, following in the way of the Christ to live the imperatives of the kingdom of God. It is to the church as the people of God that the task of assisting the disciple process is given.[1] Ministry formation is the development of disciples whose specialized function within the body of God is to give leadership to the calling out and developing of others in the same pilgrimage toward the kingdom. Thus, spiritual formation begins with the call of Jesus Christ to the individual. It is the task of theological institutions and local congregations to develop this inherently theological process in the lives of the people of God.

Spiritual Formation as the Development of Ethical Persons

The first priority in Christian ministry is that of spiritual formation, which is the cultivation and acquisition of the values and perceptions of reality that are consistent with the will of God as revealed in Jesus Christ. Spirituality is not a parading of pious postures or a proclaiming of pious platitudes. It is not a particular style of walking or talking, as if cultivating a resonant voice or a sweetness of speaking, or even a humble posture, were a sign of being spiritual. Nor is it an outward display of humility through facial expression or pious bearing. As Bill Leonard points out, these are more likely signs of one's own pride and self-centeredness rather than genuine spirituality.[2] Spirituality involves practicing the presence of God, not making an effort to achieve status as the spiritual elite of the church.

As a free moral agent, each individual is the focus of God's love and the object of divine care. The Christian gospel gives balance to the pragmatist's moral value scale. The pragmatist is interested only in what one produces, the effectiveness of one's role performance, or the success one is able to attain in ministry. Such pragmatic issues are not without concern to the Christian, but they are consequences of character, not ends in themselves. Character is the sine qua non of spirituality. Being is the primary concern of formation, since it is from being that action flows. The specific functions of ministry derive from growth in virtue. The authenticity of ethical actions is a consequence of Christian nurture.[3]

Formation in Identity

The first component of the kind of person we are is a sense of identity. Who we are is rooted in understanding *whose* we are. Loyalties shape and define our perceptions of reality, our interests and allegiances. Christians are those who live in conscious and consistent relationship with God. Thus the initial step for the formation of ethical consciousness is commitment to Christian discipleship. The task of the teacher or the spiritual guide is to teach the discernment of divine truth.[4] Efforts to develop ethical behavior without the foundational work of biblical teaching and the historical understandings of the Christian tradition will prove ultimately to be inadequate. Faith is active trust in and steadfast loyalty toward God. These grow from a living tradition. Faith in God establishes the center of value around which all other loyalties are structured.

The radical monotheism of the Old Testament forbade obedience or fidelity to any lesser loyalty.[5] The elect were identified by covenant loyalty. They were conscious of their special relationship to God. The New Covenant sharpens this awareness by relating obedience to God's revealed character in Jesus Christ. God's character of love and mercy is to be emulated in the life of God's people. As the divine Parent is, so we are to be. Karl Barth, speaking of the character of Jesus' followers, put it well: "Their 'state,' their 'form,' their 'bearing,' must therefore here and now already be under the invisible discipline of that kingdom, must be in accordance with the 'state' which is to be reflected in their conduct, 'worthy' of the gospel."[6] Identity and character are thus distinguishable but inseparable.

The Bible constantly points to the profound insight that conduct grows out of and reflects one's character (Matt. 7:16–17). This relationship of act and being is underscored and affirmed in the incarnation—Christ was the perfect image of God. Jesus embodied the will of God for human life and thus became both the true revelation of God and the true model of personhood. He is the ultimate model of discipleship. Growth toward Christlikeness is the goal of Christian ethical formation.

Bonhoeffer referred to this process as "formation," which he said resulted from "being drawn into the form of Jesus Christ."[7] The minister's perception of reality revolves around Christ as spiritual center.[8] We affirm this in our hymns, prayers, confessions of faith, and theological discussions, but it is often denied in daily experience. Those who rely on personal charm, youthful enthusiasm, or native gifts instead of spiritual depth will wither away inwardly, facing fear of failure and the guilt of hypocrisy. The minister is to model the difference that being a Christian makes in all areas of life, from devotional depth to public appearance.

A sense of Christian identity cannot be established apart from coming to terms with one's self-identity. Charles Blair's *The Man Who Could Do No Wrong*[9] poignantly portrays a pastor who compulsively pursues his tasks but has no inner sense of self. He is not centered and thus is driven by ambition and a need for power. Unfortunately, many ministers are terribly insecure persons who work out of a need to acquire power and prestige or simply to achieve acceptance.

A primary need of the minister is to move from being driven to a sense of calling. Rediscovering our call will result in such a centering of self that both personal authenticity and spiritual growth will be the result. Daily self-examination in the light of God's righteousness and the admissions of personal finitude and limitations will be required.

Coming to terms with one's past is also necessary. Many ministers come from economically deprived backgrounds or struggle with unresolved moral conflicts. Such inner tensions affect one's relationships with people and perhaps explain the will to power that lies behind so much compulsive activity. Growth toward self-understanding can be facilitated by encounter groups or support groups. Sometimes professional therapy is needed to ferret out and relate maturely to the formative experiences of earlier years.

Of greatest importance, however, is the devotional life. There is nothing genuine in Christianity that does not begin and end in prayer and devotion. An intensive study of scripture is an enormous aid to discovering who we are and to becoming whom God intends us to be.[10]

Bonhoeffer once reflected on the transformation wrought in his own life through intensive studies of scripture. He had, he said, thrown himself into this work in an unchristian and proud manner. "Then," he recalled, "something else came along, something which has permanently changed my life and its direction. . . . I had often preached, I had seen a lot of the church, I had talked and written about it, but I had not yet become a Christian."[11] A study of the Bible, especially the Sermon on the Mount, freed him from compulsive activity. As he said, he was set free to be who he was. Knowing he belonged to Christ liberated Bonhoeffer from the need to acquire acceptance from the wrong people and gave him spiritual strength and courage to resist the Nazi demonism. Knowing who he was enabled him to do authentic Christian ministry in the world.

Formation in Integrity

Integrity is the second focus for understanding ethical formation. The word refers to wholeness, entireness, or completeness. The process of ethical formation involves the convergence of the outer and inner life, achieving harmony of thought and act— being and doing. The biblical term is *teleios*, which means whole, mature, or complete.

The opposite of integrity is deceit, deviousness, dishonesty, or pretense. The devious person lives in contradiction; without an integrating core, one's conduct is marked by inconsistency.

Christ is the Christian's model of integrity. He could declare, "I and the Father are one" (John 10:30). His will was so integrated with that of the One whom he called Father that there was no division of mind or heart. We are all called to be so integrated, to be conformed to the image of God in Christ. As Henri Nouwen put it, "The goal of the Christian is to be a living reminder of God . . . by seeking a life of total integrity."[12]

Jesus pointed to the wholeness that is required of God's people by reminding them that the central commandment was to "love the Lord your God with all your heart, and with all your soul, and with all your strength, and with all your mind" (Luke 10:27; cf. Matt. 22:39). The picture is one of committing all the powers of one's life—the affections, spiritual capacities, physical abilities, and intellectual powers. Bringing every area of life under the lordship of Christ and into harmony with faith commitment to God is the task of ethical formation.

The crisis in contemporary ministry, best illustrated in the moral failures of highly visible television evangelists, can be traced to confusion about what really matters in ministry. Jesus demands both moral and intellectual integrity on the part of his followers. The call to ministry is itself a call to integrity. Plagiarized sermons, bogus seminary degrees, cheap substitutes for quality theological education, ostentatious life-styles, yellow journalism, sexual promiscuity, and fanatical patriotism wed to zealous religion and open misrepresentation of others all indicate a crisis of integrity of major proportions among what are supposed to be Christian leaders.

The crusade to establish power within a given denomination or religious institution often involves tactics that have little integrity. The end of winning seems to justify any means that might be employed. Assassinating character, encouraging strategies of deceit, implying guilt by association, stereotyping, and acting surreptitiously against "the enemy" all seem acceptable to people who have apparently forgotten the first word in ministry: integrity. The apostle Paul addressed young Timothy and every minister when he said to "make yourself an example to believers in speech and behaviour, in love, fidelity, and purity" (1 Tim. 4:12, NEB).

Intellectual integrity is also crucial. Jesus' concern was that his disciples "know the truth, [for] the truth will make you free" (John 8:32). Such truth is not merely doctrinal or propositional; it is relational, moral, and spiritual. Its first and foremost sign in the believer's life is that of moral and intellectual integrity.

As Augustine rightly noted, faith seeks understanding. The Christian's life is a process of growth, change, and development. New insights and more profound wisdom should emerge from the pilgrimage one shares with God and in the context of the Christian community. The life that is not growing in understanding and expanding in moral wisdom is either stagnant and frozen at an immature stage or is arrogantly parading immaturity as maturity, ignorance as knowledge.

The problem is as old as Christianity. Paul confronted it in Corinth (1 Corinthians 13) and Galatia (Gal. 1:6–7). Belief systems based on authoritarian dogmatism rather than dynamic creativity are the crutches of an inadequate and immature faith. Coercion in religious matters is guilt turned in anger toward another who is perceived as a threat. Jesus' warning about being angry with a brother (Matt. 5:22) should be a constant reminder against the temptation to compromise intellectual integrity. Paul admonished his friend Timothy "to study to show yourself approved of God, a workman that does not need to be ashamed, rightly dividing [straight cutting] the word of truth" (2 Tim. 2:15, KJV, adapted). His stress is on "study"—honest, diligent, intellectual pursuit of God's truth as revealed in Christ. One of the best-educated people of his day, Paul viewed study as the guide for "rightly dividing the word of truth." The word is integrity. Without it there is no Christianity.

Formation as Pilgrimage

The third crucial word for spiritual formation is pilgrimage. Contemporary moral and faith-development theorists have shown clearly the importance of understanding the psychological processes of development in ethical and theological formation.[13] No one is born or reborn ethically mature. Formation itself denotes the concept of growth. A part of the frustration of participation in the growth process of Christian disciples is the recognition that moral failure is inevitable. None of us has achieved the highest levels of Christian maturity; thus, our judgment of unethical behavior is constantly a judgment of ourselves.

The spiritual guide must recognize that the teacher is also on pilgrimage. Ethical formation requires an environment of learning in which the leader of the formation process is also a disciple who is related to another as guide and spiritual friend.

Such a pilgrimage assumes a level of emotional maturity and commitment to the process of growth. One of the major sources of difficulty in contemporary theological education is the student who has never made a commitment to pilgrimage. Such lack of commitment may be the product of many factors. Some have never made the emotional journey of differentiation from parents. They remain dependent on the financial support of the family for education. Others come from church environments in which faith has been so prescribed by rigid systems of doctrinaire teaching that growth is a threat to all they have learned about Christian faith. Still others lack any experiential understanding of the cultural context within which faith must be applied today and live with a naïve assumption that ethical character is a matter of intellectual understanding only. Many presume philosophies of education based more on indoctrination of propositions than that genuine learning in which faith is owned through the struggle of growth. Finally, a new reality for the formation process is evident in those older students whose values are shaped outside of theological assumptions and who may cling to an overcommitment to secular, corporate models of the church.

The consequence of this situation is that the process of developing character and integrity is an intimately personal process that requires knowledge of the persons in pilgrimage, their family histories, and other factors that shape present value commitments. The first task of ethical formation is often the difficult task of unlearning the very value system that has motivated involvement in ministry. Such a process is extremely threatening to most of us, but it is an essential part of formation. None of us can be growing individuals until we have confronted the barriers to our growth.

The second aspect of the ethical formation pilgrimage involves relearning new values. Models of learning that stimulate integration between study and experience are needed. Studying the scriptural values of peacemaking will be an essential part of any ethical formation. But if such study is not more than an academic approach to the subject, the concepts will not be lived out in the crucible of life. Participation in a peacemaking community—embodied, for example, in a peacemaker's group in a local congregation—will shape the ideal of scripture into an integration of understanding and application. Experiential approaches to ethical formation are necessary.[14]

The pilgrimage toward ethical formation is not complete until new values have been adopted by the disciple. It is one thing to be exposed to ethical truth; it is another for such truth to be appropriated into one's being. For such a development to occur, ethical formation must develop in the process of community development. Approaches that focus only on individual development lack the social power of the community. As individuals participate through worship, and in the struggles of community decision-making, as they interact with the pilgrimage of others, a tradition of ethical consciousness emerges. Individuals need the power of group support for the maintenance of those behaviors that challenge the values of a culture whose ethos is not rooted in the consciousness of the kingdom of God.

Spiritual Formation as the Development of Ethical Actions

Ethical formation is also growth in ethical behavior. Being without upright behavior is not true being. There is a consequence of Christian character and integrity: namely, action consistent with the will of God.

How does one know what God's will is for a specific form of action? The first response to such a question must be rooted in the teachings of scripture. The will of God is always consistent with the vision of the kingdom of God set forth in the Bible.

Living a Kingdom of God Ethic

The whole of scripture is concerned with the nature and coming of the kingdom of God.[15] Its fullest expression can be found in the teachings of Jesus. The kingdom dominated his teachings, which cannot be dismissed without doing damage to the gospel message. Few passages portray more dramatically the central concern for the kingdom of God than Luke 9:57–62, where the all-consuming nature of the disciple's commitment to the kingdom is portrayed. At least three points are driven home: (1) a passion for the kingdom is more important than striving for material security, (2) pursuing the kingdom takes priority over other obligations, and (3) proclaiming the kingdom requires constancy of commitment. Concern about economic security, investments of time in otherwise important social customs, and a divided mind all contradict the attention required by the kingdom.

Jesus set forth the vision of the kingdom of God as the apocalyptic vision of a coming world that calls us to see beyond the present. The motivating vision of the Christian in the modern world is a vision of participation in it as a parable of a kingdom that is to come. Jesus acted out demonstration projects of the kingdom in his world. Every time he touched a person with the power of healing, every time he cast out a demon, every time he told a story of how the kingdom reverses the status of the rulers and servants, every time he raised up an outcast, and every time he forgave sin, he was bringing into human life the hope of the kingdom of God. We shall have little impact on the world until our values are shaped by the overarching ethic of the kingdom.

A biblical theology of the kingdom is a radical acceptance of persons, whatever may be the dominant valuing system of the culture. Thus, a transforming Christian stance in the contemporary world would affirm the personhood of all without regard to sex, status, income, or ethnicity. The statement "Christ died for your sins" is the most radical value statement in human history, for it affirms the worth of every individual. As Georgia Harkness puts it, "the Kingdom is both our ultimate challenge and our ultimate hope."[16] The goal of the minister's life is to perfect the righteous reign and rule of God in one's own life and to hold that goal before those to whom and with whom he or she ministers. All Christians are to be people who seek "first the kingdom of God, and his righteousness" (Matt. 6:33, KJV) above all other pursuits.

Efforts to define the kingdom are futile if not misleading. It is a vision—a picture—of the way life is to be and could be lived in the human family when God is crowned Lord of life. Jesus did not so much carefully define the nature of God's kingdom as he declared the urgency of its realization and the vitality of its presence when people "saw" what it was all about, "entered into" it with abandon, and discovered the difference it made in human relations.

Several errors should be avoided at all costs. One error is to identify the kingdom with a geopolitical entity, as theocrats and revolutionaries are inclined to do. "My kingdom is not of this world," Jesus declared (John 18:36), meaning both that the kingdom does not have its origin in the world and that it is not a political or national entity. The kingdom is "of God" and transcends all geographical boundaries and nation-states. No human entity can claim divine correspondence to God's kingdom. All such associations are idolatrous. No economic system or political structure can claim God as its source.

Another error is to dismiss the importance of the kingdom as apocalyptic imagery or imply a future expectation. Both Albert Schweitzer and C. I. Scofield made this mistake, although in different ways. Schweitzer thought Jesus' teachings were largely irrelevant for modern people because they were based on an expectation for the inbreaking of the kingdom. Jesus' exaggerated demands of love for enemies and lack of concern with material security were based on the short time before the end, according to Schweitzer. Since Jesus was wrong about the kingdom, Schweitzer reasoned, the very foundations of his moral commands collapsed.

Dispensationalists, following J. N. Darby and C. I. Scofield, argued that Jesus' teachings were not normative for us because they were given for life in a kingdom yet to come! Living the requirements of the Sermon on the Mount awaits a millennial reign of Jesus on earth during which all Christians will be able to love their enemies, share their goods generously with the poor, and never go to war.

Both approaches dismiss too quickly the importance of Jesus' teachings for contemporary Christians. Understanding the kingdom as a powerful moral vision and Jesus' teachings as illustrations of the sacrificial life required by God recovers the power of his teachings without succumbing to a slavish literalism. "The kingdom of God is in the midst of you," Jesus declared (Luke 17:21). It is there to challenge the ways of the world and to offer the hope that people will choose the way of God's kingdom.

Applying Love and Justice

Moral directions for priorities in ministry are provided by a commitment of love and justice. These twin axioms of biblical faith help to shape the basic religious perspectives of the people of God. Love and justice are characteristics of God's nature and are basic requirements of God's followers. They form the basis for God's commandments; all other commands are explications of the meaning and requirements of love and justice.

Baptists and other conservative Christians have been inclined to stress the importance of love and diminish the requirement of justice. Two patterns have been followed. The first identifies love in emotional terms, stressing the relationship between persons. Strong attachments are cultivated that involve powerful sentiments, emotions, and affections. Acts of charity and missionary zeal are based on the reaction of the heart to personal needs. Thus, evangelism and social ministries to individuals and small groups become the forms of application of this love ethic. Justice, in this pattern, is largely regarded as the processes of law. To do justice is to be fair in the administrative processes of the civil and criminal legal codes. Thus, justice often has a stern and harsh element allowing killing in war or capital punishment without the need of sentiment or emotion. Even God is portrayed as "just" in the sense of requiring or exacting punishment for sin.

The second tradition relates the exacting requirements of love to the transcendent kingdom of heaven and justice to the necessary, if messy, details of power politics. Love of enemies is a nice ideal but unrealistic and impossible on earth, by this construct. Justice is attempting to balance power between various groups so as to avoid having the powerful take advantage of the more vulnerable. In this view the state emerges as a structure of Christian justice, often resulting in an uncritical support for the actions of the state and an idolatrous civil religion that lacks prophetic power.

The Bible seems to hold justice and love together in a more subtle and sophisticated way than either of these. Love is neither pious sentiment nor vacillating emotion. It is a determination of will and intention. That is why it can be commanded.

The command to love God and neighbor summarizes God's will for human life together. Love embraces and includes all other requirements; no other rule or principle rivals its impact or importance. It is universally valid and absolutely binding. To love is to pattern one's life after God's redemptive work and intend one's will toward doing the will of God.

Justice is love at work seeking the good of the other through social policy. Equity, fairness, and equal regard are aims and characteristics of this social posture. Justice is love seeking political power to serve the neighbor. The negative aspect is that justice-love constrains all attempts to use political or social power that is destructive or harmful.

Holistic ethical action calls for the practice of social action as a process of transforming the economic, social, and political structures of the culture to meet the criteria of both love and justice. A kingdom ethic can ask for no less. Thus a truly biblical consciousness formed in the mind and heart of the minister calls for training in understanding structures, their frameworks and processes of change. Spiritual formation that is ethical in its framework is inherently political in the best sense of understanding the application of imperatives of love and justice in the real world of complex social realities. Thus, Micah could rightly say, "God has told you what is good; and what is it that the LORD asks of you? Only to act justly, to love loyalty, to walk wisely before your God" (Micah 6:8, NEB). Without a commitment to justice, the minister neglects a major cause of person-damaging injuries from social structures and fails to give adequate account of a great deal of scripture.

Jesus' concern for people included dealing with sociopolitical institutions, as the inaugural sermon (Luke 4:18–20), the cleansing of the Temple (Matt. 21:12; John 2:13–16), and scathing denunciations of economic practices (Matt. 23:13ff.) make clear. God's message of salvation included deliverance from the oppression of unjust social structures.

Placing justice concerns squarely in the center of priorities makes considerable difference in the way ministers interpret and relate to reality. Karen Lebacqz argues forcefully that the minister's use of power and authority is related to his or her ability to define reality.[17] The "power of definition" gives significant control over a person's life. The individual is often manipulated, controlled, and denigrated by well-meaning ministers who interpret problems in ways that do not take social forces into account. Focusing simply on the individual's faults is most often a tunnel-vision approach that neglects significant aspects of any issue, from problem pregnancy to poverty.

A commitment to justice in the service of love is required of any minister concerned with the truth of Christ. A stress on being good, loving, and kind is not enough. Power realities in social structures also need to be brought under the moral scrutiny of the servant of God. Wielders of unjust power are to be called to repentance no less than are those who fall victim to personal sin.

Study-Action-Reflection Training for Ethical Formation

Ethical formation is clearly a learning process of both understanding the ethical imperatives of biblical faith and learning to put those imperatives into practice in the real world. The processes of ethical formation call for integrative approaches that unite thought and action. Seminaries and churches have generally done well at the task of imparting the conceptual knowledge needed for forming ethical consciousness. They have not been as successful at the equally important task of preparing persons to apply such insights in action.

Models of learning that are themselves integrative of thought and action are needed if ethical formation is to occur in theological education centers. One such possibility of this is a modification of the action-reflection training approach of the past two decades. In this approach, students were sent into the settings of ministry—congregations, hospitals, jails, community agencies, and streets—to engage directly the social problems calling for gospel responses. After such encounters, students were led in reflection on the meaning of the gospel for such settings. Inadequate study of the theological basis for meaningful reflection often preceded such action, however. Thus this method was often too shallow in theological and historical content to provide the spiritual depth to sustain the difficult questions of such settings.

The approach still has validity, however, if rooted in an adequate conceptual base. Thus we have modified this approach into what we call a study-action-reflection model. Ethical formation calls for in-depth analysis of the theological mandates of scripture. But until such consciousness has been tested in the marketplace of the real world, it has not become a genuine commitment. The cycle is complete when the biblical mandates are restudied in the light of personal experience.

An example of formation training using this model would be a study of the biblical teachings on concern for the poor. Following in-depth study, an experience designed to put the disciple, student, or minister in action contexts with the poor would be essential. Serving in a soup kitchen, living for a time on the street, working for legislation to reform welfare benefits, or living in a shelter for a month provide the contemporary framework for giving life to the biblical text. Following such an experience, the reflective process must reexamine the biblical teaching for new practice in the interpretive process of applying it to the present world context. Reflection becomes a restudy of the biblical content to understand its freshness as a word for today.

Conclusion

Spiritual formation is at the heart of the Christian life. Without growth toward the mind of Christ (Phil. 2:5) or the striving of Christian maturity or perfection (Heb. 6:2), all activity is misguided and superficial. There can be no Christian growth apart from spiritual depth. Personal character and integrity are the signs of such personal maturity.

Similarly, there can be no spiritual maturity without ethical formation. Any growth that is genuinely spiritual is also genuinely ethical. There is no dichotomy between that which is "of God" and that which is "right." The process of formation is foremost one of humbly seeking to know the will of God; it is not the learning of techniques in the latest art of meditation or community organization. It may involve the use of techniques that foster openness to the discovery of God's presence in the midst of complex ethical issues.

"Seeking the kingdom" is both a personal preoccupation and a professional orientation. The church as organization lives to proclaim the kingdom of God and witness through its structures, presence, and message to the transforming power of God in human relationships.

Love and justice are indispensable commitments if the Christian minister is rightly to guide the work of the church in the world. The problem with so much public Christianity is that the leaders are confused as to their own identity and show little understanding of the nature and requirements of love and justice.

Formation is a pilgrimage of commitment and learning. On the one hand, spiritual formation is a gift of grace that flows from the bounty of a gracious God. On the other, it is a seeking of the kingdom of God first, to which all other concerns are secondary. That quest is a commitment to the process of learning the practice of the presence of God in personal life and the doing of the will of God in the world. Thus learning how to be ethical and how to do the works of the One who sends us into the world are part of such a quest.

5
Story and Spirituality

James Hyde and Glen Harold Stassen

In Nikos Kazantzakis's *Saint Francis,* Brother Leo has taken up his pen to write the life and times of the saintly Francis. "When you first met me," Leo recalls,

> I was a humble beggar, ugly . . . my eyes were frightened and naive . . . and you, in order to ridicule my ugliness and abasement, you named me Brother Leo the Lion! But *when I told you my life story you began to weep*; you clasped me in your arms, kissed me and said, "Brother Leo, forgive me. I called you 'lion' to ridicule you, but now I see that you are a true lion because only a lion has the courage to pursue what you are pursuing."[1]

When people trust each other to tell and hear parts of their untold life stories—hitherto untold because they feared the judgments of others or did not sense the presence of a community of trust—revelation happens. The teller is revealed in a new way. The hearers reveal their way of hearing in surprising ways. A new sense of community between tellers and hearers is disclosed. As the anxious teller had feared and hoped, God who hears our cries and sees our needs is present in the telling, in the hearing, and in the community.

This was the experience of seven members of the Southern Seminary faculty who participated in a weekly story group. The group began as a part of a faculty-wide semester-long spiritual growth project stimulated by the support of the Lilly Endowment and by their own interest in spiritual growth and community. The group met once a week for an hour to tell stories—stories of their lives and their continuing experiences. When the semester was finished, however, and the formal project ended, the members did not want to disband. They were an unlikely and disparate group from diverse disciplines: music, theology, pastoral care, library science, Christian education, and Christian ethics. Surely no one would suggest that they were selected for their storytelling abilities, their similar disciplinary specialties, their natural gregariousness, or their previous close friendships. Yet the group kept on telling stories, and more stories, and still more stories. They are now the same unlikely seven, still meeting weekly, several years later.

What is it about telling stories in community that has so linked the group's members? They have come to believe that telling and hearing stories can be a nurturing process of spiritual growth. They are not a group that meets "to talk about God"—or a therapy group, a prayer group, or a Bible study group, although such groups are beneficial. They are a story group. Storytelling has bonded them together in unexpected spiritual growth.

An essential part of the group covenant has been to protect the confidentiality of the stories and the storytellers. Furthermore, the stories would not be themselves if displayed in print to prove some external point. They were stories told-in-community. The experience of community is essential to the hearing of the stories. Hence, we are shy about repeating the stories here. We do share a bit, with permission, but sometimes we illustrate our points with stories already told in print. This may seem contradictory. How can we write of the group's storytelling without recounting its specific stories? But it is true to our experience that spiritual growth through storytelling happens *in community.* Our wish for readers of this storytelling chapter is not that they be happy voyeurs, observing the group's storytelling. It is rather that you enter into the process by finding your own group and covenanting together to share *your* stories. We want you to experience your own version of what the group has experienced. If we whet your appetite enough so you complete the process yourself, it is a far better gift than had the group revealed all to you.

Knowing God by Telling Stories

H. Richard Niebuhr pioneered the effort for a narrative style in speaking of God, and he has influenced others who have emphasized story in theology and ethics. Niebuhr argued that ours is a self-consciously historical time in which we realize that our knowing is time-bound and time-filled. Our time-boundedness shows us that the way to knowledge of God is not by escape but by appreciation of what we do experience in the concreteness of our own histories. Niebuhr wrote:

In this situation, we do well to remind ourselves that the Christian community has usually—and particularly in times of its greatest vigor—used a historical method. The preaching of the early Christian church was not an argument for the existence of God or an admonition to follow the dictates of some common human conscience, unhistorical and super-social in character. It was primarily a simple recital of the great events connected with the historical appearance of Jesus Christ and a confession of what had happened to the community of disciples.[2]

Asking how history relates to faith, or how story relates to spirituality, Niebuhr says that "the history to which we point when we speak of revelation is not the succession of events which an uninterested spectator can see from the outside but our own history."[3] It is the story of our faith—the story of the event that gives meaning to our selfhood and guides us in our loyalties, perceptions, and actions.

This history is *our* story, but it is not merely a private, subjective story. It is verified by sharing and checking in community. "The history of the inner life can only be confessed by selves who speak of what happened in the community of other selves."[4] The truthfulness of what we see in our faith is checked and verified as we share in community and learn from others outside our community.[5]

The story group has been a community, entering into one another's stories and knowing—knowing themselves, knowing one another, and, in the process, quietly knowing something of God's presence in their lives.

Colleagues know each other as equals, as co-workers, who often see through pretenses. This type of knowing encourages us toward honest realism and truthfulness without exaggeration. In reflecting on the group experience, one member wrote, "The group provided the context for shared community, and the intensity and integrity of that community surprised me."

Stories Call Forth Compassion

It is a common experience: We learn a dramatic new depth of respect for someone when we hear a story disclosing a previously unsuspected dimension of struggle, suffering, or achievement. We see Christ in the other, not merely in theory but experientially. The compassion we learned in the story of Jesus is now experienced in another's life. We may also gain awareness of another's understanding of God, of God's presence, of God's compassion in Christ, through listening to the stories told by others.

All of us enjoy a good story because we recognize the basic narrative quality of human experience.[6] We recognize our common pilgrimages. We see our own image in the images of others. We know something of how they felt as their story unfolds. We, too, have been in similar situations.

In experiencing dimensions of struggle in the stories of others, we have also learned to see parallel dimensions in our own stories—dimensions we were not aware of before. One member wrote:

> I gained a new understanding of my father and his struggle with my mother's death through hearing two other men talk about their deep sense of loss. Because it has been necessary for me to learn to live alone, it has been hard for me to understand the difficulty of my father's struggle to learn to live alone, but that is another story. Though I *have* tried, perhaps I cannot understand the depth of the loneliness that he feels because I have not experienced that relationship. I will be a more understanding daughter as a result of hearing your stories.

Another wrote:

> I was deeply moved by what other members shared from their own struggles and growth—not simply moved in a momentary way, but in a way that has made an ongoing difference in my own life. As I listened to others' stories, it made me aware of parallel stories in my own life, and put me in touch with some major turning points in my own personal and spiritual pilgrimage which I had not thought about in years. I was now able to recall them and rethink them with new depth from the viewpoint of new insights learned since.

Stories Give Integrity

Stories connect; stories bring together; stories unite what would otherwise be disparate events unrelated to meaningful actions. Thus Stanley Hauerwas concludes that a story "is a narrative account that binds events and agents together in an intelligible pattern."[7] Our relationship to God is most incisively portrayed in story form in the story of Jesus Christ of Nazareth, which connects the actions and responses of his life with our actions and responses.

When told a story, listeners may experience the "aha!" of insight into why a crucial event occurred. Listeners connect it with why they themselves act or suffer as they go. They see a new light that discloses the pattern of their own lives. Tension, stability, and change can be held together by a story that connects the tenses of time, capturing meaning and letting it live for the hearer. Similarly, Jesus' parables, loaded with tension, anticipation, surprise, reversal, and confrontation, show how stories are capable of holding multiple points of view together while containing and supporting many emotions.

A story does not merely illustrate or symbolize meaning; meaning is embodied in the form of the story itself. Sallie McFague TeSelle states, "We learn who we are through the stories we embrace as our own—the story of my life is structured by the larger stories (social, political, mythic) in which I understand my personal story to take place."[8] Our stories give us the integrating unity of our lives.

One group member responded:

> This retracing of growth-points has given me new awareness of what blocks growth in me and of what enables growth to take deeper root. It has pointed me in directions of ongoing pilgrimage and of new inner tasks to wrestle with.

Everyday-Life-Experience Stories Disclose the Sacred

Stephen Crites distinguishes between three dimensions of stories we tell. One dimension concerns our everyday life experiences. These are the stories people usually tell when they are talking about how things are in their world. Through them we make sense of our world and organize its meaning. Through them we instruct our children in the "ways of the world." Crites says that "in order to be told, a story must be set within a world. . . . The stories of an age or a culture take place within its world."[9]

Another dimension of story is the sacred. Crites says that the sacred stories define the meaning for those everyday-life-experience stories we usually tell. Mostly, he says, we do not tell the sacred stories. We may not be able to tell them. Instead, the sacred dimension of stories is revealed as the faith that defines the meaning of our everyday stories. When we listen to everyday stories carefully, we can hear the sacred stories whispering meaning, direction, and limits like a prompter hidden behind the curtain in a high-school play.

For example, the story of the two disciples traveling on the road to Emmaus, joined by the resurrected Jesus, begins as they talk about what has happened in their world: their leader was crucified, their hopes shattered—although the women report that the tomb had somehow become empty. They do not recognize Jesus; they walk along talking. Yet when "their eyes were opened and they recognized him," the sacred dimension of the story transformed their understanding. They reflected to one another, "Did not our heart burn within us, while he talked with us by the way, and while he opened to us the scriptures?" (Luke 24:32, KJV). They had been discussing what had happened in their world. It was not until they recognized him, however, that the everyday story became a vehicle for the sacred.

When the everyday story disclosed the sacred, chronological time was intersected by *kairos* time, the time of God's disclosure and deliverance. God alone has command over the *kairoi* (Mark 13:32–33), but those in Christ have the insight "of the mystery hidden for ages in God who created all things" (Eph. 3:9). On the road to Emmaus, the presence of God became known in the collision of horizons between the everyday story and the sacred. This is the third dimension of story: temporality. Time is understood as past, present, and future. It is content, not sequence. Stories hold the tenses of time together through their structure. When Jesus repeated a past practice they had shared in community, eating at the table with them, breaking bread and giving it to them, their present experience of storytelling and eating together disclosed surprising new meaning. It transformed their past, their present, and their future.

Time in the Emmaus story suggests that everyday stories disclose the underlying faith of the storytellers. It sometimes takes a detective, a theologian, or a highly intuitive person to notice the underlying sacred story that determines the parameters of meaning. Other everyday stories surprise their tellers and hearers when the underlying sacred story discloses itself, no longer in hidden form but in a quiet explosion of insight. Then one sees what has been present and hidden all along. This rings true for the stories told in the story group. For the most part members did not tell stories directly about God, Jesus, or the work of the Holy Spirit in their lives. They told stories of their past, present, and future. But with eyes of faith they saw that the Spirit has been prompting them, whispering from behind the curtain. One member, reflecting back on the stories, said:

> I was surprised at the extent to which the stories we chose were not so much intense religious experience as they were intense life experience which became the context for theological construc-

tion. Spirituality is nurtured by viewing life in its theological categories, and using experience as the occasion for reflection.

In other words, stories were told about life experiences. Because the stories were genuine, faith that is usually hidden showed through in ways that led to genuine sharing and mutual growth. The group did not do extensive theologizing about stories. They thought about them, asked for more information about them, and commented briefly—perhaps too briefly. They seemed reluctant to analyze the stories very much, not wanting to intrude on another person's sacred space. But they were all aware that the sacred was there. Storytelling became a way to know God. They told stories about the context of their lives, and behold, God was there! Spiritual growth has to do with knowing God and being known by God in the context of the whole of life.

When we reflect on our everyday stories, we notice clues that point to the sacred. The group told stories of caring for students and children, of caring for truth and integrity, of continuing pilgrimage within vocation, of commitment to serving others versus the struggle not to be stretched too thin, and of experiencing guilt, grief, and forgiveness. Is it too much to suggest that these ingredients seem to point to a story of One who gave his life in caring for others, who calls us to commitment, gives us forgiveness, and suffers with us when we suffer? We have been timid—perhaps too timid—to make such claims.

One life-experience story that several have told in different forms is the story of painful tragedy and grief: death or devastation to a loved one. Following the experience, there is self-questioning as to whether the guilt was a cause ("Rabbi, who sinned that [this man] was born blind?" [John 9:1–12]); or whether the person could have done any differently. The experience and self-questioning may be held secretly, the story remaining untold for a long time. Sometimes it is first told in prayer and meditation—first told to God before being related to anyone else. There is some assurance: Jesus comes in a dream and says, "It is all right." In the meantime we invest ourselves in caring for the development of others, especially children and students.

One member wrote:

> We did not expect to learn that grief, serious and long-lasting grief, had played such a powerful subterranean role in the lives of each member of the group. We had not known one another. We had known only the usual sharing of opinions and work and the usual gripes. Only in story group have we learned something of

the selves behind the chitchat fronts. Telling stories has proved to be remarkably revealing of the shape of our own behind-the-front lives. What is behind there are some powerfully life-shaping narratives. Even now, we only have glimpses.

We also tell stories of our struggles to say the right word, do the right thing, and be present in the right way in the struggles of others we care about.

Stories Disclose Hidden Selfhood

The Greek word *kenōsis* means to "empty oneself" or to "pour oneself out." In the Old Testament, Hannah pours out her spirit unto the Lord (1 Sam. 1:15). When we tell our personal story, we are actually emptying ourselves and sharing our spirit with others. This sharing makes us vulnerable. We are exposed to the perception of others. Telling our story discloses much about our conscious self. It also reveals our unconscious self.

Not everyone is comfortable with telling his or her personal story. For many it is quite frightening to reveal information that has remained packed away for years. The risk of trusting someone with personal information creates intensity as the story unfolds. The fear of rejection and the risk of exposure heighten the disclosure process of storytelling.

One group member recalled the early days of our meeting:

> Participating in the group did have its threatening prospects (given our primary academic and professional setting) because I knew that if the sharing were to be meaningful it would have to be open, honest, and not superficial. Those who shared their stories, however, encouraged me. Hearing others' stories drew me closer in love and understanding for each narrator.
>
> After sharing my story, I did not feel that the group had the negative responses which I had anticipated, though I was still not entirely free of them myself. I did feel some sense of joy in sharing myself (how else can it be said?) with a small, respected, trusted group of friends and fellow workers. I invariably felt a new and deeper appreciation for each person who shared life experiences.
>
> Did it impact and enhance my own "spirituality"? It confirmed my deep feeling that everybody is beautiful in his or her own way, and notwithstanding the very real and important differences and uniquenesses in each person, deep down we all share very similar needs, threats, hopes, and strengths.

H. Richard Niebuhr writes that one test of a valid under-standing of the Christian story is that it entices and enables us to recall parts of our story we had suppressed. It includes the stories of others hitherto foreign to us as part of our story. The story of Christ is a story of forgiveness and acceptance that enables us to disclose what we had kept repressed in our un-conscious. It is the story of God who is Creator, Ruler, and Redeemer of others we have called our enemies. It is the story of others whom we have not called anything at all because we have not cared enough about them. Their story is now our story because they are part of the story of Christ. Through Christ, *all* were created and *all* have received grace; in Christ, God became incarnate, affirming the bodily reality of all hu-mankind.[10]

One member of the group, who confessed to having felt ini-tially intimidated by the status of colleagues, wrote:

> I was surprised at the depth and extent of experiences we have in common. It is a source of strength to realize that others have experienced similar difficulties and emotions. There is a sense of "not being alone" when you realize that others have similar struggles. There is also a sense of relief in the realization that it is all right to admit that there are difficulties. My tendency has been to suppress those feelings, pretending all is well even though there is a great deal of pain.

There is delicious irony in this statement. James McClendon writes that one of the three essential strands of narrative, of character, and of the story of Jesus Christ is incarnation or em-bodied selfhood. A story approach to Christian ethics and theol-ogy includes our whole selves better than other approaches because our stories include our bodies and our bodily emotions. The kind of spirituality that avoids acknowledging our bodily concerns is gnostic, not incarnational.[11] McClendon's insight may suggest that the group has been guilty of some of the Gnos-ticism or Victorianism still loose in our culture. They mostly avoided concerns about their bodies in the stories they told. But the irony is that the member who felt most intimidated led the group out of their inhibition by sharing intimate concerns about bodily health. When they realized what had happened, they laughed, celebrated, and sensed a new victory.

Stories Transform

James Loder uses story as a way to express the experience of "convictional knowing." This type of knowing is a sudden life-changing burst of spiritual insight that comes when our every-day stories are intersected with the sacred. Loder tells of his transformation when he experienced a serious automobile accident. He was returning from a trip with his family when he stopped to assist a middle-aged woman who had a flat tire. As Loder attempted to get the jack to work properly, he heard the sound of metal striking metal. A sixty-four-year-old man had fallen asleep at the wheel and rammed his car into the parked vehicles. Loder, pinned under the car, called for help. Only his wife, Arlene, a small woman hardly five feet tall, was able to respond. She lifted the car from him, repeating all the while, "In the name of Jesus Christ." Arlene recalled later that she seemed briefly to lose consciousness, then refocused her thoughts and was surprised when Loder was freed. In the process she broke a vertebra but did not realize it. In the midst of this catastrophe, Loder suddenly became aware of

> two solid assurances. First, I know how deeply I felt love for those around me, especially my family. My two daughters sat crying on the embankment, and deep love reached out from me toward them. The second assurance was that this disaster had a purpose. . . . I never felt more conscious of the life that poured through me, nor more aware that this life was not my own. . . . When our three-year-old daughter, Tami, came to sit on my broken chest, I was able to comfort her with a story.[12]

Loder spent several years reflecting on this story before he was able to write about it. From his experience he concluded that there is another way of knowing. This involves the process of *conflict,* such as his accident; *scanning,* the ability to search the conscious and unconscious resources of one's context; *imagining,* a preconscious awareness that offers intuition, insight, and vision for solving a problem; *releasing energy* in response to the imagination, an opening of the knower to oneself; and *interpretation* of the imaginative solution within the original context of the person. This process represents the transformational logic of "convictional knowing." The result is a spiritual awareness that is not available to us through a more rationalistic and non-narrative way of knowing. The combination of theological awareness, human sciences, and convictional knowing enhances the opportunity for spiritual awareness and formation.

Stories Give Spiritual Identity

James McClendon argues that narrative is not primarily about principles but about identity, or embodied character in its social setting, and about responding faithfully to events.[13] Forming spiritual identity is foundational for Christian theology because truthfulness depends on character. Seeing the truth depends on having a truthful perspective, a truthful spiritual identity.[14] Seeing with a clear vision is contingent on having a pure heart, which relies on investing one's interests in the right place (see Matt. 6:19–24). As we tell stories in community, we disclose our interests and our identity in community. As a result, our stories change us.

Will Campbell's writings provide an example of how storytelling leads to change and growth in spiritual identity. Campbell tells about his family history in the rural setting of the Mississippi farm country, where people grew their own food and lived off the land. "Country people were not impoverished. They were simply poor." In the country a person knew who he was by the stories told about him. Campbell set out to tell the story about his relationship to his brother Joe, but the surprise of the story is that he discovered more about himself than about his brother.

Campbell was active in the civil rights movement in the South in the turbulent years of the fifties and sixties. He was determined to confront his Mississippi culture with his understanding of the gospel. This understanding led to conflict and confrontation with his family and lifelong friends.

In the middle of this personal journey Will struggled with his relationship to his brother, Joe. Joe was known as the worker in the family. He graduated from college, became a pharmacist, and eventually became addicted to drugs. His addiction led to the destruction of his family, friendships, and business and eventually of his own life.[15]

Will had so identified himself with the gospel as expressed in the civil rights movement that he failed to attend to the gospel present in the less immediate struggle of his own family. His brother brought him up short. Joe was in the hospital for his addiction to pills. Will was visiting Joe when the conversation turned to Will's adamant determination to confront the human rights issues of the blacks in the South. Finally, Joe confronted Will:

> "You think you are going to save the goddamn South with integration, with putting niggers in every schoolhouse and on every five-and-dime store lunch-counter stool, and locking them up in the same nut hatch with white folks. . . . What you are saying is that you are going to use the nigger to save yourself. What's so Christian about that?"

My protest was less than enthusiastic. He knew that he had hit a nerve and moved in strongly. "Well, I thought I was going to save myself with pills too. With speed. And, man, it worked for a long time. They took me a long way down the road. God, how great I felt. Sailing around in the clouds. Nothing big enough to worry about. But look at me now. A self-admitted nut! Your niggers are like my pills. They prop you liberals up and make you feel good. All fresh and clean like a dose of Black Draught. But then you crash!"

Will was dumbfounded by his brother's confrontation. Joe continued, "You're going down a dead-end street . . . just like I've been doing." He started to walk away but then thought of something else to say. Forcing a grin, he said, "Anyway, Brother, you've got your hands full being brother to me. Don't try to be brother to the whole damn world."[16]

Will recognized the power in Joe's words. This story became a "convictional knowing" experience for Will. All those years as a crusader for civil rights paled in comparison to this new insight. Later he reflected, "It was the beginning of a process — the process of coming to terms with one's own history, whatever that history might be."[17] Indeed, it was a process of coming to terms with Will's own story. The spiritual impact was felt over and over as he searched for his identity with the blacks of the civil rights movement and the whites from his family and community.

Campbell's story helps us to recognize that we are participants in a larger story that includes the members of our family and our local culture. Our own identity in relation to family, selfhood, and gospel, though different in particular respects, is named and brought to recognition for us. Now we see our own identity, in reaction to our own family, to Will Campbell's family, and to all families, black and white, as part of our inclusive gospel story. This story not only yields spiritual identity for Campbell and his family, it offers us an opportunity to discover who we are and whose we are.

Stories Illuminate Social Setting

James McClendon argues that social setting is one of the three key ingredients of narrative. How a person relates to the social setting is a key ingredient of character.

The story of Jesus Christ is normative for Christian narrative and Christian character. And an essential ingredient of Jesus' story is how he related to his social setting. Because Jesus criticized the authorities for seeking authority and places of honor for themselves, for loving to lord it over others, and for not lifting a finger for justice and mercy or aiding those who were burdened, the authorities plotted to kill him. Because he included the poor, the sinners, the lepers, tax collectors, and foreigners in his community, and advocated relating to them in a forgiving and peacemaking way, many plotted to kill him. He was crucified as an insurrectionist, with two insurrectionists. Thus, Jesus' crucifixion points to his relation to his social setting; he died for our sins, and that includes our injustice and our enmity. Christian narrative that overlooks social setting is not faithful to Christ. Furthermore, community with the needy, the poor, the oppressed, the guilty, and the hurting is essential if our community is to find the sacred story in the Christ story.

The group may be guilty of avoiding stories of their encounters with injustice and their involvement in peacemaking. One member avoided telling poignant stories in his life because they might have been "political." The apolitical tendencies in our society may have inhibited our storytelling from taking up all that concerns us. We hope this insight may free other groups from being so inhibited.

Yet several group members *have* told stories of involvement in church programs concerning justice and injustice, peacemaking and reconciliation, discrimination and unfairness. One member told of a wonderfully creative education program he is assisting in at an innovative Roman Catholic church. The focus includes clear themes of peacemaking and ethics. In many different ways, youth and adults are involved in role-playing, symbolic actions, discussions in small groups, reading, and studying. Hundreds of members are participating, bringing about exciting renewal in the church. The group rejoiced in this story of a Southern Baptist seminary professor, a creative Roman Catholic church, peacemaking and renewal, and the presence of the Holy Spirit in worship.

Stories Establish Spiritual Community

John Claypool is a master storyteller. He invites the listener into his private world through his sermons. One such invitation is the powerful series of sermons on the death of his daughter, Laura Lu Claypool. He ushers the hearers into his world of anxiety, ambivalence, and pain with the story of Laura Lu's struggle with cancer. True, other families have struggled with the death of a child, but Claypool's eloquence at telling this story immediately transforms his experience into a community experience. The listeners are quickly captured by a human drama that is common to us all. The everyday story becomes a vehicle for the sacred as Claypool searches for God in the terrible tragedy. He articulates the questions to God that form in the minds and on the lips of his listeners. God is no stranger. The spiritual encounter is a life-and-death struggle in which God appears as the enemy. The question that intrudes into every person's life at some point stands stark for all to see. Is there a God? When life has become unbearable, is there Someone there? When there is nothing but darkness, is there Someone there? Claypool tells of his "wintery spirit" and the truth he discovered for himself: "I can report that strength to walk and not faint was given. No ecstasy. No great energy. Just the gift of endurance—that was all that met me in the depths of darkness."[18]

The community that formed around the Claypool family identified with and joined in the larger story of humanity and suffering. The spiritual agony of one man was transformed into the spiritual struggle of a community of faith. John Claypool and his family did not stand alone. They found community in the sharing of their story. When we reach our limits and the world we have constructed crumbles, it is then that we find spiritual community in storytelling. By sharing our story with one another and with God, we encounter the Mystery of our everyday story. We find a new vision, insight, and intuition for making reality tolerable.

One of the group members wrote:

> I began to realize that people with whom I share the present do not share a past—especially its more personal dimensions. Community develops, in part, as people share years of experience and come to know each other both in the present and from a shared past. Sharing personal stories gave us personal histories that re-shape present perspectives, and so community that might have emerged over years was accelerated. Community is a fundamental element in spirituality. Story, as we experienced it, facilitates spiritual development because it breeds meaningful community.

Yet it was not always easy. Some told stories about their children's struggles with school, with becoming adults, and with the challenge of life's tasks, and about their own struggles to be good but not domineering parents. Those stories did not always build community. Some members have experienced the tragic death of a loved one, or are single and without children, or know the pathos and pain of having children who are chronically handicapped or experience destructive defeats in the formative years of childhood and adolescence. Some experienced anger, grief, guilt, and resentment as others told of their children. The group has had to learn a new awareness of one another's sensitivities. They have had to learn how a story can function not to include others but to exclude them painfully. One person's celebration sometimes brought forth another's grief. Yet all agreed that avoiding such stories would exclude other members. So the group proceeded to share their diverse stories with a new level of empathy and sensitivity.

Stories Heal

Implicit in the stories already shared is the process of healing. Spiritual growth does not always fit the conventional ways of healing. What often appears as reasonable solutions to our conventional knowing becomes inadequate to face the ultimate concerns of our lives. The meaning of suffering and death requires more than a life-experience story to give meaning to life. An everyday story can facilitate the entrance of the Sacred, the Holy, and Mystery. It is the presence of Mystery that gives expression to our deepest yearnings: to be healed of our sense of abandonment and alienation. Stories bring us together as people in relationship to one another and people of God in relationship to Mystery. When we cannot find meaning in our conventional ways of knowing, we turn to stories.

Each of the previous stories speaks of healing: Will Campbell through his brother Joe, James Loder through convictional knowing, John Claypool in community with his congregation, and our story group through disclosure. Whereas the everyday story may bring intellectual and emotional healing, the sacred story transcends our insights. Loder directs us to spiritual healing that has ultimate significance. He found a "new" way of knowing God that brought healing. This healing was more than intellectual insight. It transcended the everyday stories he had previously depended on.

Myron Madden describes the healing power of story. He writes:

> When children must face a death of a family member or even a pet, often they express their grief in ways other than crying. They develop phobias of the dark or of some object or idea. This is a time to let them tell you a story.[19]

Madden recalls that when one of his sons was six years old, he became nervous, unable to sleep, and difficult to live with, all this shortly after the death of the boy's grandmother. In response, Madden showed the child a picture of a castle on an island in the middle of a lake. He asked his son to tell a story about the future. The boy replied, "There is an old mean king and queen that live in that castle and they have a little boy. They are very mean to the little boy."

When Madden asked what the boy was going to do, his son answered, "He is going to kill the king."

Having said this, the child produced a rubber knife and stabbed his father in the heart. Next he climbed into an imaginary little boat and sailed away. After a few moments the boy returned to the room, took an imaginary needle, and pretended to sew his father back together. Then he kissed his chest where the imaginary wound had been made. His father was made whole once again.

Madden observes that his son was healed almost instantly from whatever it was that made life impossible for him and all the family.[20]

Stories do have a power to bring spiritual healing. Whatever the dynamics, the story told by Madden's son offers a new way of knowing.

In the group, members have needed healing for grief, for loneliness—and for guilt. One participant wrote:

> Seminary faculty are a species with hyper-developed consciences. We feel painfully guilty about failures in responsibility that normal people might shrug off forgetfully. Without a story group, we would hold our sense of guilt tightly in our chests where they could turn into bad hearts, bad consciences, or bad anger. Confession is good for the soul—and the heart, too. We have been able to find common wavelengths, to resonate understandingly, with each other's experiences of guilt. We have received relief, acceptance, understanding, and mutual support. And we have talked about how difficult it is to receive forgiveness, and how it seems too shallow or too quick simply to ask another to forgive us.
>
> We've experienced some of that kind of healing community as we have hesitatingly revealed parts of our stories and responded with questions, probings, and honest reactions—and continuing and growing community with one another.

Conclusion: Our Stories Are Part of a Larger Story

Spiritual formation is a personal growth process in relationship to God. Prayer offers us an opportunity to share our stories with God and to be enlightened by Mystery as stories become another way of knowing God. Spiritual growth occurs

when we find ourselves open to the everyday stories that structure our world. Life-experience stories become the vehicle f ·
sacred story to emerge. When we do encounter our sacre..
story, a disclosure takes place. The "truth sets us free." In our
fears of disclosure we often view our stories with an approach/
avoidance duality. We become concerned that we will be rejected, abandoned, or alienated. The sacred story, however,
confronts our fears and releases us into a community of faith.
Our stories not only give community identity but transformation and healing. For the Christian, the Christ story becomes
our dominant organizing story. We find our identity in the relationship with Jesus Christ. His story ushers us into a community of faith that transforms us. His story intersects with ours
and heals our wounded spirits. This way of knowing God transcends our conventional way of knowing. It affirms our humanness and transports us to another place from which to view the
world.

6

Christian Spirituality and the Arts

William L. Hendricks and Robert Don Hughes

Look at the stained-glass windows of Chartres. Listen to Handel's *Messiah*. Watch as the chorus of *Godspell* flips acrobatically from one part of the set to another. In each case, we feel intuitively that art is expressing Christian spirituality. Certainly the arts express other ideas and attitudes. We know tacitly that art can interact with Christian spirituality; we also know that this is not always the case. How then do the arts—literary, visual, kinetic, structural, theatrical, musical—*relational*—connect with spirituality?

Toward a Definition of Spirituality

There is no possible interaction between spirituality and the arts if we mean, by Christian spirituality, contemplating a heavenly kingdom that has no relationship to this earth. It is equally impossible to relate the arts to an interior life that causes us to reflect on God, with mystical devotion, as an ineffable presence related only to our consciousness. Certain methods of Eastern meditation and some exaggerated Western views of Christian experience have promoted these mistaken notions of spirituality, with disastrous results. Meditation with a view to undermining awareness of the physical brings a loss of life's most immediate reality—the material form and content of our existence. Spirituality based on perceptions of religious emotionalism leads to a distinctly non-Christian notion that we do not have to relate faith to the world around us. Both of these inappropriate notions lead to a hopeless concentration on the self, which may result in a stagnant spirituality.

A third mistaken notion of spirituality is the primitive belief that spirit is a separate entity or being inherent in every life, a kind of "zippered inner lining" deep inside the individual. Modern spiritualists and the mercurial New Age movement assume that spirit is an outer aura, an astral force that radiates from the body. Early Gnostics and Neoplatonists felt it was spiritual for the "inner spirit" to desire a release from matter that was inherently sinful. Spiritualism, which includes New Age practices and ideologies, desires to bring the superimposed spirit in tune with the universal or cosmic spirit, an entity that remains essentially undefined and indescribable. Much mischief occurs in the name of spirituality.

Definition of the elusive word "spirit" (*ruach* in Hebrew, *pneuma* in Greek, *anima* in Latin) lies at the heart of the matter. Spirit may be understood as a refined element or a being similar to a material being, only thinner (spiritualism). Spirit may be defined as a vaporous substance floating and unformed (ghost). Animists view spirit as an invasive force that comes on, overwhelms, or fills people and things. Since the Enlightenment, spirit has often been understood as a cultural attitude (*Weltgeist*) or as a psychological state (a mean-spirited person). Such misdefinitions have led to misapplications. When spirit is seen as purely otherworldly, escapism results. When spirit is not integrally related to the physical, the apparent realities around us are ignored. When spirit is privatized, the social and the ethical are excluded.

The Bible provides a more complete understanding of the terms "spirit" and "spirituality." It is better to stay with biblical descriptions as to what spirit does than try to define precisely what spirit is. In scripture, spirit is related to God. Spirit is related to life: its force, its form, its dynamic. Spirit keeps people from reducing all of reality to the material by pointing to a dimension of existence that goes beyond the material. The great crisis of existence is that divorce of matter and spirit called death. God enlivens all else through the Spirit in the creation of the material world. God as Spirit unites the spiritual and the material in the incarnation and its physical acts of redemption. Things that are certain in a biblical understanding of spirit include:

1. The world, as an expression of God's Spirit, exists as physical and spiritual (Genesis 1).
2. Humans must discuss earthly existence in terms of both the physical and the spiritual.
3. God deals with creation in such a way that the whole of it is made possible, is preserved, and is redeemed (Ephesians 1).

4. None of God's ways with the world are designed to separate the physical and the spiritual; all divine activity is geared to the fulfillment and the enhancement of all creation (Rev. 21:5).
5. Indeed, quite a case can be made for saying that separation (death), distortion (sin), and seduction (the evil one) of the world are attempts to rend the physical and the spiritual.
6. All reality is the concern of God.

Adequate biblical spirituality must be concerned with all reality, all people, all places, and all things. In the light of these affirmations, we propose the following definition of Christian spirituality: *Christian spirituality is the total activity of a fully integrated person cooperating with God in Christ to accomplish God's good and ultimate purpose.* To accept such a definition means that spirituality involves all of life all of the time. Anything less is an inadequate view of Christian spirituality.

Toward a Definition of the Arts

Defining the arts is an equally demanding task. According to Aristotle's classification, art is the application of a science. Such a broad designation certainly requires further divisions. Today we hear of medical arts, applied arts, fine arts. These are recent refinements unknown in biblical and classical times, when all art was applied and practical, serving some good purpose toward the enrichment of life. This chapter discusses the so-called "fine arts." Within this broad genus are several species: literary arts (literature, drama, poetry), visual arts (painting, sculpture, photography, graphics), the art of architecture and its attendant embellishments, kinetic arts (ballet, classical dancing, athletics, mime), theater arts (production, puppetry, readings), musical arts (vocal, instrumental, opera), and the communication arts (television, radio, multimedia).

These categories have only recently received positive attention from representatives of the so-called evangelical tradition. These descendants of the Radical Reformation and the Free Church traditions have tended *not* to value these arts in conjunction with spirituality. This is a grave omission and a grievous error. It is our hope in this chapter to point out ways in which the arts may be used to develop a healthy spirituality.

Seeking a Theological Starting Point

If we accept the above definitions, it would be possible to see all creation as God's art and all human fabrications as humanity's art. But such a general view—although it is a good conclusion—is altogether too vague and too uncritical as a starting point. We must ask if there is some supreme moment when the ultimate will of God is accomplished in bringing together the physical and the spiritual, the material element of life and the motivational force that lies behind it. Such a moment would have to combine the physical and the spiritual in such a way that the evils of matter are cured and cared for and the concerns of spirit are adequately expressed and embodied. Such a point of union of the will of God for perfecting and completing creation must involve tangible time and space to prevent unformed spiritualism and to involve the dimension of God's kind of being as Spirit to stand as a redeemer and correction of crass materialism.

A majority of theological aestheticians would begin with creation. The argument is familiar: God is the original artist. God has made all things beautiful. Humans must love beauty because God is its author. We must appreciate the beauty of nature. We must imitate nature and produce beautiful things. This is a strong and powerful appeal. It is not incorrect; it is incomplete. Resolutions to problems are often unsatisfactory because of what they omit. Such is the case of the argument for beauty, the arts, and Christian spirituality, which starts from the created order. What is omitted is the reality of the world as it actually exists. There are some few unspoiled spots of beauty in the natural world, and Christians must strive to preserve and protect them as parables of the divine intention. Indeed, from the horror of the twentieth-century ecological crises a more forceful argument can be made: that beauty, the arts, and nature have become cosmic victims of greed, exploitation, and commercialism.

Moreover, if we begin Christian spirituality with a general and vague notion of God as creator, we will of necessity find ourselves with a vague and general idea of God. Historical focus and specific criteria for determination are required at the beginning in order that, in the light of this specificity, we can work our way back to beginnings and forward to conclusions.

Others might choose the incarnation as the starting point for relating Christian spirituality to art. The incarnation can satisfy the requirements of uniting the physical and the spiritual. We see this in the sweetness of the Madonna and child, a favorite theme of many artists. But the incarnation alone cannot resolve the problem of evil and the ugliness so blatantly proclaimed by the porno theater or the most recent hack-and-slash movie. This is why most playwrights deem it almost impossible to write a good Christmas drama. The events surrounding the nativity are less dramatic when Herod's slaughter of the innocents is not included. Herein is true horror, true evil—but no resolution. The incarnation begins the resolution of these problems, but that must wait for the true climax. The crucifixion and resurrection of Jesus Christ represent that specific Christian moment when the material and the spiritual are united, threatened, reunited, and melded together indissolubly.

These events—a crucifixion and resurrection—viewed as a single whole establish the beginning of Christian spirituality and the constituent principle that sets up a theological rationale for the relationship of Christian theology and the arts. When one begins with this Christ event and its dramatic conclusion in the cross and resurrection, it is then possible and necessary to work outward toward human artistic activity in the world. A Christian spirituality that begins with cross and resurrection is under mandate to work backward to the creation and God's purpose in it, and to work forward to the consummation and the completion it implies. When the cross/resurrection event is accepted as a criterion for beauty, no less than for truth and for goodness, it is possible to neutralize evil and ugliness—at least, that is the promise of the resurrection and the hope of those who look and wait for the kingdom of God. To rephrase a Pauline metaphor, when Christ dies on the cross he receives the curse of the law (of the condemnation of sin, the blight of ugliness). By Christ's very assumption of the ruin with which the law tries to deal, he overcomes the law. In the resolution brought by the resurrection, therefore, the law is sublimated and the conditions it sought to correct are adequately obliterated. By beginning with the cross/resurrection event as the specific criterion of goodness, truth, and beauty, we take adequate account of the reality of sin, the lie, and ugliness. When this specific and "scandalously historical particularity" is made the point of union of the physical and the spiritual, the rending of what God has joined together is seen as the major problem of the world. Christian spirituality must start from the intention of the divine will and work toward the unifying accomplishment of it. It was both the glory and the guilt of Christian visual art from the fifth century through the sixteenth century that its major focus was on crucifixion scenes. Paintings depicting Christ's passion are the glory of Christian art because the cross is central to an understanding of Christianity. Passion pictures without a resurrection scene are the blight of truly Christian art because they leave unsaid what must be said. Christian art, while embodying the cross/resurrection event, must move out from it to the original intention of creation and onward to the visionary hopes of completion. Likewise, Christian art must portray a realistic picture of the existential struggle of flesh and spirit. Christians should be able to appreciate the work of Rembrandt (*Christ, with the Sick Around Him, Receiving Little Children,* in the National Gallery), in which the spirit radiates from the physical, and recognize the truth of its counterpart in Ivan Albright's work (*The Portrait of Dorian Gray*), in which the physical seeks to dominate and disguise the spiritual.

All subjects and all types of artistic representation can be related to a Christian spirituality that begins with the cross and resurrection, that attempts to define the outworkings of God in uniting the physical and the spiritual, and that examines the concomitant activity of evil that seeks to wrench them apart.

It may well be asked if, by starting with the cross and the resurrection of Jesus Christ, we have not de facto excluded secular forms of art and the art of other religious traditions. Such artistic expressions are not at all to be excluded. Rather, by an expanded meaning of the cross and resurrection, a process begun in the New Testament itself, we have criteria for recognizing the genuinely sacred in the secular and the Christly elements in other religious traditions. If one objects to starting with specific criteria for determining the good, the true, and the beautiful, remember that human knowledge and understanding all start from specifics and not from universals.[1]

It may even be argued that all religious stories—the originating point for graphic illustrations, films, plays, and novels—derive from a single plot line, that of the sacrificial hero. From Beowulf to Arthur, from St. George to Luke Skywalker, the elements are essentially the same. "Here is what writing is trying to tell: The answer to any possible problem or question you could pose is always in some fantastic manner the diametric reversal of the question. . . . [This] is the essence of Christianity, it is the secret of sacrifice, and it is supremely exemplified in the whole life of Christ. It is the secret of fiction, of the tales told by the makers of literature of all ages and all nations."[2]

Thus, a biblical view of Christian arts best begins with the cross and resurrection of Jesus Christ, works back to creation beauty (*cosmos*), and moves on to the ideal beauty of consummation (*eschaton*). Nor can Christian spirituality or Christian art ignore the wrenching implications of *chaos*.[3]

With this in mind, we turn to specific application of the arts to Christian spirituality.

Application of Arts and Spirituality to Ministry

We now ask how these two determinants, one so general and the other so specific, may be applied to the particulars of ministry. Every science must have an art to bring it to fruition. Every art must have a science to constitute and inform its substance. Christian ministry is the art of which theological education is the science.

Ars gratia artis. The old Latin motto "Art for art's sake" may be understood in two ways. It may mean that the arts are pure sciences that do not have to justify their place beyond the fact of their existence. This imperial definition would exclude any conversation about the application or function of arts.

In the imperial interpretation the arts have no specific purpose beyond the expression of beauty. This view promotes an understanding of the arts as "high culture," unrelated to spirituality. Such an approach creates a gulf between the world of high culture and the world of popular religion. This dichotomy is particularly evident among certain Protestant groups, which view the arts as worldly, outside the realm of true religion. While much Protestant protest was historically and contextually necessary, Protestantism often failed to create its own artistic understanding of worship. Thus it promoted an approach to art more characteristic of the Enlightenment, an imperial view in which art is divorced from the context of worship, thereby requiring its own separate spheres—museums, exhibitions, concert halls. Church is for the practice of religion while museums are for the practice of art. Hence museums and concert halls have become the churches of a secular society while church buildings have become barren, artistically deprived places. It is a deplorable fact that many modern Protestant houses of worship are designed and decorated by secular professionals who have little theological awareness and limited appreciation of Christian symbols.

This situation can be corrected in three ways: (1) by a discriminating and informed use of classical Christian art, (2) by research for and information about the body of Protestant artistic expression that does exist, and (3) by a conscious, intentional affirmation of those contemporary Christian arts that are both ecumenical in theological outlook and professional in quality.

The imperial view of art for art's sake is a product of a Protestant separation of the arts and the context of worship and a product of the Enlightenment. So long as one maintains the imperial approach to the arts, there is no rationale for relating the arts to religion and spirituality.

There is another, more inclusive, interpretation of art for art's sake we could call the "integral understanding." It views art—the arts—as adjunctive in integrating all life experiences. In this perspective, art—the beautiful—becomes a hermeneutical mode for interpreting reality. Just as all communities and individuals require truth and justice as essential ingredients for relating to all of life, so corporate and individual selves require beauty for life relationships. Insightful theological education and healthy Christian spirituality must include elements that aid Christian churches and individuals in interpreting their place in the world. The point is not that art per se makes one a better person. Rather, art is a window for perceiving life itself and for relating to it in a higher dimension of spiritual experience. The integral view of art for art's sake sees the "sake" of art as a vehicle for an enriched and integrated experience of life. In this way art and Christian spirituality are integrally related. Essentially, both pursue common goals. To accomplish this integration, Christian art must be informed by and be an expression of the Christian story. One of the tasks of theological education is to inform the church and its ministry about the Christian story and its meaning. Art for art's sake speaks about both "the message and the situation" in order to complete the hermeneutical circle of education and action.

In performing this task, theological education points out the aesthetic—fitting, appropriate, beautiful—design of God's redemption and creation. The literary merits of scripture are noted, along with theological content. The sweep of church history and the literary expressions of its historical documents are apprehended not only for their truth but also for their beauty. The appropriate structures of the church's educational ministry are designed so as to be congruent with the Christian story. Ethical decisions and principles are selected because of their appropriateness—aesthetic—for the divine intentions for life. It is in these areas that theological education, Christian spirituality, and the arts interact and intersect.

That the people of God . . . The most explicit biblical reference to the inspiration of scripture is 2 Timothy 3:16–17. It reads, "All scripture is given by inspiration of God, and is profitable for doctrine, for reproof, for correction, for instruction in righteousness: That the man of God may be perfect, thoroughly furnished unto all good works" (KJV). It is a travesty of interpretation that modern theological discussions have dealt largely with verse 16 and ignored verse 17. The rationale for inspired scripture is "that the man [people] of God may be perfect, thoroughly furnished unto all good works." (The King

James Version in this instance is an accurate and aesthetic rendering.) Aesthetic theology must be ethical theology and ethical theology must be aesthetic theology, thus embodying the fitting, the proper, and the appropriate. Ethical theology should be concerned about good works. Good works in the church must take into account Christian social ministries. In this matrix Christian spirituality, theological education, and the arts are interwoven. This interweaving of adequate Christian spirituality involves:

1. Understanding salvation as a matter of gratitude, not guilt
2. Taking a realistic view of the human community
3. Realizing that Christology involves incarnation and declaration
4. Acknowledging the church as a redemptive community concerned with social adjustment
5. Being aware that the community of faith is an embodiment of vision and a working for the wholeness of society[4]

In an integrated theological curriculum, ethics, Christian social ministries, and aesthetic concerns are equally a part of Christian spirituality.

"In the beauty of holiness." Seldom in scripture is a thing said three times. But the injunction to worship the Lord in the beauty of holiness is found in 1 Chronicles 16:29, in Psalm 29:2, and in Psalm 96:9. Christian exegesis has placed greater emphasis on defining holiness than on defining beauty. In its definition of holiness, Christian exegesis has largely limited holiness to morality and moral conventions. Without denying that holiness includes morality, it must not be limited to morality.[5]

Moreover, it is a mistake to place all exegetical effort on defining holiness and none in explaining beauty. Holiness and beauty are coeval (equal). In the Old Testament the word "holy" (*kol*) means to be cut off, to be separate, to be set apart. The appropriate response to holiness is awe or wonder. Ours is an egalitarian age where there are no mysteries that cannot be solved. In the biblical worldview and in primitive societies mystery was a basic ingredient of faith. Mystery was that which defied explanation. Mystery was an intrinsic part of holiness. Holiness involved morality and legal sanctions, cultic rules and ritual obligations, but there was also a surplus of meaning about holiness. The surplus of meaning[6] involved in holiness was mystery. We believe that the experience of the holy involving mystery and the aesthetic experience involving awe are coeval. These categories are not only psychological and experiential, they are also essential and constituent.

However differently they may be perceived in various cultures and among individuals, holiness and beauty are substantially related. Artistic expositions of the cross/resurrection event may prove to be the most effective means of expressing the Christian message across cultural barriers. Cultural barriers fall frequently in the modern world. The interpenetration of the world's cultures has not lessened the level of evil and ugliness. Pluralism and the influx of other cultural expressions have threatened the traditional in every culture, striking bonfires of reaction often fueled by the arts. It is easier to burn a book than an idea, a film or a fashion than a philosophy. An easy next step is to regard all books, films, paintings, sculptures, and icons as suspect, even if they appear to bear some of the mark of orthodoxy. After all, if Marshall McLuhan was right, the medium *is* the message. Far more difficult than suppressing a film with a mistaken spiritual viewpoint is making a film to compete effectively in the artistic marketplace. Yet if we abdicate the arts to those with a limited notion of spirituality, we ensure the propagation of such viewpoints among a population in confused pursuit of the awe-inspiring and the beautiful. It is imperative that we educate artists theologically.

In a theological curriculum this is translated into adequate courses and studies in worship, music, drama, communications, and the visual arts. Such a curriculum for the study of religion and the arts should:

1. Articulate the aesthetic implications of Christian theology and ministry
2. Integrate the arts and theological education
3. Serve as a resource center for artistic expressions of faith: music, communication, archaeology, drama, oratory, literature, and visual arts
4. Elicit and enhance the artistic gifts of the seminary community
5. Assist ministers and churches in applying the arts in all areas of Christian ministry

In this formal way we strive to bring needed emphasis in spirituality by teaching the skills and enhancing the sensibilities needful in spirituality. We are enormously concerned about the beauty of holiness, both as it pertains to the corporate life of the seminary community and to the spiritual experiences of the individual.

Conclusion

There are many ways in which the visual arts can enhance the worship and work of the church. The beauty of holiness can be enhanced by the beauty of human creativity. Those in ministry can use the following practical suggestions to enlarge the awareness of beauty, to make use of the talents and creativity of the arts in ministry, and to recognize the gifts and abilities of the congregation.

1. Ask the preaching minister to give a message on beauty from such biblical passages as Genesis 1; Job 40:10; Psalms 8; 19; 29:2; 96:9; and 110:3.
2. Take a survey of the abilities of the congregation in such areas as music, creative writing, drama, clowning, puppetry, painting, and crafts.
3. Make the results of this survey available to those who plan the worship services and request that they use these talents in the church service.
4. Form a committee on the arts in each church to correlate the talents and presentation of the artistic gifts of the congregation.
5. Sponsor a festival of the arts. This could be done around a sacred season of the church year such as Advent.
6. Ask gifted persons in the congregation or the community to teach classes in their artistic specialty.
7. Organize performing teams in such areas as drama, mime, and puppetry that would be available for presentations in ministry situations in worship and in ministry opportunities in the community. Senior citizens enjoy puppetry no less than children.
8. Relate your concerns with the arts in the church to the broader community of the arts in your location. A senior citizens' trip to a particular art exhibit in a metropolitan area and a subsequent discussion of the spiritual implications of the exhibit would be a grand idea.
9. Enlarge and educate the congregation as to the scope and use of art in ministry. Art is not just painting. There are the culinary art of cooking, the naturalist arts of gardening and flower arranging, the artistic ability of crafts and useful construction. We use art (a skill) in a variety of ways that we do not recognize as art and classify only under the burdensome title of work. Art is work, hard work, careful skillful work, enjoyable work.
10. From the most modest circumstances of worship to the grandest cathedrals, there is one artistic expression that

can and ought to be practiced in every worshiping place, and that is the art of cleanliness that keeps places in appropriate circumstances for worship. Perhaps you have never considered cleanliness as an art; but it is!

Relating religion and the arts helps to define spirituality. It also helps to apply good theological insights in all major artistic modes and means. As Christians, it is our purpose to ensure that the classical virtue of beauty will join with truth and goodness to promote the theological virtues of faith, hope, and love.

BIBLIOGRAPHY FOR CHAPTER 6

Balthasar, Hans Urs von. *The Glory of the Lord: A Theological Aesthetics.* Vol. 1: *Seeing the Form,* ed. Joseph Fessio and John Riches, tr. Erasmo Leiva-Merikakis; vol. 2: *Studies in Theological Style/Clerical Styles,* ed. Joseph Fessio and John Riches, tr. Andrew Louth, Francis McDonagh, and Brian McNeil; vol. 3: *Studies in Theological Style/Lay Styles,* ed. John John Riches, tr. Andrew Louth, John Saward, Martin Simon, and Rowan Williams. San Francisco: Ignatius Press, 1982, 1984, 1986.

Barth, Karl. *Church Dogmatics* III/2, *The Doctrine of Creation.* Ed. G. W. Bromiley and Thomas F. Torrance, tr. G. W. Bromiley, R. J. Ehrlich, et al. Edinburgh: T. & T. Clark, 1958.

Dillenberger, Jane. *Style and Content in Christian Art.* New York: Abingdon Press, 1965.

Dillenberger, John. *A Theology of Artistic Sensibilities: The Visual Arts and the Church.* New York: Crossroad Publishing Co., 1986.

Harris, William F. *The Basic Patterns of Plot.* Norman, Okla.: University of Oklahoma Press, 1959.

Moltmann, Jürgen. *The Theology of Hope: On the Ground and the Implications of a Christian Eschatology.* Tr. James W. Leitch. New York: Harper & Row, 1967.

PART TWO

Communal Dimensions of Spiritual Formation

7

Learning Environments and Spiritual Formation

C. Anne Davis and John D. Hendrix

In the book *The Educational Imagination,* Elliot Eisner says that every institution teaches both an explicit and an implicit curriculum.[1] The explicit curriculum refers to what is consciously taught and verbally addressed. In contrast, the implicit curriculum is less obvious but is still powerfully present in the environment and atmosphere of the learning setting. The implicit curriculum refers to what is really going on in the forms, patterns, and organization of the environment. It centers not so much on what is taught as on the environment of the teaching and learning setting.

The environment is the context or the situation in which spiritual formation takes place. Environments either enhance and encourage or impede or frustrate. They speak to us of places, settings, and situations. The setting may be a classroom, but the effect of the environment is also seen in families, workplaces, churches, retreat settings, and mission enterprises. Much of the environment has to do with the physical setting—chairs, walls, floors, room temperatures—but it also has to do with social, political, and economic factors.

One might compare learning settings to the design of houses. The way space in a house is shaped and partitioned can be called the house's structure or design. This structure influences how people in the house normally interact with one another. For example, if all the rooms are small and closed off, it is difficult for a lot of people to move around and interact easily. Conversely, if the house is wide open, it is difficult for individuals to find privacy. Structures influence certain types of behavior, but they do not guarantee or prevent specific behaviors. For example, we know of instances where good experiences have occurred in small places; we also know of instances where ideal structural conditions have not produced positive family relationships.

Form Giving

Spiritual formation has to do with giving form to processes. It provides a perspective by which we grasp and stabilize that which shapes our experiences. This form giving influences what we see and the meanings we draw from our perspectives. The environment leads an individual to see, feel, and believe certain things. It powerfully influences certain patterns of behavior. In brief, the environment consists of those conditions that promote and stimulate or hinder and inhibit the characteristic activities of a living being.

Form giving has to do with the assumptions we make about space. This learning space may be anywhere people meet together for spiritual formation. It powerfully influences the way we think, feel, and discover meaning. The old dictum is true: "We shape our buildings; thereafter they shape us." In other words, architectural forms are allowed to restrict and determine boundaries of our involvement. Fixed space becomes a way of predicting and controlling the activities of people. Unconsciously we let our surrounding define what we are going to do. But the setting is often unhelpful and detrimental to what our purposes are. Formation is a very fluid process, whereas settings are often locked in place. Needs and settings hardly ever have a good fit, since our needs change faster than our settings.

One might feel that there are more important things to be concerned with than the arrangement of space. But some issues in spiritual formation cannot be shaped unless this issue is settled. Perhaps the confusion surrounding spiritual formation and direction is directly related to assumptions we have made about space. A people in the process of spiritual formation are in motion. Strength is found in the performance of all the people and validates itself in the process of building communities. Many learning settings are designed for private experience—settle in, sit, and listen. Biblical images show a people energized by spirit and in motion, with a sense of being called forth and on the way.

Setting Up the Environment

The task of setting up environments involves the language of teaching and learning. Those who know the language are involved in the detailed drudgery of connecting materials and processes with personalities. They are concerned with the way materials and personalities interact in a particular teaching repertoire. This includes an understanding of the different levels of a person's involvement with the various materials and the discovery of the limitations and capacities of that material. It includes the placing of table and chairs as if one were preparing a stage setting. There is a planned balance between control and freedom, between preparation and flexibility. Setting up the environment has a much more dynamic nature than stating goals, listening to materials, sequencing materials, and programming responses. It involves creating a visual picture of "meaning-full" space. Mary Tully describes setting up the environment in this way:

> By preparation I mean, in the first instance, previsualization. I previsualize. I see ahead of time what the hall, what the students, what the material may be like. I find myself summoning resources, thinking through sequences of events, such as the gestures of a model. I do not see the outcome, but I do see the situation as in a film. And as I previsualize I start preparing, and previsualization and preparation go along in concert. Simultaneously, like a director and a stage designer working together.
>
> In other words, preparation does not mean inflexibility and an ordered structure superimposed on the learner. It means setting up an environment which stimulates—which appeals to the senses and intuition, and which evokes the imagination.[2]

The atmosphere of a learning space contains many elements—thoughts, feelings, sense perceptions, and imagery. The content of the environment is available for examination. This includes an awareness of interior experiences as well as a perception of what is present and what is absent in the external environment. This kind of sensitivity is not fully teachable but grows out of being in touch with inner experience. Parker Palmer's definition of a teaching space is a classic description of the need to give attention to environments. "To teach is to create a space in which obedience to truth is practiced."[3] For Palmer, a learning space has three major characteristics: openness, boundaries, and an air of hospitality. We will concentrate our attention on space and boundaries.

Learning Space

One of the fascinations with teaching comes with using the boxlike arrangements of the classroom in creative ways. Dramatic space can be seen as a stage, and stages are like classrooms—similar in size and shape. Most stages are square or rectangular, with structures comparable to the proportions of a standard classroom. Even the performance arena and its arrangement are similar. There is an area for the main performance and an area to watch or observe.

Dramatic settings have space and boundaries that determine the type of performance. A lecture or presentation is much like the solo artist, with the boundaries marked off by desks, lectern, and blackboard. When the teacher becomes a conductor or facilitator of the performance, the setting has changed into a stage or a rehearsal hall. Although the settings may vary in size and shape, there are usually two identifying characteristics. There is a seeing area reserved for an audience to watch and listen, an auditorium. And there is the stage itself where the performance happens, often set off by being properly elevated. An invisible line—psychological, emotional, and dramatic—separates the audience from the performer.

This invisible line becomes a crucial dynamic in a setting that fosters spiritual formation—a call to form, to re-create a space. How is this boxlike area transformed into a believable representation of real life? The environmental change does not need to be elaborate. The easiest way to change environments is with media. But there is a danger of changing a classroom to a junkyard of detractors.

Teaching and learning occur best within an environment in which maximum involvement by both teacher and student occurs, where the whole classroom becomes a stage of shared activity. In such common participation the teacher is a learner, and the learner, often without knowing it, is a teacher. The less consciousness there is, on either side, of distinct roles of giving or receiving instruction, the better. Creating this kind of environment is thus done through an atmosphere of playfulness. If learning is encounter, play allows people to practice the art of encounter in a pleasant and safe context. Play is a way to practice opening the mind and heart for the real meetings with others. Meeting people different from us in the playful environment can open up authentic interchange rather than the old games of patronizing and posturing.

Play, rather than being infantile, facilitates a more sophisticated form of communication that integrates many levels of meaning. It offers a better understanding of the many frames of reference involved in conflict situations. It promotes rapid and fluid communicative feedback. It operates as a natural and enjoyable way of learning. In a playful environment the teacher seeks to give people learning opportunities, provides a warm supportive atmosphere, keeps groups small so that everyone can play, and continually eliminates judgment, competitiveness, and psychologizing.

This spontaneous dramatic environment is seen in the spirit of the new games movement.[4] Characteristic of the new games movement—and making it a powerful environment—are hospitality, good humor, and a willingness to try things. There is a great deal of involvement in a warm, casual atmosphere. There is support for one another in the face of the unexpected interpersonal confusion. There are engagement and celebration of friendship and cooperation. In this kind of atmosphere the teacher serves as a catalyst—dissecting, probing, and analyzing. The teacher is much like an orchestra conductor, who can be seen pleading, cajoling, demanding, demonstrating, clowning, ranting, and raving, encouraging freedom of individual expression and at the same time restricting this freedom in corporate endeavor.

The other extreme in an open environment is silence. Silence is multifaceted, multilayered, and richly textured. Sometimes silence is the only way to bring energy back into the environment—a process of emptying space of all the clutter and distracting elements.

Contemplative silence brings us into mystery, a sense of awe of where we are, who is present, and what is really going on. Silence becomes powerfully creative and opens our hearts to be more receptive to others. In the silence of the quiet room comes the power to think for oneself and to be receptive to oneself. In hearing silence, one hears the inner voices of care-filled listening, deep reflecting, and heightened awareness. Many of the themes of spiritual formation are developed through personal and communal silence.

The processes of listening to silence are profoundly simple. The room where you are reading will serve this purpose. Sit quietly and ask the room about itself, its history and its story. What are the most profound things that have happened in it or around it? When and how was it built, and how many people have been in it? What kinds of secrets does it hold? What stories would it tell? What does the room wish to tell you? Concentrate on one small object in the room and study it. What finally emerges in the room as a point of focus? Sit quietly and wait for the answers.

There are other ways to create an open space. Stories, dreams, prayers, songs, meditations, and activities that create self-awareness can all be used in creating openness. Openness comes from a listening spirit and a willingness to be vulnerable. Vulnerability is a susceptibility to being wounded and is the opposite of defensiveness. In vulnerability we take emotional risks. There is a willingness to be hurt, lose face, and respond with eyes open, arms open, and heart open. All of this creates a milieu, an environment, and brings about the distinction between thinking about and being in a situation.

Boundaries

Once a week (sometimes more and sometimes less), I go into an empty room with no windows and only a small door at one end. There is nothing in the room and nothing on the walls—a bare room. For an hour or more this bare room calls for all my skill, ingenuity, and energy; and most times I leave the room exhausted and exhilarated. The room is called a racquetball court. It illustrates again the two essential aspects of learning environments—space and boundaries. The good teachers in our lives create both space and boundaries. They give us room to explore but put frames around our explorations so we are able to focus attention. In other words, they help us pay attention to the world and all that dwells therein and also pay attention to ourselves and all that dwells therein. They do that by creating a space and building a boundary around it. They provide a structure for us to learn from our involvement with the environment.

Boundaries do not limit our search, but they do frame our search so we become aware of certain things. Otherwise, we might not give some very important truths a second thought. Boundaries are reminders of everything that distracts and makes possible a second thought. They urge us to look again. Boundaries call us to pay attention.

Boundaries do not necessarily change the environment, but they do change our way of perceiving it. We are called on to give our attention to people, temperature, light and darkness, color, windows, scratches on the wall, venetian blinds, chalk dust, and scraps on the floor.

Take another moment to stop, look, and listen. Listen to your own heart beating, the tremble in a voice, the pauses, the silences between sounds, the voices outside the room, the hissing through air conditioning or heating vents, the creak of your chair or desk. These are ways of becoming more conscious of boundaries.

Until very recently teachers were admonished to teach toward a single objective. But this concept is being questioned by many who are involved in teaching today. This is particularly true in a concept of spiritual formation. Teaching toward a single objective would be similar to telling a doctor to pay attention only to the way incisions are made during an operation or telling a football quarterback to pay attention only to the behavior of linebackers. To be involved in spiritual formation, we must learn how to read complex environmental situations so that a number of objectives and activities can be accomplished simultaneously. Interpersonal and group skills can be communicated right along with academic content with little additional time required.

A Theoretical Framework for Assessing Social Climates of Learning Environments

Before the 1960s little attention was given to the study of interactional outcomes of persons and environments as an important aspect of understanding human behavior.[5] Benjamin Bloom explained this lack of attention as owing to the fact that there were no instruments available with which to measure these effects.[6] The absence of measuring the effects of environments resulted from a lack of conceptual frameworks to guide a systematic analysis of social environments.[7]

While serious attention has been given to the study of social environments during the last thirty years, Rudolf H. Moos is the only person who has developed a comprehensive set of measures for use in assessing a variety of social climates based on empirical research.

Environments and Social Climates

Social environments are defined as "combinations of people, their interactions and transactions in particular geographic, socially defined and constructed spaces over particular periods of time both in the individual's and family's life and in the life of social and cultural systems."[8]

Social climates are usually thought of as clusters or selected pieces of this general definition of a social environment, usually limited to a group setting in which a limited number of people have gathered voluntarily for an explicit purpose. For example, several adults decide to meet for Bible study. The interactions and transactions of these adults within the time and space of the group create a social climate. The social climate that is created will either hinder or facilitate the group's Bible study goal.

Selected features of the general environment of groups, such as (1) physical features of the building and room arrangements,

(2) organizational policies of the setting about what can and cannot be done, (3) the characteristics of the teacher or whether or not there is a designated teacher, and (4) the collective characteristics and styles of the participants have been discussed. However, the impact of these factors on the participants of the group seems to be mediated through the social climate[9]—that is to say, the social climate of a group has the direct influence while the other environmental factors have impact only after having been put through the sieve of the social climate.

If social climates are indeed mediators of the impact of learning environments, they can have either positive or negative effects on intended learning goals. The only way to know which effects are at work is to assess the social climate of the learning environment.

Moos Social Climate Scales

In 1974, Rudolf Moos developed a way to measure the social climates of environments. Early in his work Moos discovered that three basic subdivisions seem to exist in most environments. These were: (1) those elements concerning relationships among people, (2) those items relating to personal growth and development of people, and (3) those elements involving the maintenance of and changes in the systems within the environment.[10] In other words, the social climate of an environment can be understood and measured by looking at the relationships that exist among people in the environment, the personal growth and development that take place in the people who experience the environment, and the changes within and activities designed to maintain the environment as the participants pursue their goals and intentions.

With these three dimensions identified, Moos went on to develop scales for each dimension that could be used to assess the social climate of families, workplaces, classrooms, groups, and other environmental settings.

Moos's social climate scales are based on two assumptions: (1) that the consensus of the individuals' perception of their environment constitutes a measure of social climate, and (2) that environments have personalities just as people do, and if one can be measured, so can the other.[11] The first of these assumptions is the more important for the purpose of this chapter. Moos believed that the social climate of consequence was the social climate as perceived by the individuals who experienced it. For example, if we wanted to know the social climate of the adult Bible study group, we would have to have a systematic means of gathering a consensus of the opinions of the members of the group. On the other hand, according to Moos's assumption, we would not want to rely on the teacher's opinion as to the nature of the social climate of the Bible study group.

The second assumption Moos makes is that the social climate of a setting can be viewed as having a personality. Since many instruments were available to measure personality, Moos believed that these same kinds of measures could be used as models for developing social climate scales.

Social Climate and Adult Education

Four years after Moos had published his initial work on social climate scales, Malcolm Knowles published his now-famous book *The Adult Learner: A Neglected Species* (1978). Relying heavily on ecological psychology, the work of cognitive theorists, and studies on environment, Knowles brought the importance of building an educational environment to the attention of educators in a new way. It was an idea whose time had come.

Knowles's definition of an effective adult educational environment was one characterized by (1) respect for the individual, (2) shared decision-making, (3) freedom of expression and availability of information, and (4) mutuality of responsibility in defining goals, planning, and conducting education activities.[12] This definition contains elements of Moos's Group Environment Scale.

Knowles's writing gained great popularity among educators and quickly struck a cord with those who had long held strong commitments to the tenets of progressive education. Departments of education in universities began to place more emphasis on preparing teachers to create learning climates in classrooms for all age groups. In other settings, education groups expressed increased interest in the role of the social climate in developing learning potential.

By the early 1980s, creating a learning climate had become a significant piece of the educational scene. As Knowles and others had suggested, giving consideration to the social climate is now considered an essential part of the teaching-learning transaction by the vast majority of educators.

Group Environment Scale

Moos's Group Environment Scale, developed to measure the social climate of groups, is most appropriate for assessing the mediating role of the social climate in learning environments and spiritual formation. This social climate scale is divided into three dimensions, with each dimension having several subscales, as follows:

I. *Relationship Dimensions*
   A. Cohesion Subscale measures
      1. The degree of member involvement in and commitment to the group
      2. The degree of concern and friendship members show for each other
   B. Leader Support Subscale measures
      3. The degree of help, concern, and friendship shown by the leader for the members
   C. Expressiveness Subscale measures
      4. The extent to which freedom of action and expression of feelings are encouraged

II. *Personal Growth Dimensions*
   A. Independence Subscale measures
      5. The extent to which the group encourages independent action and expression among members
   B. Task Orientation Subscale measures
      6. The degree of emphasis on practical, concrete, and down-to-earth tasks and on decision-making and training
   C. Self-Discovery Subscale measures
      7. The extent to which the group encourages member revelation and discussion of personal information
   D. Anger and Aggression Subscale measures
      8. The degree to which the group tolerates and encourages open expression of negative feelings and intermember disagreement

III. *System Maintenance and Change Dimensions*
   A. Order and Organization Subscale measures
      9. The degree of formality and structure of the group and the explicitness of group rules and sanctions
   B. Leader Control Subscale measures
      10. The extent to which the tasks of directing the group, making decisions, and enforcing rules are assigned to the leader
   C. Innovation Subscale measures
      11. The extent to which the group facilitates diversity and change in its own functions and activities[13]

Practical Suggestions

Learning environments must be structured to enhance the group's capacity to foster spiritual development. The negative or positive impact of these structures will be mediated through the social climate that the group engenders. Therefore, teachers must give attention both to the structuring of the learning environment and to the building of appropriate social climates to increase the probability of positive spiritual formation outcomes.

To assess social climates, we suggest one of two methods, either the administration of Moos's Group Environment Scale[14] or the application of a self-constructed list of characteristics that can be rated by the participants of the group.

To construct your own list, think of the characteristics identified in Moos's ten subscales, such as self-discovery or expressing negative feelings. Construct a statement from each of the subscales: for example, "In our group people are expected to talk openly about themselves," or "It's all right to express negative feelings in our group." Then ask each member to rate the statement on a scale of zero to five, with five indicating "all the time" and zero meaning "never." The average of the ratings of all the group members on each statement will give a general measure of that aspect of the social climate.

Once a rating has been determined, it will be the responsibility of the group and the teacher to decide if the rated factor facilitates the intention of the group related to spiritual formation or if it is an impediment to the goals of the group. In the first instance, the group and the leader will want to continue to develop in the direction they are now moving. If, on the other hand, this factor of the social climate is a hindrance, the group and the teacher will need to decide on corrective actions to restructure that part of the social climate.

Conclusion

Dorothee Soelle tells of a pious old man in his last years, who was sound in mind but whose speech grew more feeble with each passing day. Finally, he was limited to just one word, uttered repeatedly in a whisper: "Everything, everything, everything." He died with that word on his lips.[15] That is the meaning of learning environments and spiritual formation—giving attention to everything and forgetting nothing and no one.

Formation is a call to stop, look, and listen. "Consider the lilies of the field" is not one of the Ten Commandments, but it is an imperative, calling us to pay attention. For those sensitive to "being in" rather than "talking about," everything in the environment has the power to teach.

8

The Contribution
of Women to Spirituality

Molly T. Marshall-Green and E. Glenn Hinson

This chapter will assess the significant contribution of women to Christian spirituality. Further, it will delineate the particular dimensions of spiritual formation that women articulate and represent. It also attempts to acknowledge the role of women in promoting spirituality, a role long underestimated.

Historical Overview in Christian Tradition

The contribution of women to Christian spirituality has largely been overlooked through centuries of male-dominated history. But this contribution is significant and extensive—indeed, women shaped the directions of Christian spirituality from the early days of the church. Women were prominent in such parachurch movements as Gnosticism and Montanism. These groups maintained a keen interest in spirituality, not simply in intellectual approaches to faith. Women also played prominent roles in more distinctly orthodox segments of the church. If martyrs deserve the paramount place in history accorded them by such scholars as Louis Bouyer,[1] the role of women is particularly important. Many women not only gave up their own lives in martyrdom but also rallied others as martyrs, boldly confessing allegiance to the Christian cause. Women likewise helped to shape both the ascetic tradition that developed on the heels of persecution and the mystical tradition that became prominent in the high Middle Ages. Although their contribution paralleled that made by men, it also differed from and complemented the male approach to spirituality.

Martyrs

Women stand out alongside men among the martyrs of early Christianity who shaped the dimensions of Christian spirituality from the beginning of the church. Martyrs were distinguished by the faithfulness of their witness. According to early martyrologies, women surpassed men in the steadfastness of their faith under threat and torture. At Lyons in A.D. 177, Blandina, a slave whose mistress was also under trial, endured horrible tortures while steadfastly refusing to recant her confession that "I am a Christian." Exposed to the savagery of wild animals, she inspired others with her prayers. The most famous of the martyrs, however, was Vibia Perpetua, a newly married twenty-two-year-old noblewoman, nursing an infant child. Still only a catechumen (or learner), she ignored the anguished pleas and threats of her father. Dragging her to the altar, he commanded, "Perform the sacrifice [to the emperor]! Have pity on your baby!" When the time came for her execution, she refused to dress in the garb of the priestess of Ceres. Obviously a leader of persecuted Christians, she urged others to stand fast, and, when the executioner missed his mark, she drew his trembling hand to her throat. Her companion, Felicitas, eight months pregnant, gave birth to a daughter who was reared by one of the sisters. She too refused to revoke her confession.

Historians cannot give accurate statistics, but there is little doubt that women equaled men in their faithfulness as martyrs. Despite the tendency of ancient documents to overlook women, martyrologies list many by name. Six of the twelve persons martyred at Scillium in North Africa in A.D. 180 were women named specifically. Several martyrologies, besides the one written by Perpetua herself, celebrated the heroic acts of women.

The martyrs laid the groundwork for both ascetic and mystical piety. Although data are limited, the *Martyrdom of Perpetua and Felicitas* hints at a more affective than rational piety, which added strength to the commitment of women in the face of suffering. For women, endurance during torture was not unlike the endurance of pain in childbirth. When Felicitas cried out in anguish as she was giving birth to her child, one of her prison guards chided her. "You suffer so much now—what will you do when you are tossed to the beasts?" She responded, "What I am suffering now, I suffer by myself. But then another will be inside me who will suffer for me, just as I shall be suffering for him."[2]

Monks

We often speak of "desert fathers" when we refer to the early hermits and cenobites in the church, forgetting that there were also "desert mothers" who lived out their faith in spiritual insight and discipline. In fact, women have supplied their share of ascetics and contemplatives from the beginning. Here and there we find evidence of a powerful influence on those who shaped the ascetic and contemplative tradition. This was especially true among those from the wealthy and cultured classes who poured into the deserts during the late fourth and early fifth centuries.

Already in the primitive period the churches recognized "orders" of women devoted in special ways to prayer and ministry. In the New Testament, 1 Timothy 5:10 suggests that Christian widows performed acts of charity, extended hospitality to travelers, cared for orphans, nursed the sick, and rendered other ministries. The *Apostolic Canons,* a collection of church rules of early but uncertain date, divided widows into three groups, two to offer intercessory prayer and the other to "watch out for those who are tried by illnesses, ministering well and wisely and reporting to the elders what they need."[3] The third-century *Didascalia,* a Syrian church manual, instructed widows to pray for and anoint the sick. Related to this group were virgins who devoted themselves to prayer and charitable activities. Through virginity women exercised the same freedom of choice as men in the way they committed themselves to the service of God.

Women heard the call to solitude and prayer just as men did during the early centuries of Christian history, and some distinguished themselves as did men, not only for their piety but also for their special insight. Notable here was the saintly Macrina (c. 327–379), elder sister of Basil of Caesarea and Gregory of Nyssa. If we can trust the *Life* written by Gregory, Macrina was the person responsible for nudging virtually her whole family toward the contemplative life. Named after her paternal grandmother, who was martyred during the persecution under Diocletian (304–311), she was schooled in the Holy Scriptures rather than in Homer, the principal pagan primer. Early on, she took up the monastic regimen of reciting the psalms morning, noon, and night. A beautiful young woman, she was much sought after by suitors, and her father arranged a marriage. Unfortunately, the bridegroom-to-be died before they could be married. Macrina refused all subsequent efforts to arrange another engagement. Instead, she attached herself to her mother.

When her father died, she persuaded her mother to give up the ostentatious style of life she had pursued and form a religious community housed on one of the family estates in Cappadocia. The household was established and included the family maids, now treated as equals rather than slaves. Macrina herself became the superior of this women's community patterned after the Pachomian cenobite communities in Egypt. The sisters engaged in constant prayer and hymn singing "throughout the entire day and night" and in the regimen of daily work. When her mother died, Macrina refused her portion of the vast holdings in three different provinces, offering it instead to the church.

Macrina also steered her four brothers toward the contemplative life. Basil (330–379), the next oldest and most distinguished, made the decision first. After receiving the best education both pagan and Christian culture could offer at Caesarea in Cappadocia, Constantinople, and Athens, he visited monasteries in Syria and Egypt, settling as a hermit by the Iris River near Neocaesarea in 358. Here he fashioned the Rule that became the basis for the monastic life in the Eastern churches. Naucratius, the next oldest son, also took up the solitary life at the urging of his sister, but he was killed in a hunting accident while he was trying to capture game for the poor. During this traumatic period, Macrina stabilized the family while their mother was overwhelmed with grief. Another brother, Gregory of Nyssa (c. 330–c. 395), temporarily pursued a career as a rhetorician but then entered a monastery founded by Basil. After her mother's death, Macrina reared the youngest of the ten children, Peter, instructing him in "sacred learning so as not to give him leisure to incline the soul to vanities."[4] He, too, became a solitary, distinguished by his care for the poor.

Another influential ascetic and contemplative group of women was led by a wealthy Roman widow named Marcella, for whom Jerome served as teacher and spiritual guide during his brief stay in the city (382–385) by invitation of Pope Damasus I. Others in the group included Marcella's mother, Albina; her sister Asella; Paula, who followed Jerome to Palestine; and her two daughters, Blesilla and Eustochium. All were cultured, well educated, intelligent, and possessed of an intense desire for spiritual growth. After the early death of her husband, Marcella (325–410) turned her palace on the Aventine Hill into a center for study and asceticism. Jerome praised her highly for her "zeal and faith." When he was in Rome, she constantly badgered him with questions about the scriptures and settled for no easy answers. Instead, Jerome said, she "tested all things and weighed the matter so sagaciously that I perceived I had not a disciple so much as a judge."[5]

Paula (347–404), a mother of five children, dedicated herself at age thirty-three to a life of devotion. As Jerome described her, she excelled in her ascetic regimen. "She mourned and fasted, she was squalid with dirt, her eyes were dim from weeping. For whole nights she would pray to the Lord for mercy, and often the rising of the sun found her still at her prayers. The psalms were her only songs, the Gospel her whole speech, continence her one indulgence, fasting the staple of her life."[6] Soon after Jerome departed for Palestine in August 385, Paula and her daughter Eustochium followed. They visited holy sites, traveled to Egypt to visit hermits, and then returned to Bethlehem to found two monasteries each for monks and nuns. They tried to persuade Marcella to join them,[7] but she remained in Rome and continued to lead her *collegium pietatis* until the city was sacked in 410. When Paula died in 404, Eustochium (370–c. 419) assumed the direction of the monasteries. It was Jerome's letter to her in 384 on the subject of virginity, urging her to take up the life of the Egyptian monks, that led to his expulsion from the city.[8]

Another Roman woman, Melania the Elder (c. 342–c. 410), set the example for this. Widowed at twenty-two, she took up the ascetic life in Rome. In 372 she journeyed to Egypt, where she met and gave gifts to many prominent ascetics. When the prefect of Egypt banished them to Caesarea in Palestine, she followed, supporting them with her vast wealth. Subsequently she built two monasteries on the Mount of Olives, one for women and one for men. Assisted by Rufinus of Aquileia, she lavishly expended her wealth on bishops, monks, and nuns and wielded a considerable influence on Palestinian monasticism. A zealous Origenist, she returned to Italy when the Origenist schism flared in Palestine in 399. Despite efforts of Roman senators and their wives who opposed her asceticism, she persuaded many, including her granddaughter, Melania the Younger, to take up the solitary life. In 408 she fled the advancing Goths by way of Sicily and Africa and returned to Jerusalem. Before she died she disposed of her remaining property and endowed her monastery with it.[9]

Asceticism offered women freedom to act on their own calling. Although excluded from higher orders—ordination—they did not trail behind men at all in pursuit of holiness. Remarkable witness of that is borne by the Spanish abbess or nun Etheria or Egeria, who toured Egypt and the Holy Land between 381 and 384 and recorded rather exact impressions. A woman of high intelligence and keen powers of observation, she described holy sites from Sinai to Jerusalem. In the main portion of her *Pilgrimage* she recorded daily and Sunday services, Epiphany, Holy Week and Easter, and Pentecost as they occurred in Jerusalem at the time. Publication of her account probably influenced the shape of the Western liturgy.[10]

Mystics

Women figured prominently in the development of Christian mystical thought and practice. Although mysticism suffered a setback in the condemnation of Gnosticism and Origenism, it made a comeback in contemplative orders during the Middle Ages. To women must go much credit for the development of a rich tradition of *Brautmystick*, or "bridal mysticism," during the twelfth through the fourteenth centuries.

At the head of this stream stood visionaries such as Hildegard of Bingen (1098–1179) and Elizabeth of Schönau (c. 1129–1164). Hildegard, who became the Abbess of Rupertsberg, near Bingen, began at age forty to record visions she claimed to have experienced since age three. Between 1141 and 1151 she dictated her *Scivias* by permission of Pope Eugenius III (d. 1153). She traveled throughout Germany handing out advice and encouragement. Prelates and princes sought her counsel. Unlike some other visionaries, Hildegard did not experience ecstasies or hallucinations. Rather, like the Old Testament prophets, she felt the normal use of her physical senses suspended and received messages undergirded with biblical citations, especially from the Song of Songs, Paul's letters, and the psalms. No one, she acknowledged, experiences God directly,[11] but only "through the windows of faith."[12] Elizabeth of Schönau's visions were of the ecstatic type. At her confessor's direction she wrote them down. She also wrote a book, *The Ways of God.* Her writings circulated far and wide.

Women mystics received encouragement from Bernard of Clairvaux (1090–1153), the most influential person in the twelfth century and one whose experience fitted the affective mode characteristic of bridal mysticism. Bridal mysticism became prominent first among the Beguines, pious women devoted to prayer and charitable works in the Netherlands. Notable representatives included: Marie d'Oignies (d. 1213), Juliana of Cornillon (d. 1258), Beatrice of Nazareth (d. 1268), and Hadewijch (thirteenth century). At the base of this tradition rested the conviction that God reaches out in love toward those who reach out toward God in love. "What is this light

burden of Love and this sweet tasting yoke?" inquired Hadewijch, reflecting on Jesus' words. The reply:

> It is the noble load of the spirit,
> With which Love touches the loving soul
> And unites it to her with one will
> And with one being, without reversal.
> The depth of desire pours out continually,
> And Love drinks all that outpouring.[13]

Although the Beguines, Hadewijch included, fell under scrutiny
of the Inquisition and suffered persecution alongside the heret-
ical Cathari, they made a decided impact on spirituality during
the thirteenth century.

Among the most creative minds of this fertile period were
the nuns of Helfta, a Benedictine convent near Eisleben. Mechtild of Magdeburg (1207–1282 or 1298), a Beguine, influenced
them with bridal mysticism set forth in her *Flowing Light of the
Godhead*. She also anticipated the *Wesenmystick*, "mysticism
of essence," propounded in the next century by Meister Eck-
hart and his disciples. Mechtild of Magdeburg left her mark on
Mechtild of Hackeborn (c. 1241–1299) and her sister, Gertrude of Hackeborn (1256–1301/2), "Gertrude the Great," Abbess of Helfta, the most famous of the Helfta nuns. The latter,
"offered" to the monastery at age five, did not take the contemplative life seriously until 1285. Thereafter, however, she threw
herself into her vocation with intensity and left a record of her
experiences in her *Legate of Divine Love* and *Exercises*. Pas-
sionate devotion marks the writings of all three. Gertrude attached the greatest importance to "feeling the Beloved in
herself."[14] She played an important role in development of devotion to the Sacred Heart, a practice only lightly touched on
by Bernard of Clairvaux, William of St. Thierry, and other
men but highly developed by the Cistercian nun Lutgarde of
Aywieres (d. 1246).

Bridal mysticism had wide currency in the fourteenth century, the great century for mysticism, among men as well as
women. It was popularized in England by Richard Rolle (c.
1300–1349) and in the Netherlands by Jan van Ruysbroeck
(1293–1381). Once again, however, women distinguished
themselves through the publication of a whole row of "revelations." In England, Julian of Norwich (d. 1442), one of the
most sought after spiritual guides of her day, wrestled profoundly with such theological issues as the atonement. She is
often cited for addressing God or Christ as "our Mother," a
custom extending back as far as the third-century theologian

Clement of Alexandria, but she had a stake in other significant questions as well.[15] On the continent Bridget of Sweden (c. 1303–1373), Adelaide Langmann (d. 1375), and Catherine of Siena (1347–1380) also recorded "revelations." Catherine, a "social mystic,"[16] played a significant role in church reform during her brief life. She was largely responsible for the return of the papacy from Avignon to Rome in 1378, which, unfortunately, resulted in the papal schism.

Teachers of Prayer

No article on the contribution of women to Christian spirituality should conclude without some reference to great teachers of prayer. The example par excellence is Teresa of Avila (1515–1582), the first woman to be recognized (in 1970) as a Doctor of the Church, chiefly for her teaching on prayer. Descended from a distinguished Spanish family, Teresa was educated by Augustinian nuns. In 1535, however, she entered the Carmelite Monastery of the Incarnation at Avila. She did not excel immediately. A serious illness forced her to return home. When she recovered and returned to the monastery, she took a somewhat passive approach to religious life until 1555. Soon after that, she began to receive divine instructions and to experience her first ecstatic trance and vision of Christ. Desiring to pursue the religious life with greater intensity, in 1562 she founded a monastery in which the primitive Carmelite rule would be more strictly observed. In the newly founded convent of St. Joseph she wrote *The Way of Perfection* for her nuns and completed her spiritual autobiography. From 1567 until her death, she labored with the assistance of John of the Cross, her confessor, to establish Discalced Carmelite houses for both men and women throughout Spain.

Teresa enhanced her teaching with a down-to-earthness. In her *Life* and in *The Interior Castle* she employed simple metaphors drawn from Spanish gardens to illustrate levels of prayer, and she gave it her own design. Traditionally most teachers of prayer had followed Hugo of St. Victor (c. 1096–1141) in speaking of three levels—*cogitatio, meditatio,* and *contemplatio.* Teresa listed "four waters" and added "rapture" as a still higher experience. The first, "mental prayer," is like drawing water from a cistern with a rope and bucket. The second, "the prayer of quiet," is like water lifted by a water wheel. The third, a "sleep of the faculties," is like water running through a stream. The fourth, "the prayer of union," is like rain. The higher the level, the less human effort is needed and the more divine grace assists. In spiritual rapture, "the Lord gathers up the soul, just (we might say) as the clouds gather up the vapours from the earth, and raises it up till it is right out of itself . . . and the cloud rises to Heaven and takes the soul with it, and begins to reveal to it things concerning the Kingdom that [God] has prepared for it."[17]

In the sixteenth century, Protestantism short-circuited the opportunities for both women and men in the area of spirituality by closing the monasteries and negating the contemplative vocation. Women continued to make massive contributions to spirituality, as to other areas of church life, but we have difficulty singling out special contributions except among Quakers, "Protestant contemplatives," where Elizabeth Hooten and Margaret Fell played notable roles, and the Shakers, founded by Mother Ann Lee. Fortunately, the ecumenical era that began with Pope John XXIII (d. 1963) has again made it possible for Protestants to consider the contemplative vocation. Ecumenical exchange is generating fresh ideas again.

In contemporary feminist theology, writers of all traditions are returning to the study of women's spirituality. They are focusing on the distinctive experiences of women and the role these play in shaping the unique gestalt of spirituality in women.

Dimensions of Formation

Christian spirituality can be defined as one's response to the mystery of Christ.[18] In relation to God, "it is who we really are, the deepest self, not entirely accessible to our comprehensive self-reflection."[19] One responds, however, out of one's unique personhood, which is either male or female. New attentiveness to sexuality and spirituality is discovering the distinctiveness of male and female spirituality.[20]

We will focus here on the formation of women's spirituality. While one cannot properly think of women as an ethnic or minority group, they have remained a marginalized group in the history of the church. The uniqueness of the spirituality of women, then, must be illumined in order to integrate its contribution into the life of the Christian community more fully. For purposes of clarity, we are distinguishing between women's spirituality and feminine spirituality. The latter is not the exclusive domain of women, although it is primarily the expression of the female experience of life in faith.

Three aspects of women's experience need explication in order to understand the distinctive aspects of women's spirituality. Biological, social, and ecclesiastical experiences affect the spiritual gestalt of women. Indeed, the interdependence of these experiential spheres suggests that spirituality is not simply a privatistic arena involving only a person's interior life in relation to God. One's spiritual life—what makes one a human—has to do with God's question and the human response, according to Abraham Heschel.[21] One's response to God is most clearly seen through one's response to others in the context of God's creation. Spirituality thus is holistic, encompassing all of one's relationships.

The Biological Dimension

A woman's biological life is inextricably bound up with experiences of preparing for, conceiving, birthing, and caring for progeny. Even those women who do not experience childbirth still share in the rhythms of life that make for such a possibility. The receptive and life-bearing role of the female affects her spirituality; this role is both dependent and powerful in character. A woman does not conceive by herself; she is dependent on a male partner. Her power is seen in the nurturing matrix she provides for the bearing of the baby and the self-giving that sustains the child's life.

Accenting the biological dimension, Christian tradition has often cited Mary as the paradigm of female spirituality, holding her up as a passive instrument for God's purpose. She has been no more than a "willing womb" in the minds of many who treated her biological contribution as an isolated aspect of her personhood. Others have approached her in a more holistic way.[22] Some of the more virulent conciliar exchanges have been over the proper delineation of Mary's role in the mystery of Christ's incarnation. Never proclaimed as divine, yet given the appellation "God-bearer" (*theotokos*), Mary has been affirmed by Christians as ingredient in God's salvific purpose. Her powerful yet dependent role is not marked by passivity, however. She experiences a call to God's special service (the Annunciation of Luke 1:26–38), which is strangely akin to Gideon's call (Judg. 6:11–18), as a form-critical reading of these texts discovers. Her vital cooperation with God marks her as a paradigmatic disciple for both men and women.

Perhaps women's spirituality (integrally related to biological distinctiveness) has always been marked more by receptivity to the presence of God than by a battle to submit the will to the controlling other. When we look to male prototypes such as

Jonah, Jacob, Paul, or Luther, a recurring theme is a wrestling match in which one limps away after being subdued. This is not characteristic of women. Much more likely, as countless forebears demonstrate, is the willingness to be dependent on God's purposes, allowing the strength of the weak (according to patriarchal standards) to be God's powerful avenue for redemption.

Such receptivity to God, according to Nancy Ring, "issues in bringing forth new life in oneself and others."[23] This task involves pain, which cannot be avoided. The spirituality of women recognizes the legitimacy of suffering and blends it with hope in the task of reproduction. The travail necessary to bring forth new life could not be undertaken without hope for the future, borne in confidence that God shares the yoke of suffering. Women have intuitively understood the passion of God in ways that Neoplatonic and Aristotelian informed spirituality could not. To be free from all passion is not the mark of divinity for women; it is the legacy of a formulation of transcendence that overly values unrelatedness and impassability.[24]

Further, one must realize the interdependence of all of life—especially that which one carries in her body—to be a God-bearer in the world. While only Mary rightly deserves the name *theotokos,* many other women function as bearers of spiritual life and nurture. It is often said that women carry the faith and pass it on to the next generation.[25]

While motherhood has been exalted as the chief vocational goal for women (with barrenness seen as the sign of God's disfavor), the Holiness Code of the Old Testament proscribes full access to religious activities in the worshiping community because of uncleanness. Such frequent ambivalence toward women stains the pages of scripture. Hence, the biological experiences of menstruation, childbearing, and nursing have been given mixed reviews in the Judeo-Christian tradition. The very activities by which women fulfilled their "God-ordained destiny" rendered them unfit to serve God in the cultic sphere. Women have, accordingly, internalized a deep sense of "sacral unworthiness."[26]

Celibate women pursuing religious vocations have addressed the "shame" of barrenness through their caretaking activities of teaching and ministering to the sick. Nurturing life in these ways has allowed alternate expressions of God-bearing. Indeed, Macrina exercised this component of her vocation by nurturing virtually her whole family toward a life of profound spirituality.[27]

The Social Dimension

The social experience of women, denigrated to secondary status, has also had profound implications for the formation of women's spirituality. Confined to *kinder, kuchen, kirche,* and *kleiden* in most cultures, women have been relegated to the private realms of human concourse. Limited in their access to public power, they have exercised influence through the structures permitted by patriarchy. Characteristics such as silence, docility, cooperation, deference, and dependence have been encouraged in the socialization of women; initiative, resourcefulness, ambition, scholarship, competition, and the like have not. Women have been accorded derivative status through father, husband, son, or the patriarchal ecclesiastical superstructure.

Women have usually been measured by the standard of male normativity. It is not surprising that they have been found deficient, given this pejorative adjudication. A negative assessment of women has been regnant in Western society, mainly owing to the influence of that singular figure, Augustine.[28]

Recent studies have examined the predominant models of human development and their perpetration of the myth of women's inferior nature. The well-known work of Carol Gilligan (*In a Different Voice*) illumines the limitations of the developmental models constructed by Lawrence Kohlberg and Erik Erikson. These limitations result from the androcentric nature of their research and conclusions. Kohlberg describes the most mature level of moral development in terms of a person living according to universal principles of justice and respect for individual rights. Thus the moral imperative is expressed as an injunction to respect the rights of others and to protect from interference the right to life and self-fulfillment. For women, however, the moral imperative emerged as the concern to care, a responsibility to discern and alleviate the world's trouble. This is judged to be immature by the standards of Kohlberg, who prizes independent moral judgment.[29]

Women have always been involved in the struggle for the justice of marginal people—even at the risk of conflict. Self-actualization has been a lesser concern than the well-being of those whom society has victimized. Indeed, many women ascribe the existence of the marginalized to the wielding of "independent moral judgment."

Further, because of the misogyny of the Western cultural tradition, most women have internalized feelings of inferior personhood. Spiritually, this has taken the form of struggling to believe they are worthy or deserving of the grace of God. While the spirituality of men is more characterized by attempts to earn right standing before God, women often shrink from the gracious initiative that takes seriously the dignity of their personhood.

Lack of confidence in the area of vocational discernment plagues women. The difficulty of granting themselves permission to pursue a nontraditional course of study and work serves to reinforce feelings of inadequacy. Notions of personal identity and maturity based on Erikson's theory of the life cycle leave women feeling immature and indecisive. Carol Gilligan notes in the development of men the "sequential ordering of identity and intimacy in the transition from adolescence to adulthood."[30] A woman, on the other hand, defines her identity through relationships of intimacy and care and fears pursuing any goal that would threaten them. Her attentiveness to relationships must be seen as a more mature form of spirituality, rather than denigrated for not being sufficiently self directed.

Identity through intimacy thus shapes women's spirituality. While the tradition of the desert fathers was the ascetic flight to solitude and the abandonment of nurture and care, the spirituality of women has been characterized more by the desire for union with God and others than by surrender to the all-powerful Other who requires self-abasing obedience. Women's spirituality has also resisted the debasement of all that is bodily.[31] (Teresa of Avila is an example of the celebration of one's embodiment; rather than Jerome's rampant imagery of the desert's dryness, she used the imagery of the "four waters" and caring for the garden.) This intimate form of spirituality corresponds to Jesus' concern about friends, not slaves (John 15), and to a picture of God as self-giving rather than a dominating autocrat.

The Ecclesiastical Dimension

Western society—especially the Christian church—is male dominated. Many continue to argue that this is the divine plan of God; others reject it because they cannot reconcile their concepts of a just God with patriarchal hegemony. Sandra Schneiders describes the experience of women in the church as "religious marginalization, exclusion, and subordination."[32]

First of all, women's exclusion from positions of ministry has affected their self-understanding as Christians. Because their gifts and ministries were often ancillary to the real business of the church—namely, the sacramental realm—their sense of sacral unworthiness and their radical dependence on male clergy as the mediators of grace have been their primary experience of church. Prohibited from entering clerical ministry, women have been forced into a permanent second-class status.[33]

Second, one cannot begin to assess the effects of characterizing God in exclusively male terms. Man as the glory of God and woman as the glory of man (1 Cor. 11:7) has described an eternal cosmic hierarchy that always places man closer to (and thus more like) God than woman. Anne Wilson Schaef, in her helpful book *Women's Reality*, concludes that the male is to the female as God is to humankind in the religious mythology of the white male system.[34]

Women and men have, in large measure, internalized this analogy with the result that women often feel compelled to defer to men as they would to God; men, concomitantly, have demanded such subordination to their divinely instituted "headship." This convoluted relatedness has contributed to the abuse of women; many have remained in destructive relationships because "submission of the woman" is what God ordained.

The masculine presentation of God has made women feel a great alienation from God; that Jesus was male (a corroborating scandal of particularity) further distances women from the capacity to participate in divinity. The accent on the male apostolate further disqualifies women from legitimate roles of authority in God's "kingdom." It is little wonder that women and men have had difficulty in seeing women as the appropriate representatives of an exclusively "male" God.

Earlier in the chapter, we mentioned briefly the different reactions of men and women to grace. Similarly, the sexes carry a different sense of guilt. The portrayal of Eve in Christian tradition as the "seductive siren, source of sin"[35] continues to play out its destructive pattern in the lives of many women. Bearing the shadow of sin, much as the scapegoat of the ancient Hebrew atonement ceremonies, women have been viewed as the primary bearers of the curse. Because of the so-called priority in the Edenic fall, women's guilt has been somewhat assuaged but never fully lifted. Thus they are "ever guilty, a nuisance, and can justify themselves only by unrelenting service, continual performance, and lowly self-effacement."[36]

The view of God brandishing the fiery sword, barring reentry into the garden (spoiled by the tricks and artifices of Woman, as Luther put it in *Table Talk*),[37] colors a woman's ability to feel at home in the presence of God. The church has reinforced women's distance from the Holy through all sorts of ecclesiastical disability; yet, as the historical overview reveals, many women have had far-reaching influence through the exercise of their gifts. And many contemporary women are discovering the examples of their ancient sisters and are offering their lives in new ways.

It is important in the situation of Christ's church today to strive to include and celebrate the distinctive contribution of women's and men's spirituality. All gifts of the Spirit and expressions of Christian devotion are needed to nourish fully the work of God's people in a broken world.

9

Minorities and Spirituality

Donoso Escobar and T. Vaughn Walker

In *We Drink from Our Own Wells,* Gustavo Gutiérrez gives expression to the spiritual pilgrimage of minorities in the world. This is to say that, intentionally or unintentionally, Gutiérrez captures very ably the international, interracial, and cross-cultural character of the drama of the oppressed in their journey to the Father. Whether one agrees or disagrees with Gutiérrez's theological conclusions, one cannot escape the force exerted by the expression "drinking from one's own well."[1]

Alienated and denied the joy of celebrating God's gift of life, while forced to experience death, the oppressed of the world challenge Christians toward ecclesial spirituality. For it is among the oppressed that a new spirituality is emerging; one that, transcending individualism and privatization, is characterized by solidarity. Although Gutiérrez is primarily concerned with the Latin American reality, the universality of his concept is found in the fact of *social marginality,* which is the common bond of the world's disenfranchised. We would like to take Gutiérrez's seminal idea and suggest that minority groups, forced by negative socioenvironmental factors, have historically developed their own ways to quench their thirst for God. Unfortunately, oftentimes, part of those negative socioenvironmental factors are promoted and sustained by a significant sector of the community of faith.

A study of each minority group and its journey to the Father is beyond the scope of this chapter. Instead, we will attempt to explore some of the most common difficulties affecting that journey in order to provide some insights for those who have taken seriously the heterogeneous nature of their ministry in a pluralistic society. At the same time we would like to stimulate an increased level of self and church awareness among minority group members interested in spiritual growth.

Minorities and Church Growth

The anthropomorphic richness of the Holy Scriptures at times presents God as a generous entrepreneur (Isa. 55:1; Matt. 13:44–46; Luke 16:1–10) who expects success from his servants as they handle their investments (Matt. 25:14–30). A contextual reading of these passages proposes a reflection beyond the level of hard currency and material assets.

Whether it is spiritual values, personal talents, or material possessions, investment always requires the presence of two factors: something to invest and a place to invest it. Talents provided by God to God's people, all the human potential and material resources that the believer may have, are expected to be invested within the reign through its agent, the church (1 Cor. 14:12). Talent investment in the church fosters spirituality in that it contributes to an increased awareness of God, God's creation, and individual responsibility. There cannot be spiritual growth without talent investment; however, it all begins when the church accepts or avoids a potential member. Thus, when properly promoted and administered, talent investment not only fosters individual spirituality but also produces church growth (Acts 2:44–47; Rom. 12:1–8; 1 Peter 4:10–11); when hindered, deficit occurs (Rev. 3:17–18), at both the individual and church levels.

When one considers church growth and development in a socially heterogeneous community, a multiplicity of variables comes into play: age, gender, education, social status, cultural values, race, and minority group membership, to mention only a few. For a church under these conditions, the difference between growth and stagnation may very well be proportional to its ability and willingness to accept human diversity as a valid ingredient of God's creation. Let us admit, however, that concomitance with the spirit of Christ[2] is more than minority-sensitive worship services. In the United States we constantly face the temptation of treating solidarity with the underprivileged as a residual category. In our market-oriented society it is expedient to cover the walls of social exclusion with the silk of maternalism, paternalism and condescension. We see this happening not only in the secular sphere but in our pulpits, our church educational materials, our educational curriculum, and, yes, even in our prayers.[3] This is not conducive to ecclesial spirituality.

Minorities as Potential Talent Investors

James H. Davis and Woodie W. White,[4] researching the racial transitional church, found that social transition, which traditionally has been limited to the periphery, now permeates suburban areas. Their research suggests that racial transitional churches present specific dilemmas to the pastor and to the laity.[5] One of the greatest difficulties confronting young ministers is the polymorphic nature of human interaction. As a human organization, the church is one of many areas in the world where human interaction takes place. One hopes that all social exchanges that take place in the church are characterized by common goals, mutual trust, and reciprocal benefits. The word "koinonia" suggests the very essence of church life, the importance of the community of faith. In church, the community defines the individual, not vice versa; but then, community is defined by its organizer, Jesus. This is why hermeneutics and exegesis are critical factors at the church level. Ideally, all active participants in church life have surrendered their lives to Christ, and now, through Christ and in Christ, they join their talents to accomplish mutual growth and church expansion. What happens when potential participants exhibit differences based on cultural patterns or ethnic ancestry, physical or mental impairments, or different social, political, or economic backgrounds?

Society at large, the world, tends to respond to these discrepancies with racism, prejudice, sexism, and social discrimination.[6] The church, however, is clearly instructed not to resort to these practices (cf. Matt. 20:26–28; Luke 22:24–26; James 2:1–13). Referring to the black experience, Leon Chestang identifies three conditions that are socially determined and institutionally supported: namely, social injustice, social inconsistency, and personal impotence.[7] We may claim that the church is the only human organization originally designed to crush this tridentate weapon, which victimizes not only African Americans but all minority group members. Social impartiality is mandatory in the church (Eph. 2:19–22; Gal. 3:26–28; 1 John 3:10–17; 4:20). Paul describes the church in terms of a body whose head is Christ—a body in which there is no room for insignificance among individual members (1 Cor. 12:12–27). Ideally, then, the church is open to potential members regardless of socially defined differences. By the same token, the church ideally provides opportunities for development and participation equally to all its members. Otherwise, the church not only fails in its mission but misrepresents its founder.

A desire for membership homogeneity would lead a church to a selective acceptance of new participants; again, this practice would be contrary to the Master's plan. Jesus welcomed the incorporation of socially diverse people into his church even when the daily lives of those individuals exhibited poor social practices and tastes (Matt. 8:28–34); different political views and power (Matt. 8:10–13); social stigma (Luke 17:11–19); or social submission (Matt. 15:21–28). Unfortunately, history indicates that the church has not always been faithful to these commitments.[8] One of the agonizing passages in the American church history of the eighteenth and nineteenth centuries was the debate over the social status of baptized slaves; in the collision of the scriptures and a proslavery mentality, the opinion of the proslavery advocates prevailed. Proslavery churches continued strong and growing. Let us not be deceived, however—numerical growth is not always a good description of church growth.[9]

It seems that, in the economy of God, church development and individual development are coexistent, and true church development is attained when the church makes itself available to all human beings. Then solidarity with the socially marginal is no longer dressed in condescension, for we become one in Christ. Equality is no longer defined with reference to a particular sector of society but with reference to Christ and the unity of the human race. Then, and only then, does the church become a facilitator of spiritual growth for minority group members, rather than the main erector of spiritual and social hurdles.

Minorities and Church Stewardship of Human Resources

The commission of going to all nations places on the church an unavoidable cross-cultural task of international and multiethnic dimensions. For the early church, transition from a Jewish-dominated community to a Gentile-bound outreach program was a painful one. But once ethnocentrism and racism were overcome, Christianity expanded throughout the Roman empire with such impetus that neither political manipulation nor overt persecution was sufficient to stop it. To a great extent, this was because women and men of all social and ethnic backgrounds, and with differing human potential, were being used by the Holy Spirit at different places and in different roles.

In the parable of the vine, Jesus illustrates how his followers are functionally and structurally attached to him. Jesus also stresses the interdependent character of their relationship and the essentiality of this interdependence for individual growth. When the body of Christ, the church, is coerced by dominant groups into social discrimination, the attempted dismemberment produces social marginality. Minority group members, so excluded from participation, find themselves in the position of the bondswoman who, along with her child, is denied a place in the family of God (Gen. 21:8–21). Without diminishing Hagar's pain, the situation of marginal groups within the church of Christ is worsened by the superficial comradeship and the conditional acceptance offered by the dominant group. For those unfortunate marginal Christians, the desert is shaped by a multitude of people whose empty words and conditional love are more abrasive to the spirit than the dunes' sand is to the skin.

This is not the same type of desert voluntarily sought by Thomas Merton.[10] It is a forced wilderness. Minority group members find themselves devoid of biblical koinonia, unable to belong; restricted by paternalism or maternalism, unfulfilled. This type of desert is "sibling-in-the-faith" emptiness. Propelled by this emptiness, minorities develop a sharp ear for the voice of God that says, "He that heareth you heareth me; and he that despiseth you despiseth me; and he that despiseth me despiseth him that sent me" (Luke 10:16, KJV). God's voice is made audible, evident, and tangible in the person of those who boldly choose to identify themselves with the excluded sisters and brothers. A new conception of God emerges, a concept of God descending to the lowest strata of human society in order to elevate the pariah.[11] It produces the type of spirituality envisioned by Jon Sobrino, a spirituality that equips the marginal believer with a spirit of fortitude, of quest for truth, of fidelity, and of holiness.[12] In our own journey, following times when we have been left in the desert, we have come back as stronger believers because a handful of Christian women and men, enfleshing the Word, have dared to meet us in the dunes. Should we then conclude that in order to produce strong Christians we must promote social discrimination within the church? Not unless we want to pervert the mission of the church. What we may conclude, however, is that victims of social injustice within the church shall remain in history as an indictment against the church.

Minority Group Members and Human Access to God

Evidently, Christianity originated in a highly ethnocentric, male-oriented society. Jesus' innovating values and principles oftentimes surprised his followers or clashed with the religious leadership of his day: for example, in denouncing sexual exploitation (Matt. 5:27–30), asserting women's equality with men in God's sight (John 8:1–11), sanctioning women's eligibility to convey the message of salvation to men (John 4:39–40), reaching out to the outcasts of society (Matt. 21:32; Luke 19:1–10), ignoring cultural traditions in behalf of the oppressed (Matt. 12:9–14; John 5:1–18), and validating the religious outcasts (John 9:35–41). When the disciples intentionally placed themselves between Jesus and the socially insignificant, Jesus bypassed their intentions (Matt. 19:13–15; 20:30–34; Luke 7:37–50; 18:35–43). Time and again, in the Gospel's narrative, the caring hand of Jesus stretches over the heads and hearts of his sophisticated followers in order to reach out to the marginal individual. Once face to face with Jesus, the individual is offered full participation in the reign. Empowered by the Master himself, no human agency should dare to interfere (John 10:28).

It is not surprising, then, that Paul, inspired by the Holy Spirit, writes about the undifferentiated importance of the church's members (1 Corinthians 12; Gal. 3:26—4:7). Or that the author of the epistle to the Hebrews insists on a nonhierarchical arrangement in the administration of God's plan within the church. Or that James exhorts his dispersed sisters and brothers to avoid social discrimination (James 2). Or that John envisions the culmination of church history as a gathering of a classless, genderless, raceless multitude of God's children.

The perspective of equal access to God provides the church with a powerful principle to advocate for social justice; even more, it compels the church to exemplify in its own ranks the equal worthiness of all humans. The physically impaired, the socially unfit, the mentally impaired, the culturally distant, the ethnically different, the economically underprivileged, the politically questionable—in Christ we have been declared worthy of God's love and therefore of God's reign. To take spirituality seriously is to celebrate unity and, by tearing down the walls of social separateness, to live and promote the solidarity of the body of Christ.

An African Perspective

In *God of the Oppressed,* James Cone asserts that the black church taught him how to deal with the contradictions of life and provided a way to create meaning in a society not of his own making. The "grace of God" or "the art of survival" continues to be the black church's way of remaining physically alive in a situation of oppression without losing all dignity.[13]

The core of spirituality in minority cultures, but most especially in the African American culture, has focused on the centrality of Jesus Christ as the liberator of the oppressed. In too many instances, mainline churches and denominations have failed to actualize genuine liberation of the oppressed but have instead chosen the traditional mode called religious freedom. J. Deotis Roberts, James Cone, E. Franklin Frazier, and others are correct when they assert that authentic spirituality involves an understanding of the church as that community of and for the abused, neglected, forgotten, rejected, and oppressed.[14] Therefore, the spirituality expressed in the minority church, especially the black church, has always been from the posture of vindication of the poor over against the rich, the weak against the strong, the excluded against the included, and the rejected against the accepted.

Spirituality undoubtedly means a number of different things according to the culture and background of a particular individual. How God's Spirit interacts and intersects with the human spirit surely is a primary emphasis and focus. Richard H. Bell affirms that living in the spirit first involves seeing and facing the many ways in which we forget God in our everyday lives. "It means having courage to suffer the wounds meted out by our world. Beyond these things, living in the spirit is an active disposition—a formation of faith and a practice of gratitude and compassion before God. Spiritual formation and practice come as we remember God and share his presence in us with others."[15]

Gayraud Wilmore asserts that blacks have used Christianity not as it was delivered to them by segregated white churches but as its truth was authenticated to them in the experience of suffering, to reinforce an ingrained religious temperament and to produce an indigenous religion oriented to freedom and human welfare.[16] J. Deotis Roberts feels that much of the emotionalism in black worship is therapeutic. It releases the tension that oppression forces on black people. It is often an aid to psychological health in a racially pathological situation in which black people struggle for sanity.[17] The spirituals of the black church, in addition to their coded meaning as a communication medium for the underground railroad, provided the social-historical-theological context for the worshiping community. Deotis Roberts and Harold Carter[18] both insist that much of the priestly content for black church theology is hidden in the black prayer tradition. "Prayer in the black church unearths the tragic soul life of a suffering race. Prayer reaches into the depths of the human spirit—even to its preconscious level. But prayer is also conscious and potent with meaning for the oppressed."[19]

Those who would propose that the biblical record's assertion that we are to be "one body in Christ" (1 Cor. 12:13) means that there can be only one genuine interpretation of true spirituality need to consider also the very next verse. First Corinthians 12:14 says, "For the body is not one member, but many" (KJV). "Many" affirms that God encourages and supports diversity whenever and wherever it is not mutually exclusive.

The American Lutheran Church, from its Taskforce on Racial Inclusiveness, came to some interesting conclusions and set some ambitious goals. First, they suggest that the church at its best is "a harmonious tapestry of racial and ethnic diversity."

Second, the recommendations assert the possibility that one may become Christian, and therefore be spiritual, while maintaining significant elements of "traditional culture," given that each culture has ways that "reinforce the gospel of love, healing, mercy, and justice," all of which is found in Jesus Christ. The church should incorporate these ways, not abandon them.

Third, the pursuit of racial inclusiveness requires the church to provide, "self-consciously" and equitably, "presence, visibility, and representation" for individuals whose racial minority is "disproportionate to their numbers in the church's membership" until that time when the entire church is more "inclusive in thought and practice."

Fourth, the study concludes: "There are strong correlations among racism, sexism, classism, ageism, handicapism, and other oppressive systems of thought and behavior. The generic sin underlying them all is the sin of exclusion; thus the real issue is one of inclusiveness versus exclusiveness."[20]

The debate over the affirmation of cultural diversity within the church and what is spiritual as well as desirable was a problem in the first-century New Testament church and will continue until Jesus returns for the church. Dearing E. King even goes to the extent to assert that the use of the terms "white church" and "black church" is an obvious admission that

the church has practiced birth control; and in the process, it has become spiritually uncreative and unproductive. In the very nature of the Church of Christ, the purpose of authentic worship [spirituality] is to bring worshipers into a conscious relationship with God and into a spiritual relationship with all believers in

Christ. True worship reaches its highest expression in mutual group sharing.[21]

A definition of spirituality is "sensitivity or attachment to religious values." Minorities, especially those who have been the most excluded from the majority congregations, notably African Americans, want only for the most part full affirmation of the authenticity, value, and worth of their spiritual orientation and practice.

PART THREE

Personal Dimensions of Spirituality

10

The Minister as Spiritual Friend

Edward E. Thornton

When confronting the personal dimensions of spirituality, the first question may be, "So what does all this mean to me?" Perhaps the best response to that inquiry is to identify certain questions about spiritual formation that are often asked by seminarians, pastors, and lay persons. Imagine that you are in my study. Suppose we pull up a couple of chairs in front of the fireplace and give ourselves permission to talk leisurely about some of these issues. As we do, I hope we will put aside our reluctance to concentrate on our inner experience with God.

A Dialogue Between a Seeker and a Guide

SEEKER: Well, mainly I am wondering, What are my next steps toward spiritual formation?

GUIDE: Perhaps you are ready now for a formal process of spiritual direction. You have chosen to read this far in a book on the dimensions of spiritual formation, so I assume you are a genuine seeker after God. You are aware that the basic steps include grounding yourself in the scriptures, developing moral and ethical maturity, and nourishing your spirit in worship and in fellowship within a particular community of faith. Beyond these basic steps, you are aware that both spiritual health and disability are shaped by your family of origin. The primitive God-image that was formed in your preschool years is a powerful force in your spiritual development, and it must be constantly reformed by continuing life experience. At this point the quality of your Christian education becomes crucial. Openness to the varieties of religious experience

in cultural and ethnic communities and through literature, art, music, and drama shape your spiritual formation profoundly. These are important building
blocks that form the launching pad for spiritual direction on the adult stage of the spiritual journey.

SEEKER: I've heard the term, but I don't really know what you
mean by "spiritual direction."

GUIDE: Spiritual direction is a process of consultation, one-
to-one or in small groups, designed to foster spiritual
formation. The term "spiritual" points to a realm
other than the see-touch world of everyday experience. It points to the unseen realm of your inner, private sense of yourself and also to the outer, cosmic
reality of God. "Direction" suggests movement back
and forth between the worlds of your inmost self and
of God. It points to a destination for your spiritual
journey as well. For in spiritual direction you are going somewhere, seeking God, developing a life of faith
and prayer. In short, spiritual formation is growing
toward godlikeness in love; spiritual direction is one
way to enhance the process.

That person with whom you consult on a regular
basis is called a "spiritual director." Such a person
helps you to be attentive to God's presence, discern-
ing the directions in which the Spirit of God is moving in your life and growing in intimacy with God as
you live out the consequences of your relationship
with God.

SEEKER: This feels both inviting and frightening. How does a
spiritual director work?

GUIDE: First, you must remember that the real spiritual director is the Holy Spirit. Only the Spirit of God can accomplish the goals of spiritual formation. A passage
in 1 Corinthians 2:6–13 calls this to our attention:

> Yet among the mature we do impart wisdom, although
> it is not a wisdom of this age or of the rulers of this age,
> who are doomed to pass away. But we impart a secret
> and hidden wisdom of God, which God decreed before
> the ages for our glorification. None of the rulers of this
> age understood this; for if they had, they would not
> have crucified the Lord of glory. But, as it is written,
> "What no eye has seen, nor ear heard,
>   nor the heart of man conceived,
>   what God has prepared for those who love him,"

God has revealed to us through the Spirit. For the Spirit searches everything, even the depths of God. For what person knows a man's thoughts except the spirit of the man which is in him? So also no one comprehends the thoughts of God except the Spirit of God. Now we have received not the spirit of the world, but the Spirit which is from God, that we might understand the gifts bestowed on us by God. And we impart this in words not taught by human wisdom but taught by the Spirit, interpreting spiritual truths to those who possess the Spirit.

A spiritual director is keenly aware that you must develop your own abilities to sense the divine Presence and discern the movement of the Spirit in your own life. No one can or should try to do this for you. Tom Brown gives us a splendid analogy in his book *The Tracker*. Brown is a master woodsman, skilled in tracking animals through the wilds by reading the signs they leave as they move about. The book begins with these words:

> The first track is the end of a string. At the far end a being is moving; a mystery, dropping a hint about itself every so many feet, telling you more about itself until you can almost see it, even before you come to it. The mystery reveals itself slowly, track by track, giving its genealogy early to coax you in. Further on, it will tell you the intimate details of its life and work, until you know the maker of the track like a lifelong friend.[1]

A spiritual director, like the tracker, can help you learn to recognize the tracks of God moving ahead of you, luring you on. A spiritual director dare not do your tracking for you. The mystery of wilderness tracking is like the mystery of living a life: "The mystery leaves itself like a trail of bread crumbs, and by the time your mind has eaten its way to the maker of the tracks, the mystery is inside you, part of you forever." Brown notes that the transformation takes place not in the finding but during the process of the search. "The tracks of every mystery you have ever swallowed move inside your own tracks, shading them slightly or skewing them with nuances that show how much more you have become than what you were before."[2]

SEEKER: I was having negative feelings about the term "director" as soon as you used it, because it sounds like extreme subjection to someone else. Now I am getting even more uneasy because this whole thing seems mystically oriented. Does spiritual direction come out of some kind of mystical cult originally?

GUIDE: The term does sound foreboding, doesn't it? For years I fought against it too. It conjured up the image of a medieval monastery with monks being required to wear hair shirts and practice flagellation. For some years I argued that a term coined in an authoritarian age should not be used today. Next, I tried out Kenneth Leech's term "spiritual friend,"[3] but friendship can turn into a mere social relationship. When that happens, the relationship loses the structure, accountability, and precision in discernment that are necessary if a person is to learn the art of tracking the Spirit of God in the midst of a secular, materialistic, and humanistic age.

Also I tried out the name "spiritual guide." It feels less authoritarian than "director," but it also presumes a superiority to those who are being guided that can be misleading. Furthermore, a lot of progress has been made in redeeming the classic term "spiritual director" from one who gives orders to *one who points a direction.* So I am comfortable with spiritual director now, knowing that I must take pains to clarify its meaning in each new relationship and that the true meaning can come clear only as I embody both the discipline and the friendship of such a companion or tracker on the spiritual journey.

GUIDE: Now let us turn to your concern that there is something bizarre about spiritual direction—"mystical and cultlike," I think you said.

SEEKER: Mystical, yes. Cultlike, no.

GUIDE: Jesus corrected a primitive God-image held by the woman of Samaria, saying, "God is spirit, and those who worship him must worship in spirit and truth" (John 4:24). The worship of God is a mystical act, an act linking our spirits with the Spirit of God. Prayer is a venture into mysticism. The search for God is a mystical quest. Finding God or being found by God is mystical experience.

As for cults, nothing could be more alien to the Christian tradition of spiritual formation and the function of spiritual directors. The earliest writings we have about Christian spirituality outside of the Bible are the writings of the spiritual directors of the fifth and sixth centuries.[4] They are writing to young men and women who are in training for the religious life. The contents include interpretations of scripture and exhortations about morals and ethics but are concerned primarily with the practice of interior prayer, or what the writers call "the prayer of the heart." The prayer of the heart is at the center of spiritual formation in the early church. It flourished during the Middle Ages within monasticism. With the Reformation, our Puritan forebears attempted to incorporate monastic spirituality into the corporate life of the family and the churches. The early church fathers and mothers suggest that the tradition was from the apostles, who received it from the Lord. Far from being a fringe or fad movement, spiritual direction, focused on the discipline of interior prayer, is in the mainstream of Christian spirituality.

SEEKER: Well, that interpretation raises even more questions for me. But first I need to know what you mean by the prayer of the heart.

GUIDE: There are three forms of prayer: verbal prayer, mental prayer, and interior prayer. Everybody is acquainted with verbal prayer. It is done in public worship, as a blessing at meals, and the like. It is conscious, and it relies on spoken words. It has its place, but it is a limited place. It captures the feelings of the group and helps to focus them toward God.

Mental prayer is done silently by subvocalizing words. You are consciously thinking words and composing sentences in your mind. Most people who pray rely on mental prayers. Mental prayers have a certain range of usefulness as well. The difference between these types of prayers is not between good and bad; it is between powers and limits. Certain things can be accomplished with one form that cannot be done with another. Mental prayer can heighten your conscious awareness of needs and reinforce your faith. I believe, however, that "answers" to prayer are rather limited with the use of mental prayer.

Until recently interior prayer has been largely forgotten in mainline Protestant denominations. The Quakers maintained the discipline of silence as a way into communion with God, but insofar as rationalism and science shaped the cultural religions of Western Europe and America in the twentieth century, the discipline of interior prayer faded away.

Interior prayer is not the same as verbal or mental prayer. It is different in its method and in its results. Communication between you and God occurs at a deep level, a level right on the edge of ordinary consciousness. You can speak of it as an alternate state of consciousness. You have a strong sense during interior prayer that the Spirit of God is praying through you, using you to pray the prayers that empower the work of the Holy Spirit in the world. Thus interior prayer often becomes intercessory prayer, though it may simply be pure joy or adoration, thanksgiving, or genuine confession, penitence, and cleansing.

SEEKER: You l p raising more questions with every word. I am going to return to my skepticism soon, but right now I've got to know what kind of answers to prayer you are alluding to in using the term "prayer of the heart."

GUIDE: Let me document some of the outcomes of interior prayer that I observed while leading retreats and ongoing groups learning the prayer of the heart.

1. The first result of interior prayer is that people leave the prayer experience more relaxed than when they entered it. That is about the only thing I can guarantee to folks when they are in a prayer-of-the-heart retreat. They leave more refreshed and spontaneous, more awake to their inner selves. As you continue to give yourself to interior prayer, you gain ability to experience deep relaxation at will, any time, anywhere.

2. A second outcome is that people develop the ability for centering. Centering is a word that comes primarily from the experience. It means concentrating the mind on a single point. As you center the mind in a relaxed body, you enjoy an increased sense of being at peace in your body, more in touch with your feelings. You develop greater capacity for mental concentration. Best of all, you become more accessible to the "still small voice" of God.

3. A third outcome is that people experience the trustworthiness of their intuitive wisdom. You relax your dependency on external authorities for "the an-

swers" as you learn to listen to your inmost self. You discover again and again that the deeper you go into your own subjectivity, the more likely you are to be met by the objective reality of the living God.

4. Fourth, people experience the joy of being connected with others in a deep and profound way. You are often more ready to seek reconciliation with people with whom you are estranged as a result of the journey you are taking.

5. Fifth, many people report health benefits from the regular, joyful practice of interior prayer. These benefits include improved physical health, better mental health, or both. The relaxation aspect of interior prayer fosters optimal organismic functioning, strengthens the immune system, and reduces the ill effects of stress on body and mind alike.

6. Finally, and most important in terms of spiritual formation, people become more willing to be loved by God. What is happening is that you are overcoming the fear of the terrifying aspects of God.

Let me expand on this a bit. God presents God's self with two faces in human experience. You see this clearly in sculptures of the deity in ancient cultures as well as in everyday experience. One face is the face of a God of horror—intimidating, terrifying. The other face is the benevolent, smiling, nurturing face of the God of love.

I find that people who are trapped in their ego selves, who are still locked into the see-touch realm and the inner world of keeping up appearances, are likely to be met by the God with a terrifying face. It is terrifying because it threatens to remove the ego from the throne of life. It threatens to change your center radically from your public image to your inmost self, from status, success, and approval of others to your relationship with the Spirit of Truth who is Christ, the Lord.

So as you travel the journey of spiritual formation, you open your inmost self to the face of God and you see the loving face of Jesus that is described in the gospels. You see with your inner eye that the eye of God is full of delight in you. Your heart leaps up with the courage to accept God's acceptance just as you are. And, of course, the miracle of grace happens again—this time it is happening to you! Best of all, you become more and more willing to be loved, aided, and guided by the living God.

SEEKER: All of this about the prayer of the heart is terribly exciting—almost overwhelming! But it is almost too good to be true. What I want to know is, Why have I never heard about this kind of prayer before? The truth is that I have never known a minister or a teacher to say anything about spiritual direction or interior prayer.

GUIDE: What you say is true for many people, and I find it sad. I have puzzled over this a lot. "Why?" I ask myself. "Why has the ancient Christian wisdom about prayer been so forgotten in the churches, and access to the Power-Source of the Christian life been left to chance discoveries by believers?"

For example, my father was an earnest Christian and a diligent student of the scriptures for the last thirty years of his life. He had become a person of prayer as well. Yet, on his deathbed he told me in a whisper, as if he were imparting a secret that might be considered a heresy, "It is as if there are two realms. When I pray I am in a realm where God is so real and so fully present. But when I am not praying I am in the realm of the ordinary world." At that time I had already discovered the prayer of the heart. Tears came to my eyes. I was glad and sad all at once—glad that my father had stumbled into the mystery and delight of interior prayer before his life was over but sad that, in spite of his having been a missionary, a teacher in a church college, and a devout Christian all his adult life, he had never received so much as a hint that there is a quality of prayer that produces a stable state of God-consciousness, such as he found at the last.

SEEKER: Do you have any hunches as to why?

GUIDE: Yes, I suppose I do. I think that when we are taught that we are spiritual because we "believe correctly," we get oriented to words and ideas and lose sight of the Presence of God toward which the biblical words point.

When we learn that we are secure in God's grace once we are "born again," we neglect the call "to work out [our] salvation with fear and trembling" (Phil. 2:12). An exclusive emphasis on the moment of spiritual birth may lead us to neglect the processes of growth in grace throughout our entire life span. John Bunyan understood that the Christian life is a story of a pilgrim's progress, and it is the "progress" theme that leads us beyond the "milk" of the word to the "solid food" of faith (1 Cor. 3:1–2). When the doctrine of salvation is stressed more than that of sanctification, the quality of the Christian life deteriorates and the empowerment of the Holy Spirit is replaced by willpower. Soon the secrets of the Spirit's empowerment are forgotten as well.

Another factor is the assumption that spiritual growth is nourished best by attending meetings where inspiration is the goal. Inspirational meetings have a place in Christian experience to be sure, but opportunity for sharing personal struggles and victories is rare. As a result we do not learn to trust one another to be channels for the Spirit's guidance in our own lives. In fact, we do not even get comfortable talking about our sacred moments with God in the presence of others. One of the ironies of life in many churches today is that church school classes and small groups of many kinds are the last places in which people risk exposing their inmost selves and their most deeply held religious experiences. In some churches you feel free to talk about such happenings only so long as you use certain "in" words. In others, you can talk about your faith comfortably as long as you hide your doubts and your anger about what seems the absence of God in your life.

Perhaps we have made too much of our advocacy of "the priesthood of all believers," or have been too careless about it. We use this phrase often in the service of extreme individualism, as if our access to God is such a private and exclusive relationship that we can do it alone. The flip side of a Lone Ranger spirituality is that we are accountable to no one, not even to the Spirit of God, who lives and moves most powerfully within the community of faith as it is gathered in earnest prayer. The priesthood of believers needs to be held in one hand and Pentecost in the other. Pentecost is the sign of promise for spiritual empowerment, and Pentecost comes as believers join together, share the deepest longings of their souls, and enable one another through many days of mutual discipline to "pray without ceasing." I suspect you will realize at once that the only form of prayer that may be done without ceasing is interior prayer.

SEEKER: Your mention of Pentecost prompts another concern for me. Is there not some danger that interior prayer and all this concern about spiritual formation will lead people into the charismatic movement?

GUIDE: You are listening well. Yes, the charismatic movement seeks direct experience of God above all else.

Those who are able to relax their need for conscious control of their minds sometimes speak in tongues. The experience of tongues may happen first in public worship and be received as a sign of special blessing by the Holy Spirit. Some call it the second baptism. Soon, however, the tongues experience moves into the private prayer life of the believer and becomes a form of centering prayer. Deep relaxation and a profound sense of being at one with God characterize such prayer. Clearly, the similarities with interior prayer as taught by the early church are strong.

I find that people who practice interior prayer develop bonds of trust and friendship with charismatics, as with others whose spirituality differs from their own. But they do not abandon their own way for that of another. Neither do they hesitate to speak the truth in love when they see dangers in the charismatic way. For example, many devotees of the charismatic movement constantly struggle with the problem of ego inflation and self-righteousness. No group that is serious about spiritual formation can avoid these problems. But charismatics are especially vulnerable because of the dramatic impact of their worship services and the public expression of those spiritual gifts they cultivate and display. Perhaps charismatic and noncharismatic Christians alike would do well to see themselves as brothers and sisters who have grown up in a healthy family but who, as adults, develop quite different ways of living, while at the same time enjoying occasional family get-togethers. For my part, I enjoy family gatherings in which we can discuss our differences— even argue about them—with mutual respect and openness to learn. The Spirit works in such discussions for the enrichment of both parties.

SEEKER: You may not like my next question at all, but in all honesty I must ask it. What about the claim of some sincere preachers that mysticism opens the door for Satan to enter and take over a person's soul?

GUIDE: Every time I hear that question asked, I sense a spirit of fear in the person asking it. So I have begun in recent years to take such persons very seriously and inquire about their experience with meditation, or altered states of consciousness, or mystical prayer—whatever it is on which they are basing their judgment.

Nearly all those with whom I have talked about this issue tell me that they learned to fear such things during a time in their lives before they became Christian. Lured by the enticement of gaining special psychic powers, or simply of trying out a new high, they got involved with a psychic of some kind, and occasionally with occult practitioners as well. They may have combined their exploration of psychic phenomena with drugs and literally had a bad trip and a crash landing. Even without drugs, they may have felt exploited by the guru or group with which they were involved. Never have I talked to a person who, as a mature Christian, was working with a spiritual director, learning the classic disciplines of interior prayer, fasting, and spiritual reading, who has personally felt in danger of being possessed by the Evil One.

What Christians do fear is giving over control of their lives to the Holy Spirit. We fear being required by God to make some sacrifice or some act of surrender involving our work, an important relationship, or the use of time or money. Make no mistake about it—it is a fearful thing to be in the hands of the Living God. Most of us fight long and hard to stay in full ego control of our lives. We do not want to make fools of ourselves in the life of the church anymore than in the life of the world.

A fear-ridden person needs wise and compassionate care. Above all, you need to stand fast in your faith. Remember that when you give yourself to the disciplines of spiritual formation, you are giving yourself to the Spirit of God, who is the Lord! (2 Cor. 3:17). It is Christ into whose hands you commit your spirit, in order that you may be "changed into his likeness from one degree of glory to another" (2 Cor. 3:18). Such fears may be put to rest by praying sincerely, "Lead us not into temptation, but deliver us from evil" (Matt. 6:13).

One passage in the ancient book of Sirach says it all:

But stay constantly with a godly person
  whom you know to be a keeper of the commandments,
whose soul is in accord with your soul,
  and who will sorrow with you if you fail.
And establish the counsel of your own heart,
  for no one is more faithful to you than it is.
For our souls sometimes keep us better informed
  than seven watchmen sitting high on a watchtower.
And besides all this pray to the Most High
  that he may direct your way in truth.

                                    Sirach 37:12–15, adapted

SEEKER: I confess that my skepticism and fears are beginning to be put to rest now. So suppose I decide to enter spiritual direction, how do I find a spiritual director?

GUIDE: Let's divide your question into two parts. I want to suggest some objective criteria. Then we will come to the personal side of the matter.

First, you want to attend to the bedrock of faith. Does your potential director have a solid faith in God, a deep commitment to the truthfulness of scripture, and is he or she at home in the community of faith and its traditions? You need to know these things about your spiritual director at a deep level. The point is not whether or not the person can talk a good line or fill a prestigious religious role, but whether you sense that faith permeates the person's whole life.

Second, look for a growing person and a person of prayer. I put these two features together because growing persons can be open to their inner world, integrating the many fragments of their selfhood, but not yet be facing their religious conflicts. For example, I was serious for years about the Second Commandment: to love my neighbor as myself. But only in a major shaking of my foundations did I awaken to the life of the Spirit and to the First Commandment: to love God with a whole heart.[5] Others may be active in the life of prayer but not genuinely open as growing persons—open to the dark, shadow side of themselves, including mixed motives, angers, sexual needs, and veiled needs to control or to appear important. A prayer life can be pressed into the service of self-deception as well as self-knowledge, surrender to God, and simplicity.

Next, I look for a cluster of qualities that I sum up in the phrase "taking delight in others." I am not pointing to gregarious extroverts necessarily, though they often possess delightful traits. I have in mind those persons who relish God's extravagance in creation: extravagance in the varieties of flowers and birds, rocks and insects, cloud patterns and moods, body types, psychological types, and ways of making meaning out of life. These are people who are genuinely delighted about the growth of persons, open to an infinite variety of patterns by which God may accomplish God's will in people, deeply respectful of each person's uniqueness. A spiritual director who takes delight in others in these terms will enjoy being God's channel in the work of direction, will be relatively free from the need to control the outcome of the Spirit's work in your life, and will give God the glory for whatever God brings to pass through the process.

The only other criterion I would suggest is that a spiritual director be old enough to have experienced conspicuous failures and some of the losses and griefs as well as the healings and hope that test and sustain us in the tides of life.

I do not say that a spiritual director must be gray-haired or even middle-aged. Spiritual directors usually serve you for a time, and then you move on until you come to another critical turning in your life, when you may want to find another guide. After all, Jesus would have qualified in his late twenties or early thirties, right? Some people may be well advised to consider a spiritual director who is close to their own age in early adulthood. Others may need someone near the age of parents or grandparents. It is the qualities of a person, his or her own spirit, that matter in the nurture of your spirit. For this is what spiritual direction is about.

SEEKER: I believe you were going to say something about the actual finding of a spiritual director as well as the criteria.

GUIDE: Oh, yes, indeed. Thank you for reminding me. The answer commonly given by spiritual directors is this:

"When you are ready, your guide will appear." As a casual answer these words are an insult to the questioner. As a call to faith they are true. The core reality in spiritual direction is that "God is at work in you, both to will and to work for his good pleasure" (Phil. 2:13). God who wakens you to the spiritual journey will provide you with guides from time to time as you need them.

The passage from Philippians just cited follows the exhortation, "Work out your salvation with fear and trembling." The question, then, is what is your "work" in finding a spiritual director, other than waiting for your guide to appear? Henri Nouwen notes that while it is true that spiritual guides are hard to find, it is also true that often we do seek out such mentors of the spirit. He writes, "There are many men and women with great spiritual sensitivity whose talents remain dormant because we do not make an appeal to them." Nor do such spiritual directors have to demonstrate greater intelligence or experience than those who look to them. Rather, they accept the invitation to help us draw near to God and to enter "into the scriptures and the silence where God speaks to both of us." Nouwen insists that those who seek after the life of prayer and the meaning of the prayer of the heart also will be able to discover a particular type of guidance and a particular type of spiritual guide. Such guides often "receive the gift to help us and grow with us toward prayer." Thus, Nouwen concludes, "the openness and the honest seeking of the directee are of primary importance to both individuals in a spiritual direction relationship." It is the "openness of the directee that calls forth and creates the power and gifts of the director."[6]

SEEKER: Well, I am just about ready to take the leap of faith into spiritual direction. But I cannot keep from feeling that there may be some cautions that you could point out to me in advance—sort of like some last-minute reminders before starting out on a journey over an unfamiliar route.

GUIDE: You are right. There are a few cautions and pointers I would like to offer.

First, I want to stress again a caution about what I call the "cut root syndrome." By this I mean cutting yourself off from your own faith tradition. It is extremely important as you travel the inner way of spiritual formation that you be integrally, dynamically, and wholeheartedly involved in a tradition that carries the wisdom of the generations who have taken this journey ahead of us.

Second, we should be cautious about going public too soon with teaching about spiritual formation. Seminarians and ministers are especially vulnerable at this point. While ministers should provide guidance in spiritual matters, many find it easy to go beyond their own proven experience in talking with others or in teaching and preaching.

Seminarians often confront the problem of intellectualizing about spirituality. Talk can mask an empty heart as well as an empty head. Early in my teaching career, while conducting a training conference, I was challenged by a military chaplain who remarked, "Thornton, some people use words to reveal thoughts, others to conceal thoughts, but you are using words instead of thoughts." He was right! I have been less prone to intellectualize ever since. I recommend that students wait six or seven years after starting an intentional journey of spiritual formation before going public or seeking to guide others as a spiritual director. The time gap allows us to internalize the inner experience without the contamination of performance anxiety. It allows time for the fruit of the Spirit to ripen.

A major obstacle to spiritual growth is the tendency to make too much work of it. This is also a paradox. The harder we work at it, the less progress we make. The alternative is learning to not-do. You avoid not-doing by relaxing, by not making a performance of our spiritual disciplines, and by not being in a hurry. We learn to trust the Zen saying, "Don't push the river." The river of life and the river of the Holy Spirit flow on to their appointed ends. We need to work at removing the obstacles to the flow, but we do not need to push the growth process. Keeping the current strong is God's problem, not ours.

A final caution I would offer involves the risk of ignoring the power of our primitive God-image. We form our first God-image largely through experiences in our family of origin long before entering kindergarten. We call this experience primitive because it is the earliest experience and because it is not influenced by mature mental processes. Our primitive God-image forms itself out of our feelings about the world we find ourselves in as an infant and child. We all form such a primitive God-image, whether or not formal religion has been a part of our childhood. Primitive feelings are rarely conscious, which gives them immense power over us as we grow up.

A brief story illustrates my point. Recently I worked with a group of adults, all of whom had a history of sex abuse during childhood. They had been exploited, oppressed, and abused in their early childhood by ministers, by parents who were in the public eye, by paragons of religious virtue, or by other trusted "religious" persons. Their experience of God, therefore, involved experiences of cruelty, exploitation, punishment, and untrustworthiness.

One day I happened to say to the group, "You know, I am really impressed that some of you people have been coming to this group for four or five years. What is it about the other members of the group that keeps you coming so faithfully?" They began to describe what it was about one another that made the group so important. They used words like "love, care, understanding, acceptance, faithfulness, coming to our aid in times of trouble," and so on.

Then I said, "All right, now take the qualities you have just described and make a mental enlargement of your experience in this group and create a God-image out of it. What kind of God would you have if your God were like this group?" Sounds of "Oh!" "Wow!" and "You've got us!" came from the group. One member said in jest, "You tricked us. Of course our God-image based on experience in this group would be radically different."

After we laughed together, I began to point out that their new God-images were precisely what we have in Jesus of Nazareth. We talked about the way a primitive God-image can bind and enslave a person if it is not revised on the basis of new experience in a community that embodies the God revealed in Jesus Christ.

So you can see why it is very important for persons to explore their primitive God-images and then to risk developing new images based on positive life experience in settings other than those in which they were oppressed or abused. Once that transition is made, their energies are freed for constructive living and they are well on the journey of spiritual formation.[7]

SEEKER: I realize that we are about out of time, but before I leave, could you give me a quick look at a spiritual direction session? What would it be like? Would it be like counseling?

GUIDE: I doubt that any two people would conduct a spiritual direction session in the same way. I will be glad to tell you how I might do so, hoping that you will pay more attention to the attitudes and flow process involved than to the particulars.

To begin, you may enter spiritual direction on a one-to-one basis or in a small group. I follow pretty much the same process whether I am meeting with one person or a group of persons. I try to schedule the place and time of meeting so as to offer a relaxed and confidential atmosphere for sharing and for learning to pray together comfortably.

Assuming that you and I are talking individually, I might begin by reminding you that we are here to be attentive to God during our time together and to serve each other in our spiritual growth. I would outline briefly the plan for the time we have scheduled. (I am careful to stay within the time frame we have agreed on—usually one or one and a half hours for an individual and two hours for a group.) Outlining the plan, I suggest we begin with a few minutes of silence and a brief meditation that I will offer (no more than five to ten minutes in all). I will then invite you to begin with your concern, saying that I may ask questions for clarification as we go (usually fifteen to twenty minutes). Next, one or the other of us may suggest going back into the silence to listen for the leading of the Spirit, being receptive to the images that come to mind, to metaphors and stories that seem to relate to your concern (another five to ten minutes). Returning from the silence, we share images, stories, suggestions, possible interpretations, and clues about the next steps. Advice giving is taboo, so impressions are shared to be received or not, as seems best. We try to respect the basic premise of spiritual direction, that the Holy Spirit is the Guide (twenty to thirty minutes are typical at this stage). As we come to the end of the session, I will invite you to sum up the session if you wish, noting various issues that stand out, seem useful, or call for further attention (five minutes or so). And then we usually check our schedules and determine a time for our next session (spiritual direction sessions typically occur weekly for a few weeks, while we are getting acquainted, but then move into a once-a-month pattern).

The assumptive framework in spiritual direction is contemplative. This means being relaxed but attentive to each other and to our inner responses. It means looking for the presence of the Holy Spirit in what is happening moment by moment. If need be, I will suggest that it helps the process to refrain from leaping into the discussion with the first thing that comes to mind. It is often better to stand back a bit, trying to sense and respond to the Spirit's movement within, allowing responses to surface gently rather than grasping for them.

A prayerful atmosphere and a sensitivity to the Spirit may be disrupted by self-consciousness, by the need to appear competent or make a particular point, by a fear of criticizing or being criticized, by the need to solve problems or analyze situations to gain approval or control. Such distractions will sometimes occur. When this happens, it is desirable not only to reassert the need to listen to the Spirit but also to refocus on the process when the essential center is being lost.

Problem solving and analytical "head-tripping" are common temptations—for professional people particularly. To avoid this, be ready at any time to call for a time-out from the discussion and thus an opportunity for silence and recentering. Such comments as "I'm having trouble sensing the Spirit now" or "How do you sense God to be in that interaction?" may be helpful in a group setting to remind the group of their commitment to contemplation.

You can see that a contemplative process is different from both personal counseling and theological discussion groups. Analysis and argument are minimized in an effort to hear and respond to God's presence and the moving of the Spirit in the here and now.

Well, our time is about up. I have enjoyed our discussion, and I hope the interview has fulfilled some of your hopes.

SEEKER: Indeed it has, and thank you for the opportunity.

Conclusion

At this point, the reader might choose to summarize the chapter. Note your primary impressions, delineate new information you may have received, and reflect on specific questions and concerns regarding your own spiritual journey.

11

Spirituality, Joy, and the Value of Play

Gerald L. Keown and Glen Harold Stassen

We are serious about joy. God has given us such a beautiful world, and has surprised us with such redemptive love, that "serious" joy is an essential response. The Bible knows such joyous moments. The psalms sing out God's praise even in darkness. David dances before the presence of the Lord. The Gospels are filled with eschatological joy because God breaks through to surprise everyone with transforming initiatives.[1] The people of God are called to rejoice even in suffering, yet religious people often take joy too seriously. Joy loses its exuberance when it becomes merely another spiritual category. In religious practice and theological jargon, joy becomes stuffy and pompously pious. It may therefore be appropriate to describe one element of joy by using the more straightforward and theologically less complex label of "fun." This chapter will suggest that a proper response to God's good gift of life may come in more relaxed and less formal expressions of joy than are commonly associated with religious experience.

The two authors of this piece take fun seriously. In particular, we are involved in fun running, running fun. In the several years in which we have engaged in this fun, it has provided some unexpected benefits not at all unrelated to the expression of religious joy. This joy comes serendipitously, at odd times, sometimes with "odd" people. Nevertheless, such experiences are akin to the fresh encounters with God that enrich our lives. Reexamining some of those experiences may result in a lesson or two related to spiritual formation and the practice of joy.

Work, Play, and Spirituality

We are a results-oriented society. Even in the realm of religious experience, everything has to have a redeeming purpose evidenced by concrete results or gain. Worship is turned into work. Meditation becomes an exercise in achievement. Worship leadership or Bible teaching is evaluated on the basis of the size of the crowd and their measurable responses.

Brother Lawrence learned that, when work is turned into worship, it can be fun.[2] When worship is turned into work, however, it isn't worship, and it doesn't "work." Jim Holloway, having learned much from Jacques Ellul, has pointed out that the technological work culture of our society is invading even our worship.[3] We turn our worship into a means to an efficient end, into work. But worship was not intended to be a way of manipulating God and human beings in such a way as to achieve a fficient result. There is no grace in that kind of worship. Grace, as freely given by God, has surprise and divine initiative in it. If I am too concerned about achieving some important result in worship, I may miss the outpouring of God's grace when it occurs. Worship, in both its personal and corporate sense, is not meant to be judged as the sum of a "good" sermon, significant ideas, effective music, punctual daily prayer, persistent piety, or recognizable religiosity. It is first and foremost an encounter with God's presence.

It may well be that our spiritual life needs a revolution, one that revolts against always having to produce something efficiently. We need to be open to play, to fun, to surprise, to grace, to joy.[4] The two of us, along with many others, have found moments of that in the ritual of running. We have worshiped in our running, but not by planning to do so, not by thinking efficiently. Rather, it has often come in response to our own need, by our willingness to release that which we were holding back, and by the gift of God's surprising grace. What we will share in this often rambling, "running" chapter is not a careful analysis into the theological significance of leisure. Instead, we write narratively from our experience in the same way that we sometimes run. The point is not to navigate an exact route in some "personal best" time. It is, rather, the relaxed ramble at a slightly slower pace, which allows inspirations to spring forth. Do not look for extensive documentation. The footnotes (pun intended) are grounded in those genuine, firsthand experiences.

There is something about running, and about other activities that require physical exertion outside of the daily routine, that relaxes the inhibitions. In the shared experience of the run, the bicycle ride, the game, privately held true feelings often emerge—feelings of anger, aggression, rebellion, sadness, or celebration. It is a healthy release. Acceptance, reconciliation, thanksgiving, and joy—perhaps even union with God—can be the end result. As the more rational faculties of mind and body relax, certain glimpses of the inner life may more readily appear.

Running: Some Spiritual Encounters

The first poem one of us (Glen) wrote came at the age of twenty-two while its author was jogging at dusk on Broadway near 125th Street in New York City. It expressed beautifully and sadly a sense of unity with the pathos of others walking in the rain at dusk in that city filled with the hidden depths of suffering, cohumanity, and community. To publish it, the author sent it to his seventeen-year-old sister, a wonderful writer, who lost it. The moment, however, will never be lost.

Rain can become a catalyst for one who runs. The rain surrounds you, runs through your hair, into your eyes and mouth, and becomes a part of you. Your own perspiration and the drops of rain mingle on your skin, and there is a feeling of unity with the rain, a feeling of being part of nature that seems to be crying with you. One may be present to one's own hidden—deeply hidden—sadness while running in the rain. There is a suffering dimension in nature just as there is a suffering dimension deep within each person, ready to surface when we are present to it. We have cried while running in the rain and have prayed to God, "O Lord, why have you given me this suffering?" "Why is this suffering mixed with deep joy?" "How are the two made the unitary mixture in which I am now bathed?" "I cry to you." "I cry with you."

At such moments our faith becomes more Christ-centered and we sense more of the love and suffering of Christ in nature, especially when running in the rain. We feel God's mercy in the depths where we usually hide our deepest sadness. We realize by grace that we are no longer alone. We can allow our feelings to "rain." We can know we are a part of God's merciful love, pouring rain on the just and unjust, on us and everybody else. God's mercy is like the rain. It blesses twice. It blesses the one who suffers and the one who rejoices, making us one with Christ in suffering and celebration.

We are daily made aware of our inadequacies—as minister, as one of God's people, as friend, father, husband. When we run in a "friendly" road race, we are faced with similar revelation. The younger, fitter bodies leave us in the dust. We feel something of our own mortality. There is, however, another element of mortality, a sense of satisfaction that comes from the running, struggling, and enduring to the end. And with consistent training and effort, we do improve. On some of those days when the consciousness of sinful humanity is at its height, a long run becomes a tonic, a reminder that there is more to life, more to faith, than this day's failures and frustrations. Drained of energy, we are also drained of the sense of purposelessness with which we began to run. We determine to run again tomorrow, along the road and in life, with hope and faith, peace and joy.

Have you ever experienced the grand joy spoken of by runners in hushed, exuberant tones, the wonder of the second wind? After miles of arduous effort, suddenly there is a sense of lightness, renewed strength, and invigorated muscles that perform with unexpected freshness. This may be what keeps many of us going on the long runs. You never know when the second wind may come.

One can clearly identify with the exilic Isaiah, who knew the weariness of exhausting struggle, the despair of failure, the haunting sense of the absence of God. He knew a people of a lost nation, lost hope, lost faith. But he spoke of a "second wind," the wind of God, which, for those who remain faithful, "shall renew their strength, they shall mount up with wings like eagles, they shall run and not be weary, they shall walk and not faint" (Isa. 40:31). We keep on running, waiting, hoping, for a "second wind."

Today we ran just after it had rained. The different greens of the different trees, hung with vines—blue-greens, purple-greens, subtle greens, bright green-greens, yellow sun-greens—were softly shaded. The sun singled out one patch high up where several trees commingled and were covered by shades of ivy. Our souls sang thank you.

As runners and friends, many of the best, most open conversations we have had with each other, in which we shared more of the content and caring of our teaching than at any other time, came not in Norton Hall, Southern Seminary's main building, but on the road through Cherokee Park, running side by side. Running can lower your inhibitions, not only toward yourself and toward God but also toward friends and colleagues. We think the experience of running provides a prophetic critique of our inhibitedness, the "what will others think" prestige-righteousness, and the drivenness of our culture and our selves. If running can do this much for us because it carries us beyond our usual constrained existence, what does that say about our usual constrained existence?

Our running allows us to express our inherent competitiveness (of which we both have too much) in professorially appropriate ways. It is not that we are competitive in the sense of being fast, but we have the drive to win, to run faster than before. We want to win races and debates, to show that we are right, to teach even colleagues and spouses who do not want to be taught! Running provides an outlet for our competitiveness. Without it we would be more prone to collegial competitiveness, giving in to that theological "one-up-personship" that damages human relationships all too easily.

To illustrate our competitiveness, one need only observe that we have run together several times but never have been able to finish together. One of us always speeds up for the last mile and tries to beat the other. The first-place finisher is not always the same. We are close enough in ability that we could learn to finish together if we were not so unceasingly competitive. Imagine what we would be like in interpersonal relationships if we could not successfully sublimate our strong competitive drive in the fun of running!

To raise money for summer projects in which our students are involved, the student missions committee once arranged a game between a semiofficial seminary basketball team, the Seminary Saints, and a hastily organized team of faculty and staff. The Saints practiced regularly, played local college teams, and included some rather accomplished players. The faculty hardly practiced, was older, and lacked the skill of the Saints. Both of us were on the faculty team. After the game, one of us, while running home, gave thanks for the fun of running, when we do not experience such resentment against a vastly better team, and such disappointment at not being able to give back what they gave to us—a sound thrashing!

As we run, we usually pick up recyclable aluminum beer cans and soft-drink cans. (One of us has brought back as many as seventeen or eighteen cans from a single run, in hands of a size designed for hoeing acres of tomatoes on Grandfather's farm, or for rowing Viking ships and wielding a mighty sword, not for pushing a pen.) It makes us feel good to do our small part to clean up the outdoors and save recyclable aluminum. Admittedly, this does not put a dent in the enormous wall of waste that our society is piling up, and it does not reverse the course of our rapid rape of God's gift of nonrenewable metals and fuels, but it is our way of taking a few small steps. Like the alcoholic who takes the first steps in AA, we're not cured, but it feels like participating in grace to be able to take a few steps in God's direction.

The other day one of us found several cans from a certain brand of beer. Whoever drank that beer polluted the environment by tossing out the cans and contributed his or her money to a particular beer company that is reputed to fund the war that has killed fellow Baptists and Roman Catholics in Nicaragua. One of the cans, taken to class, served as an invitation to the students to start a boycott of that brand of beer. "Let them feel the loss of our business!" Southern Baptist Seminary is an impossible place to start a beer boycott, but it was fun conceiving the idea, fun announcing it, and still fun recounting it.

It is not widely known, but Southern Seminary has had a running team. We ran in the Louisville Corporate Competition, sponsored by General Electric Appliance Park. In that competition, each team was to be composed of three men and one woman who were fast runners and one person over forty. Alternates were allowed. One of us was the over-forty member and the other was the alternate. It was a hot, hot Saturday. We passed each other at the eight-kilometer mark. Our team won first prize! We *are* competitive! We love to talk about it and to brag about our victories. At our age, where could we have such fun so successfully and still pretend to be dignified? It also provided good community with our students, four of whom really brought home the bacon on that Saturday.

Lately one of us has been running with his wife. This is his story: "We walk together to the Louisville Water Company reservoir. This seventeen-minute walk warms us up and gives us a chance to talk together. Then we run a quarter mile, walk an eighth, run a quarter, walk an eighth, and so on until we have covered about three miles. That way we can exercise together and talk too. Then one of us (guess which one) takes off running more competitively while the other walks. The reservoir is three-fourths of a mile around, so we pass each other every mile and a half, thus still being together in spite of our different paces. Day and night there are always many others walking or running around the reservoir, so there is a sense of community. On the walk back home we talk again, now more freely because the running has warmed us, relaxed us, lowered our inhibitions, and raised our spirits. It is great marriage therapy, and it's free! I give thanks for our togetherness. We have just celebrated our thirty-first wedding anniversary. I also give thanks for her good figure, the figure of an athlete.

"My running shoes are size fourteen. It's like running with

ankle weights. You would think the race officials would give me
a head start. When our seminary team ran the ten-kilometer
Hayswood Hills Run, our team member, Randy Weber, won
overall first prize, finishing in thirty-five minutes. He weighs 118
pounds. That works out to 34 kilometer pounds per minute. I
finished in a respectable fifty minutes. I weigh 190 pounds. That
is a ratio of 38 kilometer pounds per minute, 4 kilometer
pounds faster than Randy, who is twenty-five years younger! I
give God thanks for the genuine enjoyment I experience from
my competitive spirit and my happy body.

"One beautiful fall afternoon I ran along the shores of Lake
Michigan. The sun was warm, but the heat of summer was
gone. The sky and the water were both brilliant blue. Children
played in the grass along the lake shore; sailboats skimmed
across the water. As I enjoyed the beauty of the lake and the
fog-shrouded skyscrapers along the Loop, I was reminded of
the vivid contrast this part of Chicago offers. A few days earlier
I had wandered along a pothole-filled street, not far from the
University of Chicago, searching for the home of friends. The
address I had was not correct. Trying to find it nonetheless, I
found myself in a war zone. Uninhabitable buildings, once the
homes of the desperately poor, now too far gone even for them,
were on both sides of the street. It took little imagination to
consider the life experienced by the people who eyed me suspi-
ciously from the sidewalk. Here were hopelessness and despair
on a scale I had seldom seen. I finally found my friends in Hyde
Park, a few hundred yards and a world away. The exhilaration
of a bit of exercise on a beautiful afternoon is held in tension
with the knowledge that there is much in our world that is not
beautiful. That day's run was good exercise, both physical and
spiritual."

One of us is now training to run in a ten-kilometer race to
benefit world hunger relief efforts. Students and fellow Sunday
school members are pledging a certain amount of money for
each kilometer run. "While running in practice," he says, "I can
imagine I am sharing in one-tenth of 1 percent of the pain of
the world's hungry. That is my spiritual exercise for this week."

Sometimes when we run, we feel that we are soaring. It is such
a rare gift to be able to enjoy God's good earth, the beauty of the
streams and trees and sunsets in Cherokee Park, and to have the
energy to pick up the pace, to better a previous time. We say a
more joyous prayer of thanks for God's good gift of this world
and this body and the health that one day will fade like the grass.
When that happens, we will still have the memory of soaring,
and we will still give thanks for the good that was.

Prophetic detachment is a gift. We have found that it can be a gift given by fun. We get it from running. Others get it from other kinds of play. *Chacun à son jouet*—to everyone his or her own play. We hope you let your spirit play regularly. You may be surprised at the results. You will be enriched physically. You may also find that the God whom you seek, whom you worship, may be found in a very different way from what you imagined.

Conclusion: Spiritual Serendipity

This may not appear to be an appropriately serious spiritual essay. If that is your reaction, you are missing the point. This is a profoundly serious essay. We are deeply serious about joy. Joy can be the breakthrough of grace, especially in our overly serious society. If our essay seems not sufficiently serious, that is an indictment of the rigidity of our culture, even in its "spiritual" subunits, that walls us off from openness to the God of surprise and delight and fun and eschatological joy. When we meditate while running and become inspired, this is how it comes out. That it comes out this way, which seems strange to our usual comportment in society, shows the strangeness of our society to the gracious presence of God. We have become bodily alienated from God, who comes to us in the incarnation of Jesus Christ. We have become alienated from God's nature and from our nature, from God's creation. We cannot force our way back. We can only run—or ride, or walk, or play as we will—and let it come. Thanks be to God, who runs with us.

12

Spirituality and Sexuality

Diana S. Richmond Garland and Wayne E. Oates

What is the role of sexuality in the spiritual life of the Christian? One common assumption is that spirituality and sexuality are antithetical. To be spiritual is to be asexual; to be sexual is to be unspiritual. This view is derived from the heavy influence of Greek dualism and its Hellenistic expression in Gnosticism on common modes of thinking in the Western world. The body is material, dark, and evil; the spirit is noncorporeal, light, and good; the two are enemies. The early church fathers abhorred sexual behavior, even in marriage: Augustine believed that sexual intercourse was fundamentally disgusting, Arnobius called it filthy, Jerome called it unclean, and Tertullian called it shameful. "In fact there was an unstated consensus that God ought to have invented a better way of dealing with the problem of procreation."[1]

The Hebrew view of body and spirit, which is reflected throughout the Old and New Testaments, differs dramatically from this rejection of sexuality. The totality of personality—body, mind, and spirit—is central to biblical thought. The body is intimately unified with the spirit. The spirit is the living reality that holds the body together. The spiritual person is the total person—body, mind, and spirit—living in relationship to God and God's direction for life. The unspiritual person is the total person—body, mind, and spirit—living estranged and alienated from God and God's direction for life.

Sex and Sexuality—Some Definitions

When we are asked what the Bible teaches about sexuality, the passages that come to mind are those that describe how husbands and wives are to relate to one another sexually, the command in Genesis 1:28 to "be fruitful and multiply," or proscriptions against homosexuality, adultery, and lust. In short, we think of biblical guidelines for sexual behavior.

Sexuality, however, incorporates far more than overt sexual behavior. It includes our understanding of what it means to be male or female and the degree to which that understanding shapes our own identity—our gender identity. This identity includes our preferences for homosexual or heterosexual relationships, whether or not we act on those preferences. Identity also includes what it means to be female or male in our relationships with others and with God—our gender role. Finally, sexual behavior is overt sexual behavior, which most often expresses gender identity and role. Let us look at each of these in turn.

Gender Identity

Gender identity is the understanding of self as male or female and the attitudes toward self that gender assignment carries. It includes everything we say or do to indicate our gender to ourselves and others.[2] The development of gender identity begins in infancy and is firmly established in children in the second and third years of life.[3] It continues to evolve, however, throughout life, influenced in part by physiological changes in ourselves and changing relationships with others. This subjective assessment of the self also changes, according to the degree to which one embraces or challenges strong cultural stereotypes about what it means to be female or male. Every person develops gender identity, even though one may choose a celibate life-style. This aspect of self is not to be escaped for the sake of spirituality but to be embraced as a God-given dimension of our personhood. For example, Donald Goergen defines chastity not as withdrawal from sexuality but the integration of our sexual lives into our Christian lives so that we can be whole, undivided.

> We as Christians believe in incarnational spirituality and that the future life will be an embodied way of being. Living "in the Spirit" and "in Christ" does not mean an alienation of ourselves from our own physicality.[4]

Gender Role

How we see ourselves, and how we think others see us, determines to a large extent the ways we relate to others, both in what we do and in how we expect others to behave. Gender is so basic to relationships between persons that every known society has a set of beliefs that define what it means to be male or female.[5] These behavioral expectations define the respective gender roles females and males are expected to fulfill. The actual expectations vary widely across cultures, both in their content as well as in the degree of flexibility and rigidity with which they are assigned. Virtually the only role assignment that does not vary from culture to culture is childbearing and, to a lesser extent, infant feeding. Beyond those baselines, societies can assign differing hairstyles, body adornment, occupational choices, familial relationships, and a myriad of other expectations to each gender with almost complete freedom.[6]

Gender identity is expressed, therefore, in behavior, the gender roles we enact. Gender roles include stereotypical traits that supposedly influence interpersonal relationships (women are sensitive to others and emotional; men are logical and independent), role behaviors (men handle the money and the cars; women nurture children), physical characteristics (hairstyles, clothing, gait), and social behavior (women are the switchboards of communication in extended family and friendship networks; men relate to others primarily as work colleagues or as partners in leisure sports activities).[7]

Sexual Behavior

One's behavior, therefore, reflects gender identity and gender role in a myriad of ways. Often more variation occurs among members of the same gender than between all the members of one gender and all the members of the other gender. For example, a woman's hairstyle (for example, a short bob) may be more like some men's styles than it is like some women's styles (long, straight tresses). Gender behavior such as choosing a hairstyle or occupation is related to our sexuality, but we use the term "sexual behavior" to refer to behavior that is overtly and physiologically sexual. Sexual behavior is thus a subset of gender behavior.

Sexual behavior runs the continuum from the small child's masturbation to the adult's flirtation with a potential sex partner and consequent sexual contact. The biblical writers from Genesis to the Pauline letters concerned themselves with the role of sexual behavior in the lives of God's people. It is behavior, homosexual as well as extramarital behavior and the sexual behavior of marital partners, that commands central attention. Even lust, which sounds more like attitude than it does behavior, is condemned because it leads to behavior that uses another as an object instead of recognizing the other's personhood and worth as a creation of God.

For the Christian, sexual behavior is properly channeled only in a marriage relationship based on a lifelong commitment. The relationship between women and men from the very beginning (Gen. 1:27) has been one of God's provisions for spiritual development. Together, they leave father and mother—home and dependency—to begin a new family entity. It is God's provision that in the intimacy of sexual union, a woman and a man become one flesh. They are to do so without shame, guilt, fear, or inordinate spiritual pride. They are created for the joys and responsibilities of sexual behavior. Outside of marriage, however, sexual intercourse is labeled sin.[8]

The biblical texts about sex have often been misunderstood and misinterpreted. The apostle Paul's writings about sex, for example, have often been used to fuel the debate over the role of sexual behavior in the life of the Christian. In 1 Corinthians 7, Paul writes, "It is well for a man not to touch a woman. But because of the temptation to immorality, each man should have his own wife, and each woman her own husband . . . for it is better to marry than to be aflame with passion" (vs. 1–2,9). Doesn't Paul seem to be saying that the highest good is celibacy and, if that cannot be achieved, that marriage is a sort of safeguard against sin? A cursory reading of the text leads one to believe that Paul saw sexual behavior as a stumbling block, not a resource, for spiritual development.

The context in which Paul is writing, however, needs to be understood. He was writing to the Corinthians in response to wild ideas they had developed about sexual behavior. In the first verse, Paul is introducing the idea as the Corinthians had presented it to him. In other words, Paul is not saying, "It is well not to touch"; he is quoting them: "Now you are saying, 'it is well . . . not to touch.' " This is similar to several other places in the letter where Paul writes in response to their questions and begins by first alerting his readers with "Now concerning [what you wrote]" (7:25; 8:1; 12:1; 16:1). Paul then quotes the Corinthians' saying (6:12; 8:1, 4; 10:23). This passage in 1 Corinthians, therefore, is better punctuated: "Now concerning the matters about which you wrote: 'It is well for a man not to touch a woman.' "[9] Evidently, some Corinthians were trying to reach new spiritual heights by becoming celibate, even in marriage. Paul responds by arguing that sexual behavior is not optional in marriage; it is not sinful; it is something owed to the marriage partner (7:2–5, 36). Paul clearly felt, from his own experience, that celibacy was a more desired state because of the urgency of the hour (7:29): "For the form of this world is passing away" (7:31). But he makes it clear that he is giving his opinion (7:25) and that marriage and sexual behavior within marriage are no sin. Sexual behavior in marriage does not distract persons from their calling any more than do other activities: mourning, rejoicing, and dealing with the world (1 Cor. 7:30–31). "Nowhere in Paul is there the slightest hint that human sexuality is evil."[10] His concern was simply that Christians behave in fitting ways, in holiness and honor (1 Thess. 4:3–5).

Scripture also deals with issues of gender identity and role, although in somewhat more subtle ways. Perhaps the most overt reference to gender identity and role is the proclamation that there is no gender in the kingdom of God: "There is neither male nor female; for you are all one in Christ Jesus" (Gal. 3:28). Jesus, too, implied that there would be no gender or sexuality in the life to come. The Sadducees asked him the stock question about the woman who married and was widowed by each of seven brothers—whose wife would she be in the resurrection? Jesus responded that there will be no marrying in heaven, but they will be "like angels" (Mark 12:18–25). We have trouble comprehending the meaning of this, just as we struggle to understand God as Holy Other, neither male nor female. The scriptures, by using both genders in describing God, help us recognize that gender does not limit or define God. We find God likened to a hen, a nursing mother, a woman searching for a lost coin; but God is also described as Abba, Father, vineyard owner and groom.

Gender Differences

There is no gender in the kingdom; God transcends gender. Yet people are created male and female. Does one gender or the other have greater potential for spirituality? Although most of us would answer with an emphatic no for fear of being thought sexist, we need to examine the historical position of the church and social science research about gender differences that relate to our spirituality.

On our grand entrance from the womb, most of us were held upside down by the heels as someone proclaimed, "It's a girl!" or "It's a boy!" Rarely would someone exclaim first, "It's blue-eyed!" or "It's a baldy!" Practically all other differentiations between persons, except between living and dead, seem inconsequential when compared to gender. The process of careful socialization into a gender role begins with the color of the blanket in which our nakedness is first wrapped. Before we are even given a name, the hospital card hung at the head of our bassinet reads "Girl Richmond" or "Boy Oates."

As significant as the awareness of our genitalia may be in defining our gender, it is only the beginning of a lifelong process of differentiating males from females. It is not only the equipment with which we were born, but also the prenatal environment, pubertal hormones, body type and attractiveness, relationship with significant others of the same and opposite sex, and cultural norms and mores that shape our gender identities and roles throughout life.

In contrast with the ease of identifying the different physiological structures of female and male, however, other distinctions between male and female are not easily made. No matter how precise our categories of female and male are, gender-assigned characteristics, abilities, and predispositions are found in greatly overlapping distributions.[11] Women may be biologically predisposed to take a primary nurturer role with infants and children, but many men are better nurturers than most women. Men may come equipped to develop more muscle and physical strength, but many women are stronger than most men. "As day and night merge under the glare of the midnight sun, male and female merge under the scrutiny of empirical inquiry."[12] There is no set of personality traits, dispositions, or abilities that is exclusively female or male. Our judgments about appropriate gender behavior are truly judgments and not objective fact.

Despite the diffuse boundary between female and male, women and men have not been considered equally "spiritual," although who is more spiritual has not always been a matter of agreement. Greek dualism, for example, divided flesh from spirit. Flesh represented the sin of passion and was associated with women, whereas the spirit represented the purity of reason and was associated with men.[13] Clearly, within that kind of cultural framework the woman who could be considered man's spiritual equal would be rare.

This view still exists, although it more often is couched in discussions of masculinity and femininity than in gender identity and sexuality. Presumably, this takes some of the sting out of saying that one or the other is superior, since all persons are assumed to have some elements of both. For example, John Moore argues that the feminine dimension of life is associated with sexuality, whereas the masculine dimension of life is associated with spirituality. The sexual (feminine) dimension creates and nurtures life and the well-being of the group; the spiritual (masculine) dimension is driven toward individual expression, wholeness, self-realization, and personal immortality.[14] Moore argues that the first half of life is dominated by sexuality, which gradually gives way to spirituality, the dominant drive in the last half of life. He concludes that there "must be a conversion of feminine disposition to masculine as prerequisite for spiritual fulfillment."[15]

In contrast, Lucius F. Cervantes argues that "woman's constitution is established with the good of another as the obvious ideal."[16] He suggests that women are geared toward helping and nurturing others, thus concluding that "by nature" women are more attuned to love and therefore "are predisposed to be spiritually superior to men."[17] From a historical perspective, Amanda Porterfield concludes that, although American women have often been refused direct political and economic power, they have made up for this with power in the realms of religion and esthetic expression. "From the Puritan era to the present, many Americans of Christian heritage have perceived the nature of spirituality to be intimately related to feminine responses to life."[18]

A major flaw in these approaches from a Christian perspective is the assumption that spirituality is expressed primarily in our relationship with God and sexuality is expressed primarily in our relationship with others. As Christians, however, we cannot make such a distinction. Jesus made it clear that love of God and love of neighbor (presumably our partner in bed as well as our neighbor in the world outside the home) cannot be separated. Spirituality is not something we pursue exclusively in church or in the privacy of our own devotions; it is vitally connected and influenced by our relationships, or lack thereof, with others (Matt. 25:34–45), as well as by our relationship with God (John 15:4–7). Similarly, our sexuality is a key factor not only in our relationships with others but also with God. We do not become genderless in prayer; instead, we bring all of who we are, including our sexuality, into that relationship as well.

The Role of Sexuality in Spiritual Development

Sexuality is a powerful force that can either promote or hinder spiritual growth. It can result in "pro-creation" with God or destruction of God's creation. It can lead us to greater knowledge of self and others, or it can be a source of increased ignorance. It can lead us into intimacy or into alienation. It can create a relationship climate of mutual submission or of domination. Finally, it can be a sign of our commitment, or it can seduce us into promiscuity. Each of the gifts of our sexuality also has a shadow; we can choose the light or the darkness. Let us look at each of these in turn.

Procreation/Destruction

The perpetuation of humanity through the procreation of children was the basic purpose of sexuality in Judaism. We are to be fruitful and multiply with God's blessing (Gen. 1:22), sharing in God's creative activity. Jewish sources reveal the historical significance of procreation for God's covenant people. In *Mishnah Yebamot* 6:6, a rabbi said that a man must not abstain from sexual intercourse unless he has two children. (Incidentally, the rabbis disagreed over whether a daughter counted as one of the required two.) Another rabbi said that he who does not have intercourse has in essence committed murder, asserting that by avoidance he takes the life of a potential child and diminishes the image of God in the world (*Babylonian Talmud Yebamot* 63b). Consequently, birth-control measures were forbidden; barren women, women past childbearing age, and eunuchs could not marry; and divorce was recommended if a marriage remained childless more than ten years (*Mishnah Yebamot* 8:4).[19] Many Jews have continued to take the command to procreate very seriously.[20] They have been nearly exterminated as a people more than once throughout history. This concern about the perpetuity of their people is a root cause for their fierce devotion to responsible family living and family traditions. It also explains some of the severity of their teachings about forms of sexual behavior that are alien to procreation, such as homosexuality.

Despite this background, the New Testament is loudly silent about conceiving children as the primary purpose of our sexuality, or even of our sexual behavior. Jesus stated that marriage was the act of two becoming one, not three or four (Matt. 19:6; Mark 10:8; see also Eph. 5:31). Nowhere in the New Testament is Genesis 1:28 mentioned with reference to marriage or sexual intercourse. Wayne Meeks has suggested that Paul's expectation of the nearness of the end time made procreation of little consequence.[21] Nevertheless, Paul encouraged sexual activity for marital partners (1 Cor. 7:3–5), suggesting that he did not view its sole function to be procreation. He used the relationship between wife and husband as an analogy for the relationship between Christ and the church (Eph. 5:32), and the basis of that analogy is a relationship of mutual submission and love, not conceiving children.

"Pro-creation" as a function of sexuality can be more broadly defined than the conception of children, however. We can be pro (rather than against) creation in many ways. After all, God's creativity has not been limited to creating humanity. God created the world and assigned us to care for it; God created relationships between women and men so they would not be lonely. We share God's work of creation by caring for the world that God has made and by creating loving, committed relationships.

The shadow side of the procreation function—destruction—is clearly identifiable in both Old and New Testaments. Sexual behavior can physically destroy God's good creation through sexually transmitted diseases that bring death, not new life, to God's people. Cleanliness is a major concern in the Old Testament; heavy sanctions are leveled against irresponsible sex. The house of the "loose woman . . . sinks down to death, and her paths to the shades; none who go to her come back nor do they regain the paths of life" (Prov. 2:16–19). To engage in promiscuous sex creates the risk that the "fill of your strength" (Prov. 5:10) will be taken and that life will end in groans, "when your flesh and body are consumed" (5:11). The current AIDS epidemic gives new meaning to this ancient theme. Jesus also clearly notes the destructive potential of sexual behavior; adultery and fornication bring defilement (Matt. 15:19–20; Mark 7:21–23; see also 1 Cor. 6:15–20). Paul says that persons who dishonor their bodies by giving in to "the lusts of their hearts to impurity" will receive "in their own persons the due penalty for their error" (Rom. 1:24, 27). "Safe sex" in spiritual terms is therefore responsible sex with a person to whom one is faithfully committed, a marital partner. It is creative, if not through the conception of children then in the creation of a more intimate relationship between partners; it does not destroy.

Gender roles can also be a source of destruction as well as creativity. When men are constrained from certain behaviors because of gender, such as the nurturing of children or the expression of tenderness and emotion, part of their God-given potential is destroyed. When women are denied certain vocational opportunities for which God has given them gifts and to which God has called them, gender roles have become destructive of God's creation. When gifts are forced to lie dormant because they do not fit our preconceived gender roles, the body of Christ is diminished (Eph. 4:11–12). Gender roles should help us celebrate God's good gifts to us as women and men, not set limits on what we will recognize as God-given.

Knowledge/Ignorance

The biblical authors' euphemism for intercourse, "knowing" one another (e.g., 1 Sam. 1:19), describes the second role of sexuality in spiritual development. Just as an American sojourning in a foreign culture learns much about self that escapes conscious recognition while in the home culture, so a woman or a man learns much about self in a relationship with another who represents the "foreign" gender. The male learns from the female about femaleness, affirms ways in which she is like him and different from him, and takes this reality into himself. The female learns from the male about maleness, affirms ways in which he is like her and different from her, and takes this knowledge into herself. The two become "one flesh" through this process of learning about each other and, consequently, about themselves.

This kind of knowing is spiritually far more significant than merely carnal knowledge, as it is often called. We are not speaking here about knowledge gleaned from a sex manual that gives pointers on how to relate to the opposite sex. Instead, sexual behavior can be an adventure in intimacy—knowing the other person and being made aware of one's own self more vividly. A person is called on to face up to his or her own motives for having entered into a sexual relationship with a partner. Therefore, self-encounter happens whether we like it or not. Our character is weighed on invisible scales as to its integrity or lack of integrity. Our gender identity is shaped and reshaped. The capacity to form and maintain lasting relationships is put to the test, revealing the superficiality or the depth of our sense of commitment and responsibility to another person.

We not only learn about ourselves in sexual intimacy, however, we also gain knowledge of the other. In 1 Peter 3:7, for example, husbands are exhorted to be related to their wives with understanding (NEB). In 1 Thessalonians 4:4–5, each husband is exhorted to "know how to take a wife for himself in holiness and honor, not in the passion of lust like heathen who do not know God." Our knowing God, then, is reflected in the way we relate sexually to one another. The Christian husband is to relate to his wife as a partner, as a joint heir "of the grace of life" (1 Peter 3:7). She is not a thing to be possessed; she is an other to be known and treated with honor. Not to treat one's partner with holiness and honor results in one's prayers being hindered (1 Peter 3:7).

> In intercourse a couple surrender the mystery of their selfhood to each other. They share with each other their most cherished secrets. The woman allows her partner to know her as she really is. The man reveals to his mate the full knowledge of his identity. The nakedness of the couple is symbolic that nothing is hidden from the other.[22]

One aspect of knowledge, then, is the development of empathy for another. This kind of knowledge cannot be gleaned from marriage manuals or articles in popular magazines with titles such as "What your husband wishes you knew about men." This kind of knowledge comes with the spiritual discipline of learning about this particular one who is different from every other person.

Some have read 1 Thessalonians 4:4–5, "that each one of you know how to take a wife for himself in holiness and honor, not in the passion of lust like heathen," to mean that sexual relations should be a solemn, joyless interchange. The emphasis, however, is that lust, seeing the other as a sex object, should not control our behavior, but our knowing and honoring the other as a person should be the ground of our relationship. Holiness and honor can be expressed in joyful abandon with each other, celebrative of our intimacy and our mutual commitment. The sheer joy of David as he dances before God captures the essence of joyfully expressed holiness and honor (2 Sam. 6:14).

Sexuality is a source of knowledge that contributes to one's spiritual development whether or not one is part of a sexually active relationship. Gender identity and role are significant in *all* relationships with persons of the same and opposite sex, with friends and strangers as well as with one's sex partner. From the first year of life on, a significant part of knowing oneself is one's gender identity and the consequent roles that are influenced by and influence that identity. Small children quickly learn that they are either boys or girls and can categorize others by gender, using what are often rather subtle cues.

In practically all relationships throughout life, we are learning about ourselves and the ways we are like or different from others. Opposite sex friends and colleagues affirm us as women or men and contribute to our knowledge of ourselves, at least with respect to how others see us. Same-sex friends and colleagues likewise provide grist for our mill of refining and modifying how we see ourselves.

Gender is often a primary force in bringing people into relationships with one another that do not involve sexual activity. We are drawn to others of the same gender with whom we can share common experiences. A group of young mothers can talk together about the transition to parenthood and the struggles it brings. A group of women who are the pioneers of their gender in a particular vocation (engineers, army officers, politicians, church pastors), or men who have chosen to take a paternity leave, can provide support and encouragement and information resources to others in similar situations. They can confirm one another's gender identities and roles even when others may question the gender appropriateness of chosen lifeways. Whether these relationships are embedded in a formalized group of some kind or are an informal network of social support, they offer mirrors to women and men so that they can see themselves more clearly.

The shadow side of knowledge is ignorance. When people ignore one another's uniqueness, choosing instead to act out of stereotypical assumptions about "what men are like" or "what women are like," they are ignorant. Sexual techniques are relatively easy to learn; the spiritual discipline of learning to know this particular other is far more difficult. Not to learn of each other through empathy and understanding is the "hardness of heart" of which Jesus spoke as being the root cause of divorce. The New English Bible translates "hardness of heart" as "because your minds were closed" (Matt. 19:8)—refusing to learn from each other, remaining ignorant. Clearly, to relate to one's partner as a stereotypical representation of men or of women is to abort the knowledge function of sexuality and thus to hinder one's spirituality. Hardness of heart, inconsiderateness, and a lack of empathy toward one's sexual partner breed interpersonal conflict and inhibit one's relationship to God in prayer (1 Peter 3:7). Spirituality and sexuality blend into a common purpose of a newer and deeper kind of knowledge between persons and a new form of access to fellowship with God.

It is not only knowledge of the other that has ignorance for a shadow side but also knowledge of self. Just as one can choose to operate out of stereotypes about others, one can choose to operate out of stereotypes about the self that we want to project to ourselves and to others. Instead of allowing ourselves to be vulnerable and therefore to learn about self in response to others, we may try to establish some idealized image of the self. Our culture places a major emphasis on sexual performance for both women and men. Instead of a means of learning about ourselves and our partners, sexuality has become a set of skills to be mastered in order to demonstrate one's adequacy as a person.[23] Instead of learning from each other, partners practice deceit. A wife may fake orgasm in order to boost her husband's ego as a "great lover" or to mask her own feelings of inadequacy. A husband may absent himself in his mind from the lovemaking, thinking about baseball or some other distraction in order to delay orgasm and thus be considered a satisfying sexual partner. Instead of risking vulnerability with the partner and experiencing companionship and sharing, partners may find themselves trying to impress each other, even if it is with a false impression.[24]

This process occurs not only in marriage but in any relationship in which persons hide behind sexual stereotypes about themselves rather than sharing themselves with others and using their God-given talents. Men who shun feelings and behavior thought to be feminine, in order not to be seen as "unmanly," and women who hide talents and feelings that might be seen as "unladylike" are denying themselves and others knowledge—they are strengthening stereotypes and ignorance.

The knowledge/ignorance function of sexuality also has ramifications for our understanding of God. Just as we need relationships with significant same-sex others as well as with opposite-sex others in order to develop fully in our gender identity, gender roles, and sexual behavior, so we also need to be able to relate to God both as intimately familiar with our experience and as Holy Other, beyond our experience. The church, however, has been rather lopsided in its presentation of God; God is almost always referred to as "he." For most Christians, calling God "she" sounds dissonant. It is perhaps in this way that women and men differ most in their spiritual development, and this has little to do with their biological constitution and much to do with religious education. Males have seen God as "like me"; women have related to God as Holy Other. This limits the potential spiritual development of both men and women. All of us long to be understood and known, yet this may be particularly difficult for women to experience in a relationship with a male God. Women need to feel God's empathy in the most basic role of this life—gender. A six-year-old girl said wistfully after the worship service one Sunday, "I wish God was a girl." She wanted to feel that God knew her. It is even more difficult for women who have been abused by fathers and other men in their lives to relate to a male God.

The other side is equally salient; we need relationships that highlight differences as well as likeness to grow and define ourselves. A male God may be seen by men as a reflection of themselves; they lose sight of their limited vision. "There can be no religious experience of consequence without recognition of otherness."[25]

It is crucial for spiritual development, therefore, for the church to provide the means for persons to see God as intimately familiar with their life issues, including their gender identity, as well as to see God as Holy Other, transcendent of our anthropomorphisms, including gender. Inclusive language and biblical images that ascribe both female and male characteristics to God help us to see God as transcendent of gender and yet knowing us "inside and out."

Intimacy/Alienation

Sexuality at its spiritual best combats our loneliness. Men and women were created by God that they may not be alone. Sexual behavior is by nature playful, enjoyable, and focused on you and me in this moment in time. Joyfully, we give ourselves over to caressing, holding, touching, talking, and pleasuring. We are biologically designed to enjoy the behavioral expression of our sexuality, and this enjoyment contributes to deepening intimacy.

In marriage, intimacy is the procreative theme that outlasts the birthing and rearing of children. A couple beyond the child-bearing, child-rearing, and child-launching years has their sexual union as a pleasure bond in their renewed privacy as a couple. They are God's new gift to each other for the twenty or more years they have to live together after the last child leaves home. As the later years of life approach and illnesses and disabilities appear, sexual behavior becomes refined as the touching, holding, and encouraging embraces that cause a couple to celebrate each morning that they have another day to be with one another and each evening that they do not have to face the night alone. The words of the marriage vow, "to comfort . . . in sickness and health," become specific, concrete, and real.

Research with marital couples indicates that the degree to which partners can verbally share their emotions, judgments, and opinions with each other and their perceptions of closeness and emotional bonding make much stronger contributions to relationship satisfaction than does physical intimacy.[26] This is the companionship function of sexuality addressed in Genesis 2:18.

Again, although marriage is the prototype for intimacy, intimacy as a function of sexuality for spiritual development is not limited to marital partners. Some of the most beautiful images of intimacy in the Bible are between family and friends, not spouses, such as Ruth and Naomi, Jonathan and David, and Jesus and the disciples. Our sexuality by very definition points us to intimate relationships that transcend genital sex. In all religions, spirituality includes prayer life and worship, meditation, and waiting for an experience of the divine. These do not capture the vision of spirituality in Christianity, however. The gospel is not for the individual soul alone; it is a vision concerning relationships of persons with persons: "The focal point of early Christian self-understanding was not a holy book or a cultic rite, not mystic experience and magic invocation, but a set of relationships: the experience of God's presence among one another and through one another."[27] Sexuality, then, points us to intimacy with others and, in that intimacy, to God.

The shadow side of intimacy is alienation. When we relate to another based on our stereotypes about what men or women are like, the result is not intimacy; it is alienation. We have treated the other as an object, not as a unique person. When we express our sexuality in a conscious performance to build a particular image of self or to promote our own self-worth, the result is not intimacy; it is alienation. We have protected our vulnerability and have denied the other access to knowing us. Finally, when the specter of homosexuality keeps us from forming intimate friendships with others of the same gender, the result is alienation. Apart from fellowship with God and humble teachability, sexuality can become a wedge that drives persons into conflict with and isolation from each other. Children can become battlegrounds for competing parents; churches deny women the ability to use their spiritual gifts because of gender constrictions; fathers and sons are afraid to hug one another and can only punch each other on the shoulder to express affection. Persons treat one another as stereotypes rather than persons, systematically ignoring the way each is unique. We can be hard-hearted, hardheaded, and remain strangers to each other. The end result of any one or all of these wedging attitudes is isolation, loneliness, and estrangement. Conflict may become acute, resulting in broken relationships, or it may become chronic, with the unhappiness and alienation continuing as a way of life.

Mutuality/Domination

The apostle Paul spoke clearly about the power factor inherent in sexuality. He considered sexual relations to be something owed to the partner in marriage (1 Cor. 7:3). He was concerned with the "conjugal rights" husband and wife have that they "give" to each other in sexual intercourse. The relationship between wife and husband is to be based on equality and mutuality, not on domination of one by the other.

> For the wife does not rule over her own body, but the husband does: likewise, the husband does not rule over his own body, but the wife does. Do not refuse one another except perhaps by agreement for a season, that you may devote yourselves to prayer; but then come together again lest Satan tempt you through lack of self-control.
>
> 1 Corinthians 7:4–5

This does not mean that one partner can demand sexual relations from the other. Sexual expression is to be couched in loving concern and is never to be demanded. On the other hand, by refusing each other, sexual partners exercise control—they try to dominate each other. Hostility, suspicion, rejection, and distrust ensue. In giving mutually to each other in the abandonment of power over each other, they create mutual warmth, acceptance, trust, and respect. The submission here is not the submitting of the woman to the man or the man to the woman but their mutual submission to each other. Thus we have in mature sexual love a metaphor for all relationships. The mutual submission of wife and husband to each other is a model of how *all* Christians are to relate to one another (Eph. 5:21, 32). Paul is echoing Jesus' teaching that whoever would be first must be the servant of all. Power is not to be grasped. Christians are to outdo one another only in kindness.

The struggle for power and control of one sexual partner over the other is the genesis of the larger sociocultural phenomenon of the discrimination against women by a male-dominated society. Women are treated as a means toward the purposes of men rather than as persons in their own right. In more subtle and less blatant ways, women come to respond in kind and treat men as means to their own ends. Immanuel Kant was right when he said that everything in creation except personality "can be used . . . as a means to an end; but humankind itself, the rational creature, is an end in itself. Humankind is the subject of the moral law and is sacred by virtue of its individual freedom."[28] Lust is destructive and sinful because it diminishes the other to the status of an object to be possessed rather than a unique other to be known.

In creation, we were made in the image of God, male and female. Neither was given dominion over the other. We are joint heirs of the *imago Dei*. It was not until *after* the temptation and fall of Adam and Eve that Eve was told, "Your husband shall rule over you." This initial biblical statement of male dominance is a description of humankind in the grip of sin. This was culturally institutionalized in the Law, particularly laws concerning divorce. In Deuteronomy 22:22, however, the act of adultery is stated as *both* a male and female sin for which *both* shall die. Yet in the Pharisees' condemnation of the woman taken in adultery in John 8:1–11, only the woman was to be stoned to death. They caught her "in the act" of adultery, but they let the man go. In doing so, they were disobeying the Law; even in their reading of the Law they perpetuated the sin of the first Adam. Biblical exegesis that calls for male dominance of women perpetuates humanity's fallen, sinful state. The main motive in male dominance is the love of power, the very desire that prompted Adam and Eve to sin. The apostle Paul says, "As in Adam all die, so also in Christ shall all be made alive" (1 Cor. 15:22).

Commitment/Promiscuity

The final spiritual function of sexuality is commitment. Commitment requires fidelity and generates trust between partners. Paul rejected casual sexual encounters in 1 Corinthians 6, believing that sex can never be casual. It is not simply genital behavior, it affects the deepest recesses of the soul; sexual sins come from the heart (Matt. 15:19; Mark 7:21). Commitment is not a feeling, it is a spiritual discipline. It requires an act of will, a commitment to partnership, to love even when loving feelings are in short supply:

> Couples sooner or later always fall out of love, and it is at the moment when the mating instinct has run its course that the opportunity for genuine love begins. It is when the spouses no longer feel like being in each other's company always, when they would rather be elsewhere some of the time, that their love begins to be tested and will be found to be present or absent.[29]

Again, the marital relationship models how Christians are to relate to one another outside of marriage as well as within marriage. We are to be willing to die for one another, the ultimate test of commitment (John 15:13–14). We are to forgive, even when we have been wronged so many times that we have lost count (Matt. 18:21–22). In other words, to the limits of our fallibility we are to relate to one another, both inside and outside of marriage, in the same way that God relates to us.

The shadow side of commitment is promiscuity. Commitment emphasizes looking out for the best interests of the other; promiscuity emphasizes using others for one's own pleasure. Commitment means sticking by the other no matter what; promiscuity implies getting what one can and then abandoning the partner. In commitment we give of ourselves; in promiscuity we take all we can from others. Promiscuity is normally thought of as sexual acting out with multiple partners. However, promiscuity models the shadow side of all commitments, such as "fair-weather friends" who last only as long as the good times last.

Conclusion

Sexuality plays a significant role in spirituality. The way we express our sexuality—our gender identity, the gender roles we fill, and our sexual behavior—all contribute to or detract from spiritual growth. Perhaps there is no spiritual discipline more challenging than to aim for pro-creativity, knowledge, intimacy, mutuality, and commitment in marital and other relationships in our lives in which our gender identity and roles have a significant function—which is practically every relationship in this life. However, sexuality is certainly not all of our spirituality. There seems to be little danger of the church's overemphasizing sexuality as a key shaper of persons' identities and life vocations. The danger appears to be, in a secular society that celebrates sex as a good in and of itself, that the role of sexuality in spirituality will be scrupulously avoided by the church.

13

Spirituality and Vocation

S. Milburn Price, Jr., and William B. Rogers, Jr.

A community of faith is called a crucible of love. It is also the crucible of what is going on in the culture generally, whether it be the narrow culture of the denomination or . . . the culture at large. [Communities] are like psychic or spiritual zoos. They tell us a great deal about ourselves.[1]

With those words Alan Jones offers an analysis of spiritual formation and vocation. The environment of any faith community struggles to maintain a caring for persons. How shall we care for persons and nurture them toward vocation while avoiding this caricature of a spiritual zoo?

Caring: For Persons

Craig Dykstra discussed caring for persons in this fashion:

There is nothing that people need and want more than to be loved and found worthy—just for who they are. But in most American early childhood training, affection (the concrete sign of love) is not given unconditionally. Affection is used as a manipulative device. . . . This same pattern continues, and indeed is intensified, in the school situation. In school, the ones who develop a sense of self worth are those who produce. They get the grades or social rewards.[2]

Such a pattern leads to destructiveness. Those who produce and are purposeful also tend to manipulate others in the direction of that ego-centered purposefulness. We pay the price by repressing the yearning to be loved unconditionally.

> In the achievement-oriented life-style, people become utterly, deeply, existentially convinced that they cannot be loved just as they are—with all their failures, inadequacies, and finitude. We are driven to earning love. . . . We have here, then, a pattern of socially acceptable, mutual self-destruction.[3]

Unfortunately, this pattern can be pervasive in theological education. Academic achievement, acceptance, and competition are dominant factors in the educational environment. That factor has a perennial relation to religious environments that cherish "super churches" and "super ministers." Institutions and individuals are honored because they are accomplished, purposeful, and productive. This pattern can become institutionalized from generation to generation.

Through our experience as teachers in theological education and as parents watching our children go through elementary and high school, college and graduate school, we have drawn at least one conclusion concerning the care for persons in education. Nothing in the educational experience is more important for the student than being known by members of the academic community. If persons move through academic programs with anonymity, their lives are necessarily imprinted with an inferior quality. If they are not known by fellow students and teachers, the formation of self misses the mark by light-years. If they are not known profoundly through intimate friendships, many social handicaps threaten. Without that knowing expression of care, persons develop strategies to force people to take notice; they operate to secure power by devising strategies that destroy others. Such a dynamic may be observed in organizational environments at every level. God's loving gifts must be mediated in the community of faith. God's sustaining presence must be mediated to those within the community of faith. God's caring direction must be mediated in the community of faith.

Parker Palmer has expressed the need for this mediation and has recommended three spiritual disciplines to enable our care for persons toward a discovery of vocation: "the study of sacred texts, the practice of prayer and contemplation, and the gathered life of the community itself."[4]

What more compatible list could one devise for a community of faith than this one? Such disciplines seem so inherently obvious in a church or seminary community! Unfortunately, this is not the case. In our nurturing environments we have allowed the elevation of such words as fact, theory, reality, and objective, when the more accurate word to be elevated and honored should have been "truth."

Educating toward truth does not mean turning away from facts and theories and objective realities. If we devote ourselves to truth, the facts will not necessarily change. . . . What will change is our relation to the facts, or to the world the facts make known. . . . In truthful knowing, the knower becomes coparticipant in a community of faithful relationships with other persons and creatures and things, with whatever our knowledge makes known.[5]

Hospitality: For Diversity Among Persons

Perhaps the most moving and powerful scene in the musical *Godspell* occurs as the Christ-figure is bidding farewell to the major personalities in the drama. The audience is reminded of the unique relationship Jesus has enjoyed with each follower. Therefore, the farewell with each is exceptional and reminds every observer of a previous event or scene or conversation or gesture that was witnessed earlier in the production. The message that diversity among the believers is acknowledged is communicated with extraordinary power! Such hospitality is far more than good manners. Such acceptance is beyond toleration. If spirituality and vocation converge, a caring for persons must be amplified into a hospitality for diversity among persons.

"All true formation must have within it room for contradiction and revolt."[6] If we provide environments in our communities of faith that allow for divergent as well as convergent thought, we shall encourage this diversity. If we maintain a corporate sensitivity to the revolution that shaped the earliest Christian communities, we shall continue to enrich our heritage. Of Martin Luther it has been observed that it was such a shame someone did not get hold of him when he was young and chop off his highs and fill in his lows so that when he became an adult he might have been capable of managing his father's business and living a quiet, productive life!

Whenever we struggle with what we are to do in life, we are reflecting the desire for a sense of being in the right place, finding our unique role, and celebrating diversity. Finding the will of God is a high priority. Yet we miss the internal clues written into our very existence. The parable of the talents in Matthew 25 is a story of the journey inward. It is filled with hope and encouragement. We are taught that we need not compare ourselves with others, that if we lose our lives we will find them again, that equality of gifts and equality of the distribution of gifts is not a valid issue, and that to be cautious and protective of our uniqueness will bring on hopelessness and discouragement.

One of the reasons we have difficulty celebrating diversity, finding our unique role, and being in the right place is that we have had no one to listen to us or even to look at us. Through the years of teaching, one particular exercise has demonstrated the truth of this difficulty. When students are given the opportunity of a public interview to state their opinions without interruption, rebuttal, or muttered editorials, they demonstrate an amazing eagerness to be the object of the interview! So few persons have experienced the sensation of having others listen to them. They do not hear others because they have had no one to hear them. They do not have the sense that their roles could be of any importance.

Thomas Merton insisted that every person has some type of vocation. Each individual receives God's call to experience the divine life and the divine kingdom. Only in finding that "place" will human beings be truly happy. The most important thing in life, Merton believed, was to "fulfill our own destiny . . . to be what God wants us to be." Vocation is not "a game of hide-and-seek with Divine Providence." It is no "sphinx's riddle, which we must solve in one guess or else perish." Indeed, some persons go through life making a vocation of wrong choices. Destiny, therefore, is no "immutable fate" that the deity forces upon us. It is the "interaction of two freedoms . . . two loves." We cannot "settle the problem of vocation outside the context of friendship and of love." Merton concluded that, "in planning the course of our lives, we must remember the importance and the destiny of our own freedom. . . . For our freedom is a gift God has given us in order that He may be able to love us more perfectly, and be loved by us more perfectly in return."[7]

There are several clues that God seems to use regularly in helping us discover our vocation. The first clue is to determine the needs of the world in which we live. In the concluding verses of Matthew 25, we are reminded that the hungry need food, the thirsty need drink, the strangers need a welcome, the naked need clothing, the sick need visitation, and the prisoners need an advocate. By direct implication, God must have a perennial concern for medical research to cure and prevent diseases, technical work to grow more food more efficiently, efforts to provide human rights for the oppressed, projects to provide friendship and love for the lonely, and efforts to bring peace on earth. The second clue is to discover the diversity of gifts God has given to enable us to meet some of those needs. Our discovery of gifts carries us into the world, where we find vocations and affirm our purposes.

When are we most like God? When we go to church? No!
When we read the Bible? No! When we pray? No! When we
meet the needs of others? Yes! When we engage in that which
provides meaning and fulfillment? Yes! When we do that which
can be done uniquely by us? Yes! When we release and celebrate diversity among ourselves? Yes!

> No matter how much we love and accept a person, provide sup-
> port, have warmth and affection for that individual, no matter
> how much we help in many ways, unless we can actually call that
> person forth so that the individual is exercising the uniqueness
> God gave, then the love is incomplete; the person is not free and
> is less than fully human. We have said that the most effective
> thing we can do to call forth the gift of another is to imply our
> own gift in freedom. This way seems selfish at first. Aren't we
> supposed to help the other person? What does our own gift have
> to do with it? We start there. The charismatic person is one who,
> by his/her very being, will be God's instrument in calling forth
> gifts. Such a person is Good News. That one is the embodiment
> of the freedom of the new humanity. Verbal proclamation of the
> Good News becomes believable. Those who exercise their own
> gifts in freedom can allow the Holy Spirit to do what the Spirit
> wants to do.[8]

Vocational Choices: Linking Giftedness with Purpose

Acknowledging the unique giftedness of persons, then moving logically to a celebration of diversity, still leaves us short of
the goal in our journey toward an understanding of the interre-
latedness of spirituality and vocation. For diversity can be
lauded for its own sake. In a society in which the prevailing
philosophical perspective tends toward a questionable human-
ism, the value of the individual is indeed prized. What distinctive perspective, then, does the Christian faith bring to this
concept?

The answer can be found in the *purpose* for the uniqueness of
persons. The biblical view of giftedness suggests that the Creator endows various persons with abilities for the fulfillment of
tasks requiring those particular gifts. Scripture is filled with
accounts of God's calling persons to specific tasks and equip-
ping them for their respective missions. One illustration found
early in the biblical narrative relates to the building of the tab-
ernacle:

> See, I have chosen Bezalel . . . and I have filled him with the
> Spirit of God, with skill, ability and knowledge in all kinds of

crafts—to make artistic designs for work in gold, silver and bronze, to cut and set stones, to work in wood, and to engage in all kinds of craftsmanship.

Exodus 31:2–5, NIV

A more general articulation of this principle is provided by Paul in two of his letters (1 Corinthians 12 and Ephesians 4) in which the purpose of the diversity of gifts is clearly stated—"to prepare God's people for works of service" (Eph. 4:12, NIV).

Iris Cully refers to the importance of this "purpose recognition" in writing: "All people have gifts, but only some rightly recognize these as given by God. This perspective makes it possible for individuals to develop their gifts in the conscious recognition of being empowered by the divine Spirit."[9]

It is an important goal for people's faith to discover their distinctive personal giftedness and then to search for appropriate ways to use this giftedness in vocation for the good of the kingdom and as an expression of personal spirituality. Unfortunately, there has been a tendency for the church to imply a hierarchy of vocational choices that hinders the unfolding of the vocational search process in the healthiest manner. Labels such as "secular vocation," "sacred vocation," or "church-related vocation" imply that some callings are more important than others for the follower of Jesus—that those who do not opt for the "sacred" or "church-related" vocation are relegated to a lesser status in living out their spirituality. Such a distinction is not in keeping with biblical teaching. Abbé Michel Quoist speaks to this misperception:

If only we knew how to look at life as God sees it, we would realize that nothing is secular in the world, that everything contributes to the building of the Kingdom of God. To have faith is not only to raise one's eyes to God to contemplate him; it is also to look at this world—with Christ's eyes.[10]

The conversation of the church compounds the problem by reserving the title of minister to those who are "called" to church-related vocations, thereby undermining the clear expectation of the New Testament writings that *all* believers are to be ministers in the name of Jesus as a part of their "vocation" of being Christians. "All Christians are in fact called to be ministers, and to designate one class by that name is a tacit surrender of the theological understanding of baptism."[11]

In light of the difficulties enumerated, how does one approach the search for vocation in a manner that links personhood, giftedness, faith commitment, and ministry without imposing artificial boundaries that unduly limit freedom of choice? The term "lifework spirituality" as used by James Michael Lee[12] seems to offer a constructive answer to the quest. If a person perceives vocation as the place where giftedness, spirituality, and call are integrated, then "lifework" (or vocation) can become both a source of and an expression of spirituality. Fulfillment of vocational responsibilities becomes a vehicle for demonstrating one's faith commitments. Life is viewed holistically, and the compartmentalization that too often separates faith and work is avoided. Lifework, wherever it is pursued, involves one in ministry in the name of Jesus—whether the setting is church, school, office, factory, or hundreds of other possibilities. "Wherever the Father has placed us, there we must strive that his kingdom of love and justice may come. This is not a matter of choice; it is the very meaning of our Christian life."[13]

Embracing this openness to a wide variety of vocational possibilities, all of which are seen as "thoroughly Christian" in potential, can be extraordinarily liberating to a person who senses a strong compulsion (call, if you will) to incorporate Christian commitment into lifework but does not find that his or her best gifts and interests correlate closely with the needs of those vocations often described as "church-related." There is value—and health—in an inclusive view of Christian vocation. M. Basil Pennington expresses this concept insightfully:

> Every vocation is a call to grow in love and express it in a particular context. Every vocation is a call to serve in love. This fact gives every work the dignity of a vocation, a call. Each activity we undertake is a response to God's love and presence, a part of his salvific presence and mission.[14]

Having argued the case for a broad understanding of Christian vocation, we must acknowledge that for some persons the appropriate response to vocational call will be a commitment to ministry through one of those vocations that contribute directly to the work of the church. The possibilities for such involvement have expanded substantially in recent years. Technological advances in communications, age-group specialization in education ministries, the heightened awareness of the role of the arts in faith expression, and the growth of church social ministries have all contributed to the increasing number of options now available for vocation in the church. Along with the new possibilities, there continues to be the need for those who would preach, teach, and evangelize—central to the mission of the church since its beginnings.

The forces that guide a person toward such a church-invested vocational choice may be varied. As suggested earlier, this involves a search for the correlation between one's gifts and needs—in this case the needs of the church for vocational ministry. Interest and inclination are both God-given aspects of personhood that should not be discounted. And there is the affirmation of the church itself—the beckoning from within the body of believers—which can serve to encourage the investment of life and gifts in that locus. "The call to serve . . . is both internal and external—a matter of one's individual inner awareness and the ratification of that awareness by the church."[15]

Ultimately, however, the final determinant in the process of vocational choice is our best understanding of the prompting of God's Spirit, as it enables us to understand ourselves, our world, God's purposes, and the church's mission. Decisions made within that context offer the possibility of significant fulfillment, whatever the specific vocational focus, in the blending of lifework and spirituality.

> Our goal is the Kingdom, the completion of God's creative vision, and we are God's hands in bringing that to pass.[16]

Notes

INTRODUCTION

1. Thomas M. Gannon and George W. Traub, *The Desert and the City: An Interpretation of the History of Christian Spirituality* (London: Macmillan Co., 1969), p. 10.

2. Thomas Merton, *A Vow of Conversation, Journals, 1964–1965* (New York: Farrar, Straus & Giroux, 1988), p. 103.

CHAPTER 1: MAPPING THE SPIRITUAL JOURNEY

1. Unpublished essay produced by the faculty group studying the definition of spirituality. Members of the group were Gerald Borchert, Diana Garland, Glenn Hinson, Mozelle Sherman, Tom Smothers, Dan Stiver, Wayne Ward, and Ernest White. Glenn Hinson is owed a special debt because of the way he chaired and led the committee as well as for the leadership and insight concerning things spiritual he has provided for many years through his teaching and writing. This group, of course, is not responsible for the content of this chapter.

2. Gabriel Marcel, *The Philosophy of Existentialism*, tr. Manya Harari (Secaucus, N.J.: Citadel Press, 1956), pp. 18–36.

3. The symbol of a web is related to the way in which knowledge is understood as a "web of belief" by W. V. Quine and J. S. Ullian in *The Web of Belief*, 2d ed. (New York: Random House, 1978). Maurice Merleau-Ponty points out that human beings are a "network" of relationships; see *The Phenomenology of Perception*, tr. Colin Smith, International Library of Philosophy and Scientific Method (London: Routledge & Kegan Paul, 1962), p. 456.

4. Brother Lawrence, *The Practice of the Presence of God*, tr. E. M. Blaiklock (Nashville: Thomas Nelson, 1981).

5. Karl Barth, *Church Dogmatics,* I/1 (Greenwood, S.C.: Attic Press, 1975), pp. 205–209, 227ff. The reference to Barth's doctrine of reconciliation as "the way of the Son of God into the far country" is in *Church Dogmatics* IV/1, tr. G. W. Bromiley (Edinburgh: T. & T. Clark, 1956), pp. 157–210.

6. Henri J. M. Nouwen, *With Open Hands* (Notre Dame, Ind.: Ave Maria Press, 1972), pp. 12, 14, 16–17, 20, 22, 56, 154. We are indebted to our colleague Charles J. Scalise for pointing out this image, which Nouwen used in the context of prayer, and applying it to the general context of spirituality and the movement of God's Spirit.

7. Paul Tillich, *Systematic Theology,* vol. 1 (Chicago: University of Chicago Press, 1951), pp. 11–12.

8. Ibid., p. 14.

9. Søren Kierkegaard, *Concluding Unscientific Postscript,* tr. David F. Swenson (Princeton, N.J.: Princeton University Press, 1941), pp. 178–179.

10. See John A. T. Robinson, *The Human Face of God* (Philadelphia: Westminster Press, 1973).

11. Dale Moody, *The Word of Truth: A Summary of Christian Doctrine Based on Biblical Revelation* (Grand Rapids: Wm. B. Eerdmans Publishing Co., 1981), pp. 226, 232.

12. The allusions in this sentence are to John Dewey's critique of a craving for certainty in *The Quest for Certainty: A Study of the Relation of Knowledge and Action* (New York: Capricorn Books, 1929) and to C. S. Lewis's remarkable account of his conversion, *Surprised by Joy: The Shape of My Early Life* (London: Fontana Books, 1955).

13. Tillich, *Systematic Theology,* vol. 1, p. 73.

14. Daniel O. Aleshire, *Faithcare* (Philadelphia: Westminster Press, 1988), p. 15.

15. See Urban T. Holmes III, *A History of Christian Spirituality: An Analytical Introduction* (Minneapolis: Seabury Press, 1980), pp. 68–69.

16. St. John of the Cross, *Dark Night of the Soul,* tr. E. Allison Peers (Garden City, N.Y.: Doubleday & Co., 1959); Teresa of Lisieux, *The Story of a Soul,* tr. John Clark (Washington, D.C.: ICS Publications, 1975).

17. Søren Kierkegaard, *The Sickness Unto Death: A Christian Psychological Exposition for Upbuilding and Awakening,* tr. Howard V. Hong and Edna H. Hong, Kierkegaard's Writings, vol. 19 (Princeton, N.J.: Princeton University Press, 1980), pp. 52–53.

18. Barbara Kelsey and Morton Kelsey, *Sacrament of Sexuality* (Warwick, N.Y.: Amity House, 1986), pp. 257–258. See also Morton T. Kelsey, *Companions on the Inner Way: The Art of Spiritual Guidance* (New York: Crossroad Publishing Co., 1987), pp. 113–114, 156–160.

19. A number of thinkers have appealed for a more holistic, responsible understanding of knowing. For example, see Henri J. M. Nouwen, *Creative Ministry* (Garden City, N.Y.: Doubleday & Co., Image Books, 1971), ch. 1; Parker J. Palmer, *To Know as We Are Known: A Spirituality of Education* (San Francisco: Harper & Row, 1983); Martin Heidegger, *Poetry, Language, Thought,* tr. Albert Hofstadter (New York: Harper & Row, 1971); Jerry H. Gill, *On Knowing God: New Directions for the Future of Theology* (Philadelphia: Westminster Press, 1981), chs. 3, 7, 11; Michael Polanyi, *Personal Knowledge: Towards a Post-Critical Philosophy,* 2d ed. (Chicago: University of Chicago Press, 1962); Richard J. Bernstein, *Beyond Objectivism and Relativism: Science, Hermeneutics, and Praxis* (Philadelphia: University of Pennsylvania Press, 1985).

20. Kierkegaard, *Postscript,* pp. 170ff.

21. See, for a fuller discussion, Aleshire, *Faithcare*, pp. 52–59.

22. Augustine, *The City of God*, in *Great Books of the Western World* (Chicago: Encyclopaedia Britannica, 1952), XIV.9.

23. This quotation is taken from a work based on John Wesley's selection of material from William Law: *The Heart of True Spirituality: Selections from William Law*, ed. Frank Baker, vol. 1 in the series John Wesley's Own Choice (Grand Rapids: Francis Asbury Press, 1985), p. 24 (1.14).

24. James Fowler, *Stages of Faith: The Psychology of Human Development and the Quest for Meaning* (San Francisco: Harper & Row, 1981).

25. For example, see Michael Cox, *Handbook of Christian Spirituality* (San Francisco: Harper & Row, 1983), pp. 28–33.

26. Hans-Georg Gadamer has made this point powerfully in terms of what he calls "effective-historical consciousness *(wirkungsgeschichtliches Bewusstsein)*"; see *Truth and Method* (New York: Crossroad Publishing Co., 1975), pp. 267–274.

27. Holmes, *History*, pp. 8–9.

28. E. Glenn Hinson, "Seeking a Suitable Spirituality in a Sect Becoming Catholic," *Waiting for Apocalypse*, ed. Tilden Edwards (New York: Harper & Row, 1984), p. 157.

29. For example, see John Dominic Crossan, *In Parables: The Challenge of the Historical Jesus* (New York: Harper & Row, 1973), pp. 26–27.

30. Langdon Gilkey, *Reaping the Whirlwind: A Christian Interpretation of History* (New York: Seabury Press, 1976), pp. 285–295.

31. Holmes, *History*, p. 100.

32. For example, see Kenneth Leech, *Experiencing God: Theology as Spirituality* (San Francisco: Harper & Row, 1985); Holmes, *History*; Kelsey, *Companions*; and Hinson, "Seeking."

33. Hinson, "Seeking," pp. 148–152, 157.

34. Richard J. Foster, *Celebration of Discipline: The Path to Spiritual Growth* (San Francisco: Harper & Row, 1978), p. 8.

CHAPTER 2: THE BIBLE AND THE SPIRITUAL PILGRIMAGE

1. Dietrich Bonhoeffer, *Psalms: The Prayerbook of the Bible* (Minneapolis: Augsburg Publishing House, 1970), p. 15.

2. Reflecting on his study of the psalms while in a German prison camp during World War II, Claus Westermann wrote (in *Praise and Lament in the Psalms*, 2nd ed., tr. Keith R. Crim and Richard N. Soulen [Atlanta: John Knox Press, 1981], p. 6): "Whenever one in his enforced separation praised God in song, or speech, or silence, he was conscious of himself not as an individual, but as a member of the congregation. When in hunger and cold, between interrogations, or as one sentenced to death, he was privileged to praise God, he knew that in all his ways he was borne up by the church's praise of God."

3. Psalms 81:10, 109:8–9, and other examples too numerous to cite. See Walther Zimmerli, *I Am Yahweh*, tr. Douglas W. Stott, ed. Walter Brueggemann (Atlanta: John Knox Press, 1982).

4. Robert S. Bilheimer, *A Spirituality for the Long Haul: Biblical Risk and Moral Stand* (Philadelphia: Fortress Press, 1984), p. 19.

5. James L. Crenshaw, *Ecclesiastes,* Old Testament Library (Philadelphia: Westminster Press, 1987), pp. 184–185, reports two possible emendations he believes are more consistent with the message of Ecclesiastes than the Masoretic text's "your Creator." They are "your well" (i.e., your wife) and "your pit" (i.e., your grave). Rabbi Akiba's play on words in *Pirke Abot* 3:1 testifies to the antiquity of the traditional rendering and its true meaning.

6. Jon D. Levenson, "The Jerusalem Temple in Devotional and Visionary Experience," in *Jewish Spirituality: From the Bible Through the Middle Ages,* ed. Arthur Green (New York: Crossroad Publishing Co., 1986), p. 53.

7. James L. Kugel, "Topics in the History of the Spirituality of the Psalms," in Green, ed., *Jewish Spirituality,* p. 127.

8. Gerald L. Borchert, *Assurance and Warning* (Nashville: Broadman Press, 1987).

9. Edward E. Thornton and Gerald L. Borchert, *The Crisis of Fear* (Nashville: Broadman Press, 1988).

10. For example, see Marcus Barth, *Ephesians,* Anchor Bible, 2 vols. (Garden City, N.Y.: Doubleday & Co., 1974); F. F. Bruce, *The Epistles to the Colossians, to Philemon and to the Ephesians,* New International Commentary on the New Testament (Grand Rapids: Wm. B. Eerdmans Publishing Co., 1984); W. O. Carver, *The Glory of God and the Christian Calling* (Nashville: Broadman Press, 1949); S. Hanson, *The Unity of the Church in the New Testament, Colossians, and Ephesians* (Uppsala: Almqvist, 1946); John A. Mackay, *God's Order—The Ephesian Letter and This Present Time* (New York: Macmillan Co., 1956); and Ralph Martin, "Ephesians," *The Broadman Bible Commentary,* vol. 2 (Nashville: Broadman Press, 1971).

11. The question of whether or not Paul could have written Ephesians has been the subject of great debate among New Testament scholars. For those interested in pursuing the matter further, see Introductions to the commentaries by Marcus Barth, F. F. Bruce, and Ralph Martin. Also helpful will be New Testament Introductions such as Donald Guthrie, *New Testament Introduction* (Downers Grove, Ill.: Inter-Varsity Press, 1970), pp. 479–508, and W. G. Kümmel, *Introduction to the New Testament,* rev. ed. (Nashville: Abingdon Press, 1975), pp. 357–366. For more detailed arguments, see C. Leslie Mitton, *The Epistle to the Ephesians* (Oxford: Clarendon Press, 1951) and A. Van Roon, *The Authority of Ephesians* (Leiden: Brill, 1974). For those interested in other matters related to Ephesians, please see the annotated bibliography in Gerald L. Borchert, *Paul and His Interpreters* (Madison, Wis.: InterVarsity Press, IBR, 1985), pp. 69–72.

12. Sydney Cave was absolutely correct in his analysis of Pauline mysticism when he stated that the mysticism in the Pauline corpus was not one of a mystic flight to aloneness with the absolute but a new corporate mysticism that involved the church and the Christian vocation of service. See his *The Gospel of St. Paul* (Garden City, N.Y.: Doubleday & Co., 1929), p. 50. See also Elias Andrews, *The Meaning of Christ for Paul* (Nashville: Abingdon-Cokesbury, 1949), pp. 84–88. For a bibliography on Pauline mysticism see Borchert, *Paul and His Interpreters,* pp. 100–102.

13. Parental-like care for the Christian church is a hallmark of the Pauline letters. Concerning Paul's parental style, see Gerald L. Borchert, *Discovering Thessalonians* (Carmel, N.Y.: Guideposts, 1986), p. 40.

14. In the 1960s the term "the new morality" was often applied to the changing ethical norms that were associated with discussions of "situation ethics" such as in Joseph Fletcher, *Situation Ethics: The New Morality* (Philadelphia: Westminster Press, 1966).

15. For the importance of sociological studies in understanding the New Testament, see Borchert's article "Sociology of the New Testament" in the *Mercer Dictionary of the Bible* (Macon, Ga.: Mercer University Press, 1990). The bibliography there will be helpful. Or see the bibliography in *Paul and His Interpreters*, pp. 22–24.

16. Every Christian ought to read the great classic by John Bunyan. Contemporary translations of Bunyan are also available at bookstores. See *Pilgrim's Progress in Modern English*, retold by J. H. Thomas (Chicago: Moody Press, 1964) or *Dangerous Journey* (Grand Rapids: Wm. B. Eerdmans Publishing Co., n.d.).

CHAPTER 3: SPIRITUALITY AND WORSHIP

1. Ingmar Bergman, *The Magic Lantern*, tr. Joan Tate (New York: Viking Press, 1988).

2. Paul Waitman Hoon, *The Integrity of Worship* (Nashville: Abingdon Press, 1971), p. 24.

3. E. Glenn Hinson, "Commentary on the Definition of Christian Spirituality" (Faculty retreat, Southern Baptist Theological Seminary, 1986, unpublished), p. 1.

4. Donald Hustad, *Jubilate!: Christian Music in the Evangelical Tradition* (Carol Stream, Ill.: Hope Publishing Co., 1981), p. 63.

5. Kevin W. Irwin, *Liturgy, Prayer, and Spirituality* (New York: Paulist Press, 1984), p. 14.

6. E. Frank Tupper, "A Baptist Vision of the Church," *Review and Expositor* 84 (Fall 1987), p. 620.

7. Ibid., pp. 621–622.

8. Paul Richardson, "The Primacy of Worship," *Review and Expositor* 65 (Winter 1988), p. 11.

9. Reinhold Niebuhr, "The Weakness of Common Worship in American Protestantism," *Christianity and Crisis*, May 28, 1951, cited in William H. Willimon, *The Service of God* (Nashville: Abingdon Press, 1983), p. 89.

10. Martin E. Marty, *A Cry of Absence* (San Francisco: Harper & Row, 1983), p. 5.

11. Ibid.

12. Ibid.

13. Richard A. Baer, Jr., "Quaker Silence, Catholic Liturgy, and Pentecostal Glossolalia—Some Functional Similarities," in *Perspectives on the New Pentecostalism* (Grand Rapids: Baker Book House, 1976), p. 152.

14. Ibid., p. 163.

15. Lawrence O. Richards, *A Practical Theology of Spirituality* (Grand Rapids: Zondervan Publishing House, 1987), p. 111.

16. Fred B. Craddock, *As One Without Authority* (Nashville: Abingdon Press, 1979), p. 6.

17. Ibid., p. 7, citing Max Picard, *The World of Silence* (Chicago: Henry Regnery Co., 1952), pp. 26–27.

18. Frederick Buechner, *Telling the Truth: The Gospel as Tragedy, Comedy, and Fairy Tale* (San Francisco: Harper & Row, 1977), p. 23.

19. Søren Kierkegaard, *Purity of Heart Is to Will One Thing* (New York: Harper & Row, 1938), p. 164.

20. John Wesley, *The Journal of John Wesley* (Chicago: Moody Press, 1952), pp. 63–64.

21. Harold Best, "Christian Responsibility in Music," in Leland Ryken, *The Christian Imagination* (Grand Rapids: Baker Book House, 1981), p. 405.

CHAPTER 4: ETHICAL MATURITY AND SPIRITUAL FORMATION

1. Douglas John Hall, "Theological Education as Character Formation?" *Theological Education*, vol. 24, suppl. 1, (1988), pp. 53–79, suggests formation be viewed as a contemporary effort to develop a biblical theology of discipleship.

2. Bill J. Leonard, "The Spiritual Development of the Minister," *Formation for Christian Ministry* ed. Anne Davis and Wade Rowatt, Jr. (Louisville: Review and Expositor, 1985), pp. 74–75, and Hall, "Theological Education," p. 54.

3. Richard J. Foster, *Celebration of Discipline: The Path to Spiritual Growth* (San Francisco: Harper & Row, 1978).

4. Hall, "Theological Education," p. 66.

5. See H. Richard Niebuhr, *Radical Monotheism and Western Culture* (Lincoln, Neb.: University of Nebraska Press, 1960), pp. 11–18.

6. Karl Barth, *Epistle to the Philippians* (London: SCM Press, 1962), pp. 45–46.

7. Dietrich Bonhoeffer, *Ethics*, ed. Eberhard Bethge (New York: Macmillan Co., 1965), p. 80.

8. Gordon MacDonald, "Anatomy of a Spiritual Leader," *Leadership* 5:4 (1984), p. 109.

9. Charles Blair, *The Man Who Could Do No Wrong* (Wheaton, Ill.: Tyndale House, 1982).

10. See, for instance, John Killinger, *A Devotional Guide to the Gospels* (Waco, Tex.: Word Books, 1984), and E. Glenn Hinson, *Seekers After a Mature Faith* (Waco, Tex.: Word Books, 1968).

11. Eberhard Bethge, *Dietrich Bonhoeffer: Man of Vision, Man of Courage*, tr. Eric Mosbacher et al. (New York: Harper & Row, 1970), p. 154.

12. Henri J. M. Nouwen, *Creative Ministry* (Garden City, N.Y.: Doubleday & Co., Image Books, 1978), p. 97.

13. See Lawrence Kohlberg, *The Philosophy of Moral Development: Moral Stages and the Idea of Justice*, vol. 1; *The Psychology of Moral Development: The Nature and Validity of Moral Stages*, vol. 2 (San Francisco: Harper & Row, 1984); James Fowler, *Stages of Faith* (San Francisco: Harper & Row, 1981).

14. See Parker J. Palmer, *To Know as We Are Known: A Spirituality of Education* (San Francisco: Harper & Row, 1983), pp. 17–32, and Bruce Joyce and Marsha Weil, *Models of Teaching*, 3rd ed. (Englewood Cliffs, N.J.: Prentice-Hall, 1986).

15. John Bright, *The Kingdom of God: The Biblical Concept and Its Mean-*

ing for the Church (Nashville: Abingdon-Cokesbury Press, 1953), and Rudolf Schnackenburg, *God's Rule and Kingdom*, tr. John Murray (New York: Herder & Herder, 1963).

16. Georgia Harkness, *Understanding the Kingdom of God* (Nashville: Abingdon Press, 1974), p. 55.

17. Karen Lebacqz, *Professional Ethics: Power and Paradox* (Nashville: Abingdon Press, 1985), p. 120.

CHAPTER 5: STORY AND SPIRITUALITY

1. Nikos Kazantzakis, *Saint Francis* (New York: Simon & Schuster, 1962), p. 13.

2. H. Richard Niebuhr, *The Meaning of Revelation* (New York: Macmillan Co., 1941), p. 43.

3. Ibid., p. 59.

4. Ibid., pp. 72–73.

5. Ibid., pp. 84–90, 90–101, 110–114, 132ff., 141f.; see also Stanley Hauerwas, *Truthfulness and Tragedy* (Notre Dame, Ind.: University of Notre Dame Press, 1977), pp. 10–12.

6. Stanley Hauerwas, "Story and Theology," *Religion in Life* 45:3 (1976), p. 339, quoting Sallie McFague TeSelle, "The Experience of Coming to Belief," *Theology Today* 32:2 (July 1975), pp. 159–160.

7. Ibid., p. 344.

8. Sallie McFague TeSelle, "The Experience of Coming to Belief," pp. 159–160.

9. Stephen Crites, "The Narrative Quality of Experience," *Journal of the American Academy of Religion* 39 (1971), p. 296. What we here call "everyday life-experience stories" is our effort to communicate what Crites calls "mundane stories." He says, "I am uneasy about that term." And so are we. Crites means that these stories happen *within the world of experiences that make sense to people who live in our culture.* To communicate Crites's meaning, we compromised with "everyday life-experience stories." But we still aren't satisfied. You may figure out a better term and substitute it for our term. Maybe "world-of-meaning stories"? Or simply "the kind of stories that people around here tell when they're making sense"?

10. Niebuhr, *The Meaning of Revelation*, pp. 117ff. and 132ff.; and Dietrich Bonhoeffer, *Ethics*, ed. Eberhard Bethge (New York: Macmillan Co., 1965), passim.

11. James McClendon, *Ethics* (Nashville: Abingdon Press, 1986), ch. 3.

12. James Loder, *The Transforming Moment* (San Francisco: Harper & Row, 1981).

13. Ibid., pp. 328–355.

14. Ibid., pp. 41ff., 348ff.

15. Will Campbell, *Brother to a Dragonfly* (New York: Continuum Publishing Co., 1987), p. 7.

16. Ibid., pp. 202–203.

17. Ibid., p. 224.

18. John Claypool, "To Walk and Not to Faint," in his *The Light Within You: Looking at Life Through New Eyes* (Waco, Tex.: Word Press, 1983), p. 139.

19. Myron C. Madden, *Blessing: Giving the Gift of Power* (Nashville: Broadman Press, 1988), p. 90.

20. Ibid., p. 91.

CHAPTER 6: CHRISTIAN SPIRITUALITY AND THE ARTS

1. Hans-Georg Gadamer, *Truth and Method,* tr. Garrett Barden and John Cumming (New York: Crossroad Publishing Co., 1985); and Jürgen Habermas, *Knowledge and Human Interests,* tr. Jeremy J. Shapiro (Boston: Beacon Press, 1971).

2. See William F. Harris, *The Basic Patterns of Plot* (Norman, Okla.: University of Oklahoma Press, 1959).

3. See "Learning from Beauty," *Review and Expositor* 65:1 (Winter 1988), pp. 101–120.

4. For a full discussion of these points see *Review and Expositor* 65:2 (Spring 1988), pp. 221–231.

5. See Rudolf Otto, *The Idea of the Holy,* tr. John W. Harvey (New York: Oxford University Press, 1950).

6. Paul Ricoeur, *Interpretation Series: Discourses in the Surplus of Meaning* (Fort Worth, Tex.: Texas Christian University Press, 1976), pp. 45–69.

CHAPTER 7: LEARNING ENVIRONMENTS AND SPIRITUAL FORMATION

1. Elliot Eisner, *The Educational Imagination: On the Design and Evaluation of School Programs* (New York: Macmillan Co., 1979).

2. Quoted in Maria Harris, *Teaching and Religious Imagination* (New York: Harper & Row, 1987), p. 133.

3. Parker Palmer, *To Know as We Are Known* (New York: Harper & Row, 1983), p. 69.

4. The New Games Foundation, P.O. Box 7901, San Francisco, CA 94120.

5. Benjamin S. Bloom, *Stability and Change in Human Characteristics* (New York: John Wiley & Sons, 1964), p. 221.

6. Ibid.

7. P. S. Holzman and C. Pousey, "Disinhibition of Communicated Thought: Generality and Role of Cognitive Style," *Journal of Abnormal Psychology* 77 (1971), p. 125.

8. Beulah Roberts Compton and Burt Galaway, *Social Work Processes* (Homewood, Ill.: Dorsey Press, 1984), p. 107.

9. Rudolf H. Moos, *The Social Climate Scale* (Palo Alto, Calif.: Consulting Psychologists Press, 1974), p. 30.

10. Ibid., p. 4.

11. Rudolf H. Moos, *Evaluation of Treatment Environments* (New York: John Wiley & Sons, 1974), p. 4.

12. Malcolm Knowles, *The Adult Learner: A Neglected Species,* 2d ed. (Houston, Tex.: Gulf Publishing Co., 1978), p. 91.

13. Rudolf H. Moos, *Group Environment Scale Manual* (Palo Alto, Calif.: Consulting Psychologists Press, 1986), pp. 1–2.

14. The *Group Environment Scale* can be ordered from the Consulting Psychologists Press, 577 College Avenue, Palo Alto, CA 94306.

15. Dorothee Soelle, *Death by Bread Alone* (Philadelphia: Fortress Press, 1978), p. 138.

CHAPTER 8: THE CONTRIBUTION OF WOMEN TO SPIRITUALITY

1. Louis Bouyer, *The Spirituality of the New Testament and the Fathers*, tr. Mary P. Ryan (New York: Desclee Co., 1960), pp. 190–210.

2. *Martyrdom of Perpetua and Felicitas* 15; Musurillo, pp. 123ff.

3. *Apostolic Canons* 65.1; in *Texte und Untersuchungen*, LXXV:109.

4. Gregory of Nyssa, *Life of St. Macrina;* Migne, *Patrologia Graeca*, XLVI:972.

5. Preface to *Commentary on Galatians*.

6. *Letters* 40.3; *Nicene and Post-Nicene Fathers*, First series, ed. Philip Schaff, VI:59.

7. Jerome, *Letters* 46.1, 13.

8. Jerome, *Letters* 22.

9. See Palladius, *Lausiac History*, chs. 46, 54. Palladius, also an Origenist, was an unabashed admirer of Melania. The story of Melania the Younger is equally interesting, for it reflects the influence women of wealth and culture could wield. See Elizabeth Clark, "Piety, Propaganda, and Politics in the *Life of Melania the Younger*," in *Ascetic Piety and Women's Faith*, Studies in Women and Religion, vol. 20 (Lewiston, N.Y.: Edwin Mellen Press, 1986), pp. 61–94.

10. Regarding the impact of the Jerusalem liturgy on the rest of the Christian world after Etheria, see Randall Merle Payne, "Christian Worship in Jerusalem in the Fourth and Fifth Centuries: The Development of the Lectionary, Calendar, and Liturgy" (Ph.D. dissertation, Southern Baptist Theological Seminary, Louisville, Kentucky, 1980), pp. 269–278.

11. *Scivias*, Part III, Vision XI.38; *Corpus Christianorum*, XLIIIA:592f.

12. *Liber vitae meritorum*, Book II, ch. 35.

13. *Hadewijch: The Complete Works*, ed. Mother Columba Hart, O.S.B. Classics of Western Spirituality (New York: Paulist Press, 1980), p. 158.

14. *Legate of Divine Love* II.6; *Sources Chrétiennes*, II:258.

15. On Julian as a spiritual guide see Julia Gatta, *Three Spiritual Directors for Our Time* (Cambridge, Mass.: Cowley Publications, 1986), pp. 50–90; on her theological significance see Grace M. Jantzen, *Julian of Norwich: Mystic and Theologian* (New York: Paulist Press, 1988).

16. Suzanne Nofke, O.P., *Catherine of Siena: The Dialogue.* Classics of Western Spirituality (New York: Paulist Press, 1980), p. 9.

17. *Life*, ch. 20; tr. E. Allison Peers (Garden City, N.Y.: Doubleday & Co., Image Books, 1960), p. 189.

18. Nancy Ring, "Feminine Spirituality," *The Westminster Dictionary of Christian Spirituality*, ed. Gordon S. Wakefield (Philadelphia: Westminster Press, 1983), p. 148.

19. Anne Carr, "On Feminist Spirituality," *Women's Spirituality: Resources for Christian Development*, ed. Joann Wolski Conn (New York: Paulist Press, 1986), p. 49.

20. See the helpful delineations in Conn's introduction to *Women's Spirituality*, p. 3.

21. *I Asked for Wonder: A Spiritual Anthology*, ed. Samuel S. Dresner (New York: Crossroad Publishing Co., 1988), p. 38.

22. An insightful new book by Leonardo Boff, *The Maternal Face of God* (New York: Harper & Row, 1987), offers an extended analysis of the feminine in its religious expressions through a comprehensive study of Mary.

23. *The Westminster Dictionary of Christian Spirituality*, p. 149.

24. Much constructive reflection on the suffering of God is occurring in contemporary theology. See especially Paul S. Fiddes, *The Creative Suffering of God* (Oxford: Clarendon Press, 1986).

25. A point made in the new work by Kathleen Fischer, *Women at the Well: Feminist Perspectives on Spiritual Direction* (New York: Paulist Press, 1988), pp. 195ff.

26. This is Sandra M. Schneiders's conclusion in "The Effects of Women's Experience on Their Spirituality," *Women's Spirituality*, p. 33.

27. See above, pp. 5–6.

28. On Augustine as a towering, if pejorative, theological interpreter, see Elaine Pagels's *Adam, Eve, and the Serpent* (New York: Random House, 1988). In this rich analysis, Pagels illumines how Augustine's portrayal of the creation and human fall have continued to shape perspectives concerning sexuality, moral freedom, and human value.

29. Carol Gilligan compares the male and female developmental models in her article "In a Different Voice: Visions of Maturity," *Women's Spirituality*, pp. 63ff.

30. Ibid., p. 75.

31. See Rosemary Radford Ruether, "Mothers of the Church: Ascetic Women in the Late Patristic Age," in *Women of Spirit: Female Leadership in the Jewish and Christian Traditions*, ed. R. Ruether and E. McLaughlin (New York: Simon & Schuster, 1979).

32. Schneiders, "Effects of Women's Experience," p. 31.

33. See Mary Daly's epochal *The Church and the Second Sex* (New York: Harper & Row, 1968).

34. Anne Wilson Schaef, *Women's Reality: An Emerging Female System in the White Male Society* (San Francisco: Harper & Row, 1981). Cf. Barbel von Wartenberg-Potter, *We Will Not Hang Our Harps on the Willows* (Oak Park, Ill.: Meyer-Stone Books, 1988), pp. 88ff.

35. This is Bernard Prusak's descriptive phrase. See his article in *Religion and Sexism*, ed. Rosemary Radford Ruether (New York: Simon & Schuster, 1974), pp. 89–116.

36. Schneiders, "Effects of Women's Experience," p. 42.

37. *Table Talk of Luther*, tr. and ed. William Hazlitt (London: William Clowes & Sons, 1890), p. 300.

CHAPTER 9: MINORITIES AND SPIRITUALITY

This paper has benefited from the comments of a friend and colleague in the reign, Otis Turner, of the Presbyterian Church (U.S.A.)

1. Gustavo Gutiérrez, *We Drink from Our Own Wells: The Spiritual Jour-*

ney of a People (Maryknoll, N.Y.: Orbis Books, 1985). For a discussion, see Jon Sobrino, *Spirituality of Liberation Toward Political Holiness* (Maryknoll, N.Y.: Orbis Books, 1985), pp. 46–79.

2. Federico Revilla, *Usted Puede Ser un Mistico* (Barcelona: Juan Flores, 1964), p. 107. Revilla suggests that one should be addicted to thinking and living within the body of Christ without erecting personal or corporate barriers.

3. This is not to say that we Christians are totally insensitive to the issue. Major denominations are seriously searching for solutions. See, for example, *Visions of an Inclusive Church: Report to the American Lutheran Church from Its Taskforce on Racial Inclusiveness* (Minneapolis: Office of Church in Society, American Lutheran Church, 1984); Paul W. Light, "Race and Ethnicity in the ABC: Summarizing a Research Process and Report," *American Baptist Quarterly* 5 (March 1986), p. 43.

4. James H. Davis and Woodie W. White, *Racial Transition in the Church* (Nashville: Abingdon Press, 1980), p. 80.

5. Ibid., pp. 14–47.

6. Several theorists have studied the problem of prejudice in society. Classic among these is Gordon W. Allport's *The Nature of Prejudice,* first published in 1954 by Addison-Wesley, which published a 25th Anniversary Edition in March 1987.

7. Leon Chestang, "Environmental Influences on Social Functioning: The Black Experience," in P. San Juan Cafferty and Leon Chestang, eds., *The Diverse Society: Implications for Social Policy* (Washington, D.C.: National Association of Social Workers, 1976), pp. 59–74.

8. For a discussion on the subject, see David Chidester, *Patterns of Power, Religion, and Politics in American Culture* (Englewood Cliffs, N.J.: Prentice-Hall, 1988), pp. 148ff.

9. This is not to deny the validity of concern for numerical growth. My position here is that quantitative growth, purposely sought from a homogeneous perspective, is contrary to the church's original purpose. For a meaningful discussion on this issue, see C. René Padilla, *Mission Between the Times* (Grand Rapids: Wm. B. Eerdmans Publishing Co., 1985), pp. 165–169.

10. Raymond Bailey, *Thomas Merton on Mysticism* (Garden City, N.Y.: Doubleday & Co., Image Books, 1987), pp. 53–79.

11. For a discussion on the impact of the social environment on the marginal believer, see Edward P. Wimberly and Anne Streaty Wimberly, *Liberation and Human Wholeness: The Conversion Experiences of Black People in Slavery and Freedom* (Nashville: Abingdon Press, 1986).

12. Jon Sobrino, *Spirituality of Liberation: Toward Political Holiness,* tr. from the Spanish by Robert R. Barr (Maryknoll, N.Y.: Orbis Books, 1988).

13. James H. Cone, *God of the Oppressed* (New York: Seabury Press, 1975), pp. 16–102.

14. J. Deotis Roberts, *Roots of a Black Future: Family and Church* (Philadelphia: Westminster Press, 1980), pp. 39–56. For further discussion see James H. Cone, *A Black Theology of Liberation,* 2nd ed. (Maryknoll, N.Y.: Orbis Books, 1986), pp. 1–40; and E. Franklin Frazier, *The Negro Church in America.* (New York: Schocken Books, 1974).

15. Don E. Saliers, *Worship and Spirituality* (Philadelphia: Westminster Press, 1984). See editor's introduction by Richard H. Bell, p. 12.

16. Gayraud S. Wilmore, *Black Religion and Black Radicalism,* 2d ed. (Maryknoll, N.Y.: Orbis Books, 1983). For discussion see Roberts, *Roots of a Black Future,* pp. 39–56.

17. Roberts, *Roots of a Black Future,* pp. 114–116.

18. Harold Carter, *The Prayer Tradition of Black People* (Valley Forge, Pa.: Judson Press, 1976).

19. Roberts, *Roots of a Black Future,* pp. 113–115.

20. *Visions of an Inclusive Church,* pp. 3–4.

21. Dearing E. King, "Worship in the Black Church," in Emmanuel L. McCall, *Black Church Lifestyles* (Nashville: Broadman Press, 1986), pp. 69–81.

CHAPTER 10: THE MINISTER AS SPIRITUAL FRIEND

1. Tom Brown and William J. Watkins, *The Tracker* (East Rutherford, N.J.: Berkley Publishing Group, 1984), p. 1.

2. Ibid.

3. Kenneth Leech, *Soul Friend: The Practice of Christian Spirituality* (San Francisco: Harper & Row, 1980).

4. *The Philokalia: The Complete Text,* tr. and ed. G. E. H. Palmer, Philip Sherrard, and Kallistos Ware, 3 vols. (London and Boston: Faber & Faber, 1979ff.). A one-volume anthology of the same source material is *The Art of Prayer,* tr. E. Kadloubovsky and E. M. Palmer (London: Faber & Faber, 1966).

5. I write of this spiritual awakening in *Being Transformed: An Inner Way of Spiritual Growth* (Philadelphia: Westminster Press, 1984).

6. Henri J. M. Nouwen, "Reaching Out," in Jerome M. Neufelder and Mary C. Coelho, eds., *Writings on Spiritual Direction by Great Christian Masters* (New York: Seabury Press, 1982), pp. 60–61.

7. This story and some of the preceding ideas were first published in "Prayer of the Heart," *The Pastoral Forum,* Publication of the Pastoral Institute, Columbus, Georgia, 7:3 (Fall 1988), pp. 14–16.

CHAPTER 11: SPIRITUALITY, JOY, AND THE VALUE OF PLAY

1. Bo Reicke, *The Gospel of Luke* (Richmond: John Knox Press, 1964), pp. 58ff. and 75ff. Luke's "record is dominated by future expectations and colored by *ecstatic joy* that the kingdom of God will come. . . . The idea of joy at the closeness of salvation and the hope that the kingdom of God will promptly become a reality are nowhere so clearly worked out as in these birth narratives."

2. Nicolas Herman (Brother Lawrence), *The Practice of the Presence of God,* tr. John J. Delaney (Garden City, N.Y.: Doubleday & Co., Image Books, 1977).

3. From a lecture at Berea College, Berea, Kentucky, 1975.

4. Harvey Cox, *The Feast of Fools* (Cambridge, Mass.: Harvard University Press, 1969).

CHAPTER 12: SPIRITUALITY AND SEXUALITY

1. Reay Tannahill, *Sex in History* (Briarcliff Manor, N.Y.: Stein & Day, 1980), p. 141.

2. J. Money, "Propaedeutics of diecious G-I/R: Theoretical foundations for understanding dimorphic gender-identity role," in J. M. Reinisch, L. A. Rosenblum, and S. A. Sanders, eds., *Masculinity/Femininity: Basic Perspectives* (New York: Oxford University Press, 1987).

3. Virginia Goldner, "Warning: Family Therapy May Be Hazardous to Your Health," *The Family Therapy Networker* 9 (1985), 19–23.

4. Donald Goergen, *The Sexual Celibate* (New York: Seabury Press, 1974), p. 224.

5. Kay Deaux, "Psychological Constructions of Masculinity and Femininity," in Reinisch, Rosenblum, and Sanders, eds., *Masculinity/Femininity*, pp. 289–303.

6. Eleanor Maccoby, "The Varied Meanings of 'Masculine' and 'Feminine,' " in Reinisch, Rosenblum, and Sanders, eds., *Masculinity/Femininity*, pp. 227–239.

7. Deaux, op. cit.

8. Victor Furnish, *The Moral Teaching of Paul* (Nashville: Abingdon Press, 1987).

9. Diana S. and David E. Garland, *Beyond Companionship: Christians in Marriage* (Philadelphia: Westminster Press, 1986), p. 128.

10. R. F. Collins, "The Bible and Sexuality II: The New Testament," in *Biblical Theology Bulletin 8* (1978), 3–18, p. 11.

11. Reinisch, Rosenblum, and Sanders, eds., *Masculinity/Femininity*.

12. Money, "Propaedeutics," p. 13.

13. Ibid.

14. John Moore, *Sexuality and Spirituality: The Interplay of Masculine and Feminine in Human Development* (San Francisco: Harper & Row, 1981).

15. Ibid., p. 229.

16. Lucius F. Cervantes, *And God Made Man and Woman* (Chicago: Henry Regnery Co., 1959), p. 139.

17. Ibid., p. 140.

18. Amanda Porterfield, *Feminine Spirituality in America* (Philadelphia: Temple University Press, 1980), p. 6.

19. See also Garland and Garland, *Beyond Companionship*.

20. David Mace, *Hebrew Marriage: A Sociological Study* (New York: Philosophical Library, 1953).

21. Wayne A. Meeks, *The First Urban Christians: The Social World of the Apostle Paul* (New Haven, Conn.: Yale University Press, 1983).

22. Harry N. Hollis and B. A. Clendinning, *Sex Education: Resource Guide for the Church* (Nashville: Broadman Press, 1970), p. 5.

23. David M. Reed, "Male Sexual Conditioning," in Robert F. Stahmann and William J. Hiebert, eds., *Klemer's Counseling in Marital and Sexual Problems: A Clinician's Handbook,* 2d ed. (Baltimore: Williams & Wilkins Co., 1977).

24. Garland and Garland, *Beyond Companionship,* p. 143.

25. Ann Belford Ulanov, *Receiving Woman: Studies in the Psychology and Theology of the Feminine* (Philadelphia: Westminster Press, 1981), p. 91.

26. B. E. Toldstedt and J. P. Stokes, "Relation of Verbal Affectivism and Physical Intimacy to Marital Satisfaction," *Journal of Counseling Psychology 30* (1983), pp. 573–580.

27. Elisabeth Schüssler Fiorenza, *In Memory of Her: A Feminist's Theological Reconstruction of Christian Origins* (New York: Crossroad Publishing Co., 1983), p. 345.

28. Immanuel Kant, *Kritik der praktischen Vernunft, Gesammelte Schriften*, vol. V (Rumer-Verlag, 1908), p. 87.

29. Scott M. Peck, *The Road Less Traveled* (New York: Simon & Schuster, 1978), p. 118.

CHAPTER 13: SPIRITUALITY AND VOCATION

1. Alan Jones, "Are We Lovers Anymore?" *ATS Theological Education* 14:1 (1987), p. 10.

2. Craig Dykstra, "The Formative Power of the Congregation," *Religious Education* 82:4 (1987), p. 534.

3. Ibid., p. 535.

4. Parker Palmer, *To Know as We Are Known* (San Francisco: Harper & Row, 1983), p. 17.

5. Ibid., pp. 31–32.

6. Jones, "Are We Lovers Anymore?" p. 22.

7. Thomas Merton, *No Man Is an Island* (Garden City, N.Y.: Doubleday & Co., 1956), pp. 107–108.

8. Gordon Cosby, "The Calling Forth of the Charisma," unpublished sermon.

9. Iris V. Cully, *Education for Spiritual Growth* (San Francisco: Harper & Row, 1984), p. 45.

10. Michel Quoist, *Prayers*, tr. Agnes M. Forsyth and Anne Marie de Commaille (Kansas City, Mo.: Sheed & Ward, 1963), p. 11.

11. Urban T. Holmes III, *Spirituality for Ministry* (San Francisco: Harper & Row, 1983), p. 30.

12. James Michael Lee, "Lifework Spirituality and the Religious Educator," in *The Spirituality of the Religious Educator*, ed. James Michael Lee (Birmingham, Ala.: Religious Education Press, 1985), pp. 7–42.

13. Quoist, *Prayers*, p. x.

14. M. Basil Pennington, *Called: New Thinking on Christian Vocation* (New York: Seabury Press, 1983), p. 34.

15. Holmes, *Spirituality for Ministry*, p. 171.

16. Ibid., p. 190.

Contributors

*All are affiliated with The Southern Baptist
Theological Seminary.*

DANIEL O. ALESHIRE is Professor of Psychology and Christian
Education and Director of Professional Studies. He is the
author of *Faithcare: Ministering to All God's People Through
the Ages of Life (1988).*
GERALD L. BORCHERT is Professor of New Testament Interpretation. His other books include *Paul and His Interpreters*
(1985).
C. ANNE DAVIS is Dean, Carver School of Church Social Work
and Woman's Missionary Union Professor of Social Work.
She was named Social Worker of the Year, Kentucky Chapter of the National Association of Social Workers, 1984. Dr.
Davis is coeditor with Wade Rowatt of the book *Formation
for Christian Ministry.*
DONOSO ESCOBAR is Assistant Professor of Social Work. Before
joining the faculty, he was Director of the Immigration and
Refugee Service for the Home Mission Board of the South-
ern Baptist Convention.
DIANA S. RICHMOND GARLAND is Associate Professor of Social
Work. A prolific writer, she and David E. Garland have re-
cently written *Marriage for Better or for Worse* (1989).
WILLIAM L. HENDRICKS is Professor of Christian Theology and
Director of Graduate Studies. His most recent book is *A The-
ology of Aging* (1986).
JOHN D. HENDRIX is Basil Manly Jr. Professor of Christian
Education. His most recent book is *A Journey to Commit-
ment* (1989).

E. GLENN HINSON is David T. Porter Professor of Church History. He is the author of numerous books, including *A Serious Call to a Contemplative Lifestyle* (1974) and *The Evangelization of the Roman Empire* (1981).

ROY LEE HONEYCUTT is President of The Southern Baptist Theological Seminary and Professor of Old Testament Interpretation. His writings include *Exodus* in The Broadman Bible Commentary.

ROBERT DON HUGHES is Associate Professor of Communication and Mass Media. His books include *Giving Together* (1990), *The Forging of the Dragon* (1990), and a play entitled *You Cain't Just Let a Man Drown.*

JAMES HYDE is Adjunct Professor of Pastoral Care. His recent Ph.D. dissertation is entitled "Story Theology in Family Systems Theory: Contributions to Pastoral Counseling with Families" (1988).

GERALD L. KEOWN is Associate Professor of Old Testament Interpretation. He is a recent contributor to *The International Standard Bible Encyclopedia*, volumes 3 and 4.

BILL J. LEONARD is Professor of Church History. He is the author of *The Nature of the Church* (1986).

MOLLY T. MARSHALL-GREEN is Assistant Professor of Christian Theology. Her writings include "When Keeping Silent No Longer Will Do: A Theological Agenda for the Contemporary Church," *Review and Expositor* (Winter 1986), and "Women in Ministry: A Biblical Theology," *Folio* (Fall 1983).

HUGH T. MCELRATH is V. V. Cooke Professor of Church Music and a well-known hymnologist. He is the author, with Harry Lee Eskew, of *Sing with Understanding: An Introduction to Christian Hymnology* (1980).

LARRY L. MCSWAIN is Dean of the School of Theology and Professor of Church and Community. He coauthored *Church Organizations Alive* (1987) with William Treadwell.

WAYNE E. OATES is Senior Professor of Pastoral Care. His numerous books include *Behind the Masks* (1987); *Protestant Pastoral Counseling* (1962); and *The Presence of God in Pastoral Counseling* (1986).

S. MILBURN PRICE, JR., is Dean of the School of Church Music. He has written text and music for several hymns, three of which are included in the 1975 *Baptist Hymnal*, and is the author of *A Survey of Christian Hymnody.*

WILLIAM B. ROGERS, JR., is Dean of the School of Christian Education and Professor of History and Philosophy of Education. His publications include numerous articles published in *The Theological Educator, Review and Expositor,* and other journals.

PAMELA J. SCALISE is Assistant Professor of Old Testament. Her writings include "Women in Ministry: Reclaiming our Old Testament Heritage," *Review and Expositor* (Winter 1986).

PAUL D. SIMMONS is Professor of Christian Ethics and Director of the Clarence Jordan Center at Southern Seminary. He is the author of *Birth and Death: Bioethical Decision-making* (1983).

GLEN HAROLD STASSEN is Professor of Christian Ethics. His publications include *Journey Into Peacemaking* (1983) and a chapter in *Peacemakers* (ed. Jim Wallis, 1983).

DAN R. STIVER is Assistant Professor of Christian Philosophy. He is a recent contributor to a book entitled *Baptist Theologians* (1990).

EDWARD E. THORNTON is Laurence and Charlotte Hoover Professor of Pastoral Care. He is the author of *Theology and Pastoral Counseling* (1964), *Being Transformed: An Inner Way of Spiritual Growth* (1984), and *The Crisis of Fear* (with Gerald L. Borchert, 1988).

T. VAUGHN WALKER is Assistant Professor of Social Work and Pastor of First Gethsemane Baptist Church, Louisville, Kentucky.